So you Want to be a Professor?

How to Succeed in Academia

**Peter C. Hughes &
Roderick C. Tennyson**

Dedications

To the memories of my mother and my father, Annie-Edith Lenore (1911-1986) and David Duncan (1906-1963). They would have enjoyed reading this book.
—PCH

For all the students and colleagues I have met during my academic career. These interactions have provided the experiences required to write such a book.
—RCT

Copyright © 2010 Peter C. Hughes & Roderick C. Tennyson
All rights reserved.

ISBN: 1456405322
ISBN-13: 9781456405328

Preface

Welcome to the world of academia. If the prospect of being a 'professor' seems interesting, this book is for you. If you have already committed yourself to an academic career, then find out what options are available to you now, before time runs out! This book is a primer on how to succeed in this challenging—yet rewarding—vocation.

Although this book is written primarily for young professors who are near the tenure point (on either side), other audiences will discover the fascinating world inhabited by professors.

BOOK AUDIENCES — ACADEMIC DEMOGRAPHICS
Why you should read this book

A coherent academic career philosophy, as described in this book, should be of interest to many demographic cohorts:

Graduates. The "simple facts" are these: *academic career* ➜ *graduate study required,* and that *graduate study* ➜ *academic career kept open.*

Contingency Faculty: Those who aspire to a tenure stream appointment and all the options it brings.

New Tenure-Track Professors. "The rules" will require a strategic approach to survival and tenure attainment, but it's not too early for some strategic thinking about one's post-tenure stance either!

Newly Tenured Professors. The primary target audience for this book.

Mature Tenured Professors. A key demographic because, first, with today's long careers it's never too late for a mid-course correction and, second, because they should understand why it is necessary, for the vitality of their institution, that most professors consider other options within the academic milieu.

SO YOU WANT TO BE A PROFESSOR?

The critical career decisions of university and college students begin with their choice of degree programs. One of the options available to the undergraduate is that of pursuing graduate studies, either in preparation for a possible academic career or as a necessary adjunct to a professional career in the 'outside' world.

This book first describes the authors' views on an academic career, its opportunities and pitfalls, including the concept of tenure, the long sought goal of most aspiring academics. One of the benefits to an undergraduate reader is an opportunity to get inside the world of the academic and examine the many different career paths that are available, once the tenure hurdle is overcome.

This book contains the authors' frank viewpoints, but it also includes much commentary gleaned from detailed interviews with other academics who have achieved 'stardom' as leaders, scholars, researchers, entrepreneurs and teachers. Among our interviewees are the presidents of four leading universities (two American, two Canadian). Importantly, the authors and most of the interviewees have, in addition to their academic achievements, substantial experience in the public sector and private business; they can see from the outside as well as from the inside.

For the already committed academic reader, this book begins to drill down most deeply at the point where one has been granted tenure. Not because the pre-tenure years are unimportant; far from it. Indeed, much has already been written in other places concerning the pre-tenure career phases, so there is less need in our book for such commentary.

Still, not all of such pre-tenure counsel has the professor as client. Much of the pre-tenure advice, on the contrary, is based instead on what the university wants. While not suggesting that an employee who wishes to pursue a successful career should aim to do the opposite of what his or her employer prefers, it would equally be folly to suggest that the employer's interests and the employee's interests are identical!

It is interesting to note that this dichotomy of viewpoints has resulted in increased faculty unionization. Indeed, in the U.S. a high percentage of full-time tenure track faculty in public universities constitute one of the most unionized occupations, and in Canada most faculty associations are unionized, estimated to be over 80%.

PREFACE

In contrast with the *ante*-tenurial context, what one should do *post*-tenure is somewhat more mysterious. It is less written about (from the professor's viewpoint); less discussed; less codified; more based on cryptic insinuations, private discussions with mentors, and just plain guesswork—altogether hardly a solid framework within which to plan a successful career. Simple slogans—such as "just keep on doing what you were doing before tenure"—are generally not helpful, or accurate—or in the interests of the recipient. There is much more to consider, as we shall see.

We the authors have decided to assist with this career period—hardly a brief interlude, more like virtually all one's life as an academic and most of one's life on Earth. For academics to treat their post-tenure professional life as a black art is simply not acceptable. We see the achievement of tenure as the grand (creaking?) opening of very large, very heavy doors, revealing an exciting post-tenure world beyond. As for the "black art," effectively equivalent to ignorance, we hope to shed light on the many exciting possibilities that can bloom in the post-tenure world; to broaden the options seriously available; and to suggest strategies for choosing and pursuing these options.

The authors recognize that in most North American universities there exists a two-tier academic system: those on a path to tenure, and those hired on contingency contracts (non-tenure stream). It is important to the graduate student contemplating an academic career to realize that, unlike his professors who are close to retirement, tenure stream appointments are no longer the norm and are becoming less frequent. However, this book will still be of value to contingency faculty, virtually all of whom aspire to tenure stream appointments.

Not every reader will agree with everything we say in this book. As academics who lived most of their professional lives before the suffocating modern strictures of political correctness in academia, the authors welcome such doubts—not just because of free speech, but because we know that our opinions are fallible. If we help our readers to define the issues; if we provide guidance in reflecting on these issues; if we assist other professors to broaden their perspectives; and, most of all, if we help our fellow academics to plan their careers—we will have achieved our objectives for this book.

Peter C. Hughes
Roderick C. Tennyson

TABLE OF CONTENTS

Preface iii

Chapter 1: Tenure (Finally!) 1
    Chapter Overview 1

1.1 Tenure: What is It? 2
    What Is a "University" (in this book)? 2
    What Is a Contractual Academic Relationship? 4
    What Is Tenure? 7
    Computing the Tenure Score 9

1.2 Uses and Abuses of Tenure 11
    The Continuing (Tenured) Position 11
    Tenure Removes One Important "Cause" for Dismissal 12
    The Tenure Track—A Road Becoming Less Traveled 14

1.3 Tenure as Prelude 16
    Tenure: Only a Milestone 16
    A Progression Requires Progress 17

1.4 Post-Tenure Career Advice in Short Supply 19
    Sources of Academic Career Information. 20

Chapter 2: Professorial Species 23
    Chapter Overview 23

2.1 Academic Culture 24
    What Is Culture? 24
    Intellectual Strength 25
    Scholarly Activity (Deep, but Narrow). 27
    Other Views. 28
    Miscellaneous Abuses To Be Avoided 28

2.2 Why Choose an Academic Career? 32
    A Process for Career Selection 33
    Reflections from Successful Professors 35
    Factors that Underlie Career Planning 41
    The Role of Competitiveness 43

2.3 Approaches to Career Planning 45
    One Possible Career Plan: Keep On Keeping On 46
    Boy Scout Planning 47
    Refinements on the Notion of Career Planning 50
    The Four Main Paradigms 51

Chapter 3: The Advanced Teacher 53
    Chapter Overview 53

3.1 Learning and Teaching 54
    The Input-Output Balance 55
    Input (or Output) out of Balance 56
    Teaching as Output 57

3.2 Post-Secondary Teaching — Could This Be a Career? 58
    Is Teaching Even Desirable? 59
    Teaching vis-à-vis Research 60
    Post-Tenure Career Planning 61
    Can We Justify Teaching as a Post-Secondary Career? 62
    Historically, Research Was Meant to Support Teaching 64

3.3 Teaching as a Career — A Closer Examination 66
    Teaching in a University 66
    Teaching Early Undergraduate Students 68
    Teaching Late Undergraduate Students 68
    Teaching Early Graduate Students 69
    Teaching Late Graduate Students 70

3.4 Teaching — A Career that Requires Skill 71
    Other Obstacles 72
    First Principles 73
    A Profession with a Long Past 74
    Measuring Success 76

3.5　Getting Off on the Right Foot............................ 78
　　　Consider Teaching an Existing Course (at least initially)...... 78
　　　The First Day.. 80
　　　Some Suggested Do's and Don'ts 81
3.6　University Teaching Needs Innovation..................... 84
　　　Help from New Technology 85
　　　Career Opportunities in Teaching......................... 88
3.7　Insights on Teaching from Our Interviewees 89

Chapter 4: The Eminent Scholar................ 91
　　　Chapter Overview....................................... 91
4.1　Research: A Theme with Many Variations................. 92
　　　Research—A Many-Textured Word 94
　　　Research Varies Greatly Within Acadème.................. 95
4.2　High-Quality Research—Could This Be a Career? 96
　　　Is an Academic Research Career Desirable?................. 96
　　　The Normative Paradigm................................ 99
4.3　Research as a Career—A Closer Examination.............. 105
　　　Many Variations and Textures........................... 106
　　　Re-Search (Searching Again) vs. Original Research......... 106
　　　Fundamental Research vs. Applied Research.............. 109
　　　Theoretical vs. Analytical Research...................... 110
　　　Library/E-Research vs. Laboratory (Experimental) Research .. 112
　　　Platform Research vs. Incremental Research 117
　　　High-Risk Research vs. Low-Risk Research 117
4.4　Extraordinary Research Requires Two More Special Skills ... 118
　　　Good Questions Precede Good Answers 119
　　　Extraordinary Research Requires Free Inquiry, Creativity, and
　　　Skepticism 121
　　　Skepticism vs. Cynicism................................ 123
　　　Historical Examples of Extraordinary Research from
　　　Creativity and Skepticism.............................. 124
　　　What Have We Learned about Extraordinary Research?..... 131
　　　Relationship between Research Debates
　　　and the Teaching Curriculum........................... 133
　　　Closing Comments on Skepticism and Creativity 134

4.5 Some Nuts and Bolts of Successful Research 134
    Tactics vis-à-vis Strategy. 135
    Time Management: The Importance-Urgency Dilemma 138
    Regarding Luck 141
    Types of Research—Some Strategic Implications 143
    Other Stratagems for More Effective Research 148
    Grantsmanship. 153
    Escape from the Normative Paradigm. 154

4.6 Insights on Research from Our Interviewees. 156

Chapter 5: The Academic Executive 161
    Chapter Overview. 161

5.1 Careers Measured by Promotions 162
    Forethought is a Good Thing 162
    Promotion—Another Vexed Word in This Discussion 163
    Case for the Affirmative—Academic Promotions
    are Real Promotions 164
    Guest Witness for the Affirmative—Dr. Tom Brzustowski . . . 166
    Case for the Negative—Academic Promotions
    are Not Real Promotions 169
    Authors' Conclusions on "Academic Promotions". 170

5.2 Academic Management and Leadership—Could This Be a Career? 171
    Unconventional Views May Hold the Key to Success 171
    A Family of Escape Routes from The Tube—
    Academic Management 172
    Scarcity of Academic Management Positions. 173
    Academic Leadership—The Roads Less Traveled 173
    Administration, Management, Leadership 175
    A Canonical Academic Org Chart. 176
    What is an Executive? 179
    What is an Officer?. 180
    Mobility Usually a Necessity 180
    Department Chair 181
    Faculty Dean 183
    Chief Academic Officer. 184
    President 186
    Why Are These Roads Less Traveled? 190

5.3 Academic Management as a Career — A Closer Examination 191
    The Skill Set—The DNA of Professional Functioning 192
    How To Use a Skill-Set Template 196

5.4 Academic Leadership Requires Many Special Skills 197
    Soft Skills, Emotional IQ 198
    Are Meetings a Good Idea? 199
    Meetings Are Also a Challenge 200
    A Question for Self-Diagnosis 201
    The Conduct of Effective Meetings 204
    Alternative Authority Structures for Meetings 204
    Financial Awareness and Accountability 206
    Important Question No. 1 207
    Important Question No. 2 209
    Legal Fluency 211

5.5 Some Strategies for How to Play the Game 212
    Some First Steps 213
    Second Steps 214
    Next Steps 214
    Time is of the Essence 215

5.6 Insights from Our Interviewees 217
    on the Academic Management Option
    Michael Collins 217
    Molly Shoichet 218
    Tom Brzustowski 218
    Heather Monroe-Blum 221
    David Naylor 223
    Peter Likins 224

Chapter 6: The Entrepreneurial Professor ... 231
    Chapter Overview 231

6.1 What Is an Entrepreneur? 232
    Entrepreneurial—A More Precise Description 233
    Examination of the Key Ideas 233
    The Entrepreneur 235
    Wealth Creation 236
    Sweat Equity 237

6.2 Entrepreneurial Impulses Among Academics **239**
    The Paradox Inspected 240
    Entrepreneurial Professors—A Spectrum of Intensities 241
    Entrepreneurial Professors — at the Action Level 243

6.3 The Entrepreneurial Professor—Could This Be a Career Flavor? 246
    Technology Readiness. 247
    Commercial Readiness 248
    Intellectual Capital. 249
    Intellectual Property (IP) 251
    Other Intellectual Capital. 253
    Example: The Personal Computer 254

6.4 Entrepreneurship as an Academic Flavor—A Closer Examination 254
    Entrepreneurial Professors (Level 2) 255
    Entrepreneurial Professors (Level 3) 260
    Entrepreneurial Professors (Level 4) 261

6.5 Ethical Challenges **261**
    Unethical Lapses vis-à-vis Illegal Lapses 262
    How (Un)ethical are You?. 263
    Ethical Questions Abound in Academia 264
    First Encounters with Outside Research Contracts 267
    Key Contract Issues 269
    Institutional Weaknesses 271

6.6 Frequent Ethical Dilemmas and Concrete Solutions **273**
    Dilemma 1: How Do I Split My Time? — Part I. 274
    Dilemma 1: How Do I Split My Time? — Part II 276
    Dilemma 2: Do I Owe My Colleagues Anything? 279
    Dilemma 3: How Should I Treat My Students? — Part I. . . . 280
    Dilemma 3: How Should I Treat My Students? — Part II . . . 282

6.7 Insights from Our Interviewees on the Entrepreneurial Option . **284**
    Tom Brzustowski 284
    Michael Collins 285
    Dan Farine 285
    Barry French. 289
    Donald Mackay 291
    Heather Monroe-Blum 292

Chapter 7: Academic Path Planning...........295
Chapter Overview......................................295
7.1 Other Academic Career Flavors........................295
Professorship as a Career Choice 296
Mix and Match Paradigms 296
7.2 The Celebrity Professor 298
Internal Celebrity Status................................298
External Celebrity Status 300
International Celebrity Status..........................302
7.3 The Socially Conscious Professor........................302
Entrepreneur in Social Capital 303
7.4 Some Closing Thoughts................................307
Staying in The Tube..................................307
The "Doomed"......................................308
The Normative Professor 308
Out to Pasture? Or an Exciting End-of-Life Mini-Career?....309

Bibliography 313

Appendix 315

About the Authors.................................341
Peter C Hughes, PhD, PEng, MBA, FAIAA, FCASI, CDir...341
Roderick C Tennyson, BASc, PhD, PEng, FCASI..........343

Chapter 1: Tenure (Finally!)

Now What?

Chapter Overview

The academic career period between tenure and retirement is highly significant and needlessly mysterious. This period provides the chief scope for this book. To get the discussion rolling and properly anchored, this chapter first discusses what we mean by "career" and "university." Once an academic career has been selected, how does one proceed along this career path? The first major hurdle is to secure *tenure*. This chapter addresses the context and meaning of tenure and the considerations needed to achieve this status.

Readers who have already chosen academic professorship as their career will have some familiarity with the notion of tenure. They either have tenure, or are aiming for tenure, or wish they had a chance at tenure, or have some other similar interest based on career goals. Since tenure is the key that unlocks the many opportunities herein discussed, we first must say something about the subject of tenure itself, particularly to enlighten the reader who is considering the academic lifestyle.

We open the discussion by examining tenure from a contemporary legal viewpoint. (Full disclosure to skeptics: The historical aspects, while interesting, will be left to historians; and, no, the authors are not lawyers.) Professors sometimes recoil at the idea that they are employees, but of course they are. Unless they wish to emulate the celebrated ostrich, their career planning requires that they understand their employer-employee relationship. A frank discussion of the modern threats to the edifice of tenure is, we hope, one of the valuable contributions of this section, however unsettling.

In order to understand—and benefit from—the discussion in this chapter, one must check at the door one's bred-in-the bone (and largely self-serving) notions of tenure entitlement. Like it or not, tenure—in the strict academic sense—may be an endangered species. One can rant and rail against the slow demise of this academic sacrament as much as one chooses, but in the end the academic species that prevail will be those who can adapt.

1.1 Tenure: What is It?

For readers in the process of working towards a professor's career, a rather important consideration is the choice of workplace. We now look at what a university is (in this book) and the various manifestations available to the new recruit.

What Is a "University" (in this book)?

Scores of learned treatises, over centuries, have been written on the question, "What constitutes an ideal university?" We shall not attempt to add to this literature here; however, the reader does have a right to know what the authors mean by the term "university," a word that appears on virtually every subsequent page.

> University [Definition]
>
> We shall generally refer to a post-secondary educational institution as a *university* if it satisfies the following three criteria: (a) it seeks to teach, and study in a scholarly way, a wide range of the best of human thought; (b) it is regarded by most other universities as a university; and (c) its senior teachers are called "professors."

With respect to Criterion (c), this definition is in danger of becoming circular, since it is not unreasonable to define "professors" as "those who teach at universities." Another clear case of apprehended circularity is contained in Criterion (b), which says that a university is indeed a university if the consensus among other universities is that it is.

CHAPTER 1: TENURE (FINALLY!)

Despite these seeming flaws, we shall use this definition because it is brief and pragmatic. It gives high emphasis to the teaching function (a preference of the authors); it leaves it up to the institution in question to position itself in the educational spectrum by how it names its tenured teachers; and it tends to eliminate the phenomenon wherein someone with no academic credentials or merit starts up an organization, calls it a "university," and then appoints oneself as president or chancellor (or both).

Thus we restrict ourselves to "real" universities—those that teach (and usually conduct research) in a relatively comprehensive range of areas (hence "universe"); that subject themselves regularly to assessment by other universities; and that are broadly recognized by their sister institutions in the civilized world as being, realistically, universities. This system is self-correcting.

Still, the word "university" is not universal. Some universities are called "colleges" and in very large universities some divisions are called "colleges." One thinks of, say, King's College, Cambridge. There is also the phrase "going to college," when what is actually being gone to is a university. With all these sources of confusion, the above definition starts to look pretty good.

In spite of the effort to achieve some degree of conformity through the above definition, there are still institutional parameters that vary widely, primarily as to size, the performance normally expected of staff and students, the principal sources of organizational financing, and the relative degree of emphasis placed on teaching vis-à-vis research.

	Definition (USA)	Definition (Canada)
Tier I	Elite private universities (Harvard, Stanford, etc.).	Degree-granting institutions receiving more than 1% of federal granting agency funding; hospitals; not-for-profit organizations.
Tier II	High-end public research universities.	Degree-granting institutions receiving less than 1% of federal granting agency funding.
Tier III	State universities; community colleges.	Colleges that do not confer degrees.

Figure 1.1: University Tiers (USA and Canada).

Figure 1.1 shows one helpful taxonomy. In the United States, there are three categories of universities or colleges where faculty members are known as "professors," with career path options generally addressed in this book. These major categories can be described as (**Tier I**): elite private universities (Stanford and Harvard, for example); (**Tier II**): high-end public research universities (with doctoral programs and professional faculties); and last—but not less important to the general educational landscape—(**Tier III**): state universities and community colleges (with or without graduate programs). One of the most important differences from a professor's perspective is the larger salary paid and the often shorter "annual" employment period (typically, nine months) offered by many of the Tier I and Tier II universities. This may present the professor with additional income opportunities.

The Tiers are defined slightly differently for Canada, owing partly to the narrower variations and partly to the absence of private universities; the definitions in Fig. 1.1 are based on those used by the Canada Foundation for Innovation, which gives relatively large grants for research infrastructure to universities, hospitals and colleges. As a general trend, the higher the tier, the more intensive the institutional focus on research. Whether this is "desirable" is not the point for us here. It is simply a fact, one that should be taken into account as part of career planning.

What Is a Contractual Academic Relationship?

Faculty appointments in most North American universities and colleges fall into two classes: those on a tenure track, and those hired on contingency contracts (non-tenure track). It is important that the graduate student contemplating an academic career realize that, unlike professors who are close to retirement age, tenure stream appointments are no longer the norm and are becoming less frequent. Current statistics from Dobbie and Robinson [2008] show[1] that only about 35% of new faculty hires are in the tenure stream in the United States, while in Canada, the number is much higher, around 55%.

Contingent faculty fall into a variety of categories such as adjuncts, sessionals, teaching assistants, or other labels, and constitute the majority of teaching faculty in higher education in the U.S. and to a lesser extent

---

1   "Reorganizing Higher Education in the United States and Canada: The Erosion of Tenure and the Unionization of Contingent Faculty," Robinson and Dobbie, Labor Studies Journal, 2008, 33 [2], p. 117.

CHAPTER I: TENURE (FINALLY!)

in Canada. The Canadian Association of University Teachers (CAUT) uses the term "contract academic staff" to define people who perform academic work on a contract basis. Although there are differences between countries, in general they work without job security (tenure) or other benefits that are available to tenure track faculty.

Many of the contingent faculty clearly desire to become tenure-track appointments, or at the very least strive to obtain the same benefits as their more fortunate colleagues. The American Association of University Professors (AAUP) issued a policy statement on this matter (2003) entitled *"Contingent Appointments and the Academic Professions."* This document offers guidelines for planning and implementing "gradual transitions to a higher proportion of tenurable positions" along with "intermediate, ameliorative measures by which the academic freedom and professional integration of faculty currently appointed to contingent positions can be enhanced by academic due process and assurances of continued employment."

Because of the major changes in the academic workforce, it is not surprising that faculty unionization has occurred at a rapid pace. Faculty unions in both the United States and Canada are growing each year, driven in part by the demands of contingency faculty. CAUT has recognized that the issues concerning part-time faculty—salary, benefits, job security and career mobility—need to be addressed. Similarly, the AAUP is a strong advocate for both tenure track and contingent faculty, supported by the American Federation of Teachers (AFT) who claims to be "the leading organizer of part-time faculty in the United States." Indeed, most faculty associations are unionized in Canada, estimated by the Association of Universities and Colleges of Canada (AUCC) to be over 80%. Unlike Canada, however, contingent faculty in the U.S. are not well organized, although a high percentage of full-time tenure track faculty in the public sector constitute one of the most unionized occupations in the United States. Despite faculty unionization, Dobbie and Robinson state that this has not resulted in significant reductions in the growth of contingent faculty numbers. However, there is little doubt that faculty unions regard the reduction in 'casualization' (the hiring of contingent faculty) and the consequent erosion of tenure as high priority issues.[2]

The advent of faculty unions is a contentious issue, with claims and counter-claims in abundance. One university president who commented on this issue wrote as follows:

"If one examines the 20% of universities without unions, I would bet they are stronger institutions from the standpoint of their academic performance and research intensity. And I would also bet that their faculty, on average, are better compensated.

"I think the culture of a great university is best served by a strong faculty association rather than by a formal union. That partly reflects my belief that good academics tend to be strongly individualistic, regardless of whether they are left- or right-leaning politically, and whether they operate in the solo scholar mode or in collaborative teams. Put simply, excellent professors think and act independently. And that may not be an easy mix with the collectivism of a unionized faculty.

"A further reservation is that union processes tend to empower external arbitrators who may not understand academic standards and values. The very fact of unionization tends to turn off some professors who become even less engaged with broad faculty issues. There is, moreover, no guarantee that the union leaders will be the scholarly leaders of the university or the opinion leaders of the faculty at the divisional or departmental level. The result is that, while administrators can be rightly criticized for being out of touch, the same can be true for the faculty union leaders.

"Indeed, a misdirected faculty union can meddle in departmental decision-making, promote compensation based on seniority at the expense of merit pay, and interfere on egalitarian grounds with efforts by chairs and others to accommodate and retain top performers. I am all for fairness and strong

---

2   For more information on universities and colleges in the United States and Canada, the reader is referred to the following websites: www.aaup.org, www.aft.org, www.caut.ca, and www.aucc.ca.

faculty representation, but none of these side-effects strikes me as good things."

Much in this book is focused on those young graduates and faculty who are fortunate enough to have secured a tenure track stream appointment. With this in mind, we now proceed to address the issue of 'tenure.'

What Is Tenure?

The detailed legalistic meaning of "tenure" varies somewhat from place to place, but some of its characteristics are commonly understood. The first is this: Until one has tenure, one's employment can be terminated with relative ease—perhaps automatically after a prescribed interval has elapsed. In most western jurisdictions, employment law distinguishes between **(a)** a contractual relationship for labor, and **(b)** an employer-employee relationship for labor. In the former, an individual agrees to provide certain services in exchange for compensation, but without the long-term arrangement of becoming a formal employee; in the latter, an individual similarly agrees to provide services for compensation, but now the arrangement is long-term and falls under the aegis of whatever employment law is active in the subject jurisdiction.

In the academic setting, a *contract employee* is hired for a specified term—a few years at most. A variety of titles may be used, but the older one gets the more one realizes how completely irrelevant job titles are, and the present context is a perfect example. Contract employees (in general) may have agreements with several organizations at the same time, but in the academic application they typically have an agreement with only one (academic) organization.[3]

Unfortunately, many contract employees in academia, despite their sophistication in other intellectual pursuits, remain blissfully unaware that it is important to get competent legal advice **before** signing any contract, and in particular before signing the contract that defines their livelihood. When negotiating any employment contract, the value of legal consultation virtually always exceeds the cost.

---

3   The tax department may deem the "contract employee" to be, simply, an employee if the individual has only one contract.

Most employment situations, particularly those involving extensive and somewhat unproven skill sets call for a *probationary period*, during which the employer can assess the performance of the employee. Probation is a rather purgatorial state in which one is hired temporarily but not permanently.

Actually, in law, one does not refer to a *permanent* position, but a *continuing* position—the end state after probation. Death, mandatory retirement, criminal conviction, insanity, and similar egregious and unusual circumstances will generally lead to the termination of even a "continuing appointment."

> **Reasons for Grant of Continuing Employment**
> **(End of Probation)**
> This person can fulfill the position for which he or she was hired, as envisioned at the time of hiring, to a standard that is deemed satisfactory to this organization, and it can be confidently predicted that he or she will continue to do so.

Still, during probation, these cruel fates are not seen as the main issue. The central question from the employer's standpoint is this: Can this person do the job for which he or she was hired, to a standard that is deemed satisfactory to this organization and that was envisioned at the time of hiring?

In many positions, it does not take long to make such a determination. One may assume that the probationary period for a candidate for "receptionist," at even an upscale organization, could be decided in a matter of weeks at most. Academic probation, on the other hand, has a gestational period that must surely be one of the longest in polite society. The reason is plain enough: All the important performance components take many months or even years to reach fruition and be in a state where fair and reasonably complete judgments can be made.

Take teaching, for example. Can the tenure candidate prepare a new course at either the post-secondary entry level, or at the senior undergraduate or postgraduate level—probably all three? Can the candidate then successfully organize and present that course, including lectures, tutorials (if any) and laboratory work (if any)? Finally, can the candidate evaluate the students taking this course, in a rational and unbiased way? It takes at least one year, probably several years, for these data to be available for a tenure evaluation process.

Or, take research. By the time a young professor has first made a wise decision on the area(s) to be researched; written successful grant applications and received the funding; attracted suitable graduate students; conducted the research; written an archive paper that satisfies the journal's editors and reviewers—several years will have passed. Moreover, that is only the first paper, and one research paper doesn't get you tenure very many places these days.

Thus we see an unusual characteristic of academic probation: The gestational period is elephantine. This means, in turn, that the period to tenure is also unusually long.

Computing the Tenure Score

Anyone who sportingly enters a game, even for an evening, without knowing how the score is computed, can expect to exit the adventure minus a few francs—and likely minus some respectability as well. It is similarly wise to know the formula for judging your personal contributions to your academic organization. It is very difficult to generalize, but the recipes below are typical.

Here is a typical formula[4] for achieving tenure:
1. **Teaching.** Must show ability to develop and teach courses at the level required, with evidence of competence as measured by the students in the courses. (<u>Evidence categories</u>: Successful execution of new teaching assignments, especially if substantially new courses are required; above average teaching evaluations, especially if submitted by a majority of senior students; any legitimate teaching award is a big plus; letters from students, if solicited and presented scientifically, can also shed light.)
2. **Research.** Must show promise of ability to conduct independent peer-approved research, with evidence of competence. (<u>Evidence categories</u>: One or more papers published in peer-reviewed journals; and/or one or more research grants/contracts won; and/or

---

[4] This formula will, of course, vary widely from place to place. It is far from a legalistic prescription. It is, instead, meant to be, suggestive of the sorts of criteria that most universities use as a framework for their tenure deliberations.

one or more students supervised who have successfully won advanced research-based degrees. Etc.[5] At "leading" institutions, the journals must also be "leading"; and/or the grants/contracts must also be of the size to enable meaningful research progress.)

3. **Administration.** Not usually required for tenure deliberations, but any positive evidence in this category is a plus.
4. **Entrepreneurial Activity.** A terminology yet to be carefully defined in this book—see Chapter 6—but rarely in evidence in a young academic. May have pre-tenure implications in those rare institutions that hire academic staff with outside (nonacademic) experience.

The above description applies broadly to teaching-intensive institutions. For research-intensive institutions, the relative treatments of teaching and research are significantly reversed. It is generally believed that the weighting on research contributions dominate the tenure decision. At either *genus* of institution, both quantity and quality of production are important. However, there is one subtle difference: at most teaching-intensive institutions (driven by economic factors), the *quantity* of courses taught is more important than the *quality* of courses taught; at research-intensive institutions, which must, directly or indirectly, compete with the world's best scholars, one well-received research paper by a leading archive journal in the field may be worth several publications in inferior journals.

One may also find oneself at an academic institution where the tenure advisory committees are assembled from senior colleagues who don't know how to evaluate teaching or research.[6] If one can foresee such a situation, better to leave early for another employer. Competent people tend to thrive better in a milieu where important decisions are made by other competent people.

---

[5] Most book editors would advise, "Don't say 'etc.' Either list the missing items, or ignore them." Generally, that's good advice. But if one is writing for potentially thousands of institutions, each with their own credo imposed on their hundreds of staff (potential readers, all), it's wise for the authors to advise these readers that it's the general flavor of the remarks, not their legal precision, that is intended.

[6] In other words—and not to put too fine a point on it—where one's tenure committee is incompetent. In such cases, outcomes are more difficult to predict.

CHAPTER 1: TENURE (FINALLY!)

1.2 Uses and Abuses of Tenure

Once the probationary period is successfully behind the candidate, whether in an academic or a nonacademic setting, one transfers to a *continuing* position. With this (continuing) status, the employee has certain additional employment protections. Otherwise, the distinction between probationary employment and continuing employment would be a distinction without a difference.

The Continuing (Tenured) Position

Some of these protections are provided by the pertaining law of the jurisdiction—state law, for example. In the case of newly tenured professors, additional protections regarding dismissal are usually provided by the employing institution, whether from precedent and culture, or from a unionized or faculty association collective agreement, or some combination of these.

These protections vary greatly between one legal jurisdiction and another, and between one institution of higher learning and another. The two key categories are *dismissal for cause* and *dismissal for convenience*. In the former category (dismissal for cause) are reasons deemed justifiable for dismissal without any cash settlement (the *severance package*), the equivalent of damages in a civil suit. Examples might include criminal conviction, death, certifiable mental illness, or gross incompetence. (Even in the case of the latter, the employer would have to offer some explanation as to why this incompetence was not observable at the time tenure was granted, or evidence that this incompetence developed since tenure was granted.)

The authors' favorite ground for dismissal of a tenured professor for cause is "moral turpitude," and the smoking gun for this offense is a successful seduction of the university president's life partner! We are not aware of any successful actual cases, although such a circumstance is clearly possible.

Tenure Removes One Important "Cause" for Dismissal

If a tenured professor is dismissed for *cause*, the legal point is to prove cause in court (if required to do so by the dismissee); if dismissed for *convenience*, the legal point is to prove in court that the financial settlement is fair and equitable, (if required to do so by the dismissee). In some universities, for example, extreme financial hardship of the institution is an admissible cause; in others not.

Continuing (tenured) appointments in universities do have some notable distinctions with respect to continuing appointment in business or government. The most obvious of these, and easily the most trivial, resides in the semantics. The word "tenure" (*tenir*, in French, means "to hold"), used as to employment status and not as the duration of an appointment, is identified almost totally with academia. Somewhat falsely, it has come to mean that university professors, once having achieved tenure, cannot be fired for any reason, and that they have job protection not enjoyed by any other group in society. As the above discussion shows, this is an unfair interpretation—for two reasons. First, professors can be fired under appropriate circumstances and, second, there are many positions in nonacademic walks of life whose holders are extraordinarily difficult to dislodge, although they don't use the word "tenure."

Since academic tenure is identified by many with perceived special privilege, this phrase would have outlived its usefulness were it not for one special characteristic of tenure that is quite unusual and that is restricted almost totally to academics. That characteristic is *the freedom to conduct research and scholarly inquiry without strictures from either one's colleagues or one's academic seniors.*

In many college departments, viscerally held beliefs do not usually conflict with the research work of other colleagues, so such quarrels do not arise. For example, the level of agreement amongst researchers around the world in the various engineering specialties is truly astounding. This does not mean that everyone's emphasis is identical or that there are no schools of thought, but speakers at engineering conferences do not come to blows over whether Hooke's Law (or something similar) is valid. World agreement on something is more the exception than the rule, so it is worth noting and applauding.

Similarly, in the natural sciences, agreement is almost universal on most issues—although, since science is a process that continually reveals new information, there are temporary differences of opinion. As for mathematics, a correct proof in Moscow is a correct proof in New York (and everywhere else). In such departments, tenure is, in practice, used largely as simple job security, the usual view of a continuing appointment.

CHAPTER I: TENURE (FINALLY!)

However, there are areas of inquiry where the "scholarly freedom" component of tenure is actively relied upon. Subjects like religion, political economy, sociology, and even some areas in biology, psychology and medicine can lead to rancor. Some views in these areas are held with more than normal fervor; were a professor to study and promulgate certain views that were thought "incorrect" by the consensus of his department, of even just of his boss, he could be dismissed (absent the shield of tenure).

Tsunamis of political correctness wash over some university departments quite regularly and these would drown all those who wished to take a more dispassionate view of their research findings. Without tenure there sometimes would be little diversity (of ideas).

According to a recent article,[7] Canadian academics face a more hostile environment regarding political correctness and free speech than do their colleagues in the U.S. Case in point: the outcry from some members of an audience attending a 2008 meeting of the Canadian Political Science association regarding the contents of a lecture by a fellow Canadian academic. They proclaimed that the speaker should be investigated because they perceived her presentation to be a 'hate speech'. Some wanted her book and the publisher to be censured. As the article noted, apparently in Canada, "it's okay to speak your mind if what you say does not offend anyone." Of particular interest is the existence of a U.S. petition signed by over 60 "respected political scientists" claiming that the right to free speech in Canada is threatened. There is no doubt that academic freedom and freedom of the press must be protected. Such protection is provided in the U.S. by the First Amendment to the constitution. In Canada, such protection relies on the appropriate interpretation of 'tenure'.

When it comes to teaching, substantial freedom is again given to the tenured academic, although not as much freedom as for research, since a core course curriculum should reflect the consensus in the field, not the idiosyncrasies of a particular teacher. For example, a post-secondary teacher of biology who insisted on propagating "creationism" (or it's latest mutation, "intelligent design"), while refusing to learn or teach the overwhelming evidence for evolution, would be given a quiet exit, at least in most schools, on the grounds of incompetence.

---

7   A. Shimo, writing in Maclean's, Mar 2/09, 'Tough Critique or Hate Speech,' p 42.

The Tenure Track—A Road Becoming Less Traveled

In many jurisdictions, fewer and fewer academics are offered a *tenure track* position.[8] With no surprise, we note that professorial groups find this trend alarming. In one survey, forty-three percent of faculty appointments were part time, and over half of new full-time appointments were non-tenure track. "Non-tenure track" (or *contingent*) appointments include all those who will never get a tenure hearing, whether part- or full-time, and whether compensated on a per-course or a salary basis. Individuals holding such appointments are called by a wide variety of titles including "adjuncts," "lecturers," "instructors," or "visiting professors."

Why would universities act in this manner? The initial response would be for economic reasons due to on-going budget cuts. However, there are several other forces that make an assault on tenure not only plausible as an output trend, but virtually inevitable:

> **Trend #1.** A primary reason for winnowing down the tenure-track and tenured staff complements is that rates of change of practically everything in the external environment continue to accelerate. (Just because this is stated every day doesn't mean it's not true.) Academic institutions, if they are to survive—or even thrive—in these environments, simply must adapt to these changes, which are unrelenting and beyond the institution's control.
>
> Although some idealists think and act as though the cloisters of academia are somehow inoculated from external realities, these realities must eventually impinge and produce a powerful force for change. Have these idealists checked the thrival indices of monasteries lately? Administrations must be sprightlier than universities have heretofore been known for! They can't do this if a high proportion of their staff is secure behind the ramparts of tenure. Can the reader think of a way to bring about substantive and disruptive changes in his or her department if all the senior staff and many of the junior staff are tenured?

---

8   See, for example, St. Petersburg Times, 20 Nov 2007, Tenure Track in Decline.

CHAPTER 1: TENURE (FINALLY!)

Trend #2. Universities always produce doctoral graduates at a much higher rate than they absorb them. The laws of supply and demand apply here (as they always do). Doubly so in the present context since academia is both the supplier of, and a significant customer for, new PhD's. That supply has always greatly exceeded the demand.

Trend #3. Trend #2 has accelerated in recent times. Universities now manufacture PhD's at a higher rate (per professor) than they did two or three generations ago. The proof is simple. How many PhD's did your department graduate thirty years ago? How many in the past decade? How many new academic staff were hired thirty years ago? How many in the past decade? These numbers provide the rough ratios of supply to demand and also insight into how they have been changing.

Trend #4. To make matters worse, many jurisdictions have recently made mandatory retirement illegal. Now the Gibraltar of tenure forces the university into an ironclad employment commitment to tenured professors, one that must endure not just ~35 years, but perhaps as long as ~60 years. Obviously this is all one big glorious system for tenured professors. Unfortunately, precisely the opposite is true for the university's management—and for untenured professors as well.

Trend #5. As a further adverse trend to human resources flexibility, everyone is also living longer. An institution cannot be agile if virtually all its academic staff members are safely ensconced in the concrete of tenure.

We began this list of trends by asking, "Why would universities act in this manner [to reduce tenure]?" A fair and unbiased reading of the above list tends to reverse the burden of proof: "Why is academic tenure still awarded at all?"

Nevertheless, tenure is still awarded, and likely will be for some time to come, although with less frequency and more reluctance than earlier times. For this book's readers, this should only underline how precious tenure is for those who have attained it, and wise use of this treasure should be of the highest priority.

> **Brief Course in "The New Rank Semantics"**
> Authors [to an academic]: *What is your rank?*
> Academic: *I'm an Assistant Professor.*
> Authors: *That's not very responsive. What is your **real** rank?*
> Academic: *What do you mean?*
> Authors: *Are you on the so-called tenure track, either before or after, or not?*
> Academic: *Oh, I see what you mean.*

As we shall see as a major theme in this book, the traditional segmentation of the academic staff into Assistant Professors, Associate Professors, and "Full" Professors (or similar) is much more about perception than reality, much more an appeal to one's emotions than to one's intellect. Indeed, we shall select a different segmentation altogether for tenured professors (see the last pages of Chapter 2, and all of Chapters 3–6).

First, however, we must make it abundantly clear that most pronounced cleavage in all of academia is the abyss between those who have tenure (or who are at least on track to do so) and those who do not have tenure (and are not even on that path). The latter may need some books to help as well, but this book is primarily for the former.

1.3 Tenure as Prelude

With this level of career investment having already been made, it does seem reasonable to keep an eye on the health of this asset. Understandably, the probationary period (referred to in academic jargon as the *tenure-track* phase) demands a great deal of attention; little time or energy remains for career strategizing.

Tenure: Only a Milestone

Once tenure has been attained, one should not rest on one's oars and never think again about one's academic future. On the contrary, this is the perfect time to develop plans for the majority of one's career. Academic institutions encourage the premise that all professorial careers are, in principle, clones of one other; that there is nothing to contemplate; that there are no issues to deal with or plan for; that everyone does research, and teaching, and a little administration. This is, however, as our British friends say, *bollix*.

Young college teachers and university professors, well-trained as creative thinkers, might seem immune to tunnel vision. Yet, it has been the authors' observation that there is one important academic milestone that seems to lead to the sense that "There. That's over. Now my career can proceed on autopilot." That milestone is the granting of tenure. In many cases, it seems to suffocate all further thought on career reflection by its recipient. Thus, there seems to be a tendency to regard tenure as the event which ends all career planning. One has now arrived. Our advice here is, "Enjoy the moment, but use that moment also to rededicate yourself to achieving the next mileposts on the long career path ahead."

Each young professor must take charge of his career and assume *personal responsibility* for future choices, not leaving matters either to providence or to some assumed organizational process, not acting as though the future will unfold according to a predetermined map; as though there are no longer any significant career decisions. The fact that the reader has examined this book shows that he knows such willful disregard for one's own long-term career prospects makes no sense, and that at least a small fraction of one's time should be devoted to "thinking strategically about one's career."

A Progression Requires Progress

Figure 1.2 shows a typical academic career progression, including the point of tenure award. For more details on the tenure process, see the discussion by Goldsmith *et al.* [2001] (p 210). The seminal but otherwise unimportant signposts sketched at the beginning of this chapter are indicated, as are the major academic milestones[9] of more interest here. Highlighted is the *tenure* event. Many young professors feel that tenure is the end of a long voyage, and this may well be, but the academic career journey is just about to begin.

The award of tenure is doubtless a watershed moment in the life of any academic. The reasons for this view were briefly recounted above, in §1.2.

---

9   These milestones are intended to be typical, not precise for any particular academic institution.

SO YOU WANT TO BE A PROFESSOR?

Still, there should also be, at tenure, a somewhat different view—one that is more focused on the future, one that sees tenure as a beginning, not a conclusion. At tenure, one is approximately in the middle of one's life—not likely a good time to get drowsy about one's career. Even more emphatically, when one is told that one now has the security and potential of a tenured academic position, one has about two-thirds of one's adult professional life ahead, with enormous potential still to be realized. In short, the best is yet to come, but the best will truly be one's "best" only if proper planning and execution are applied.

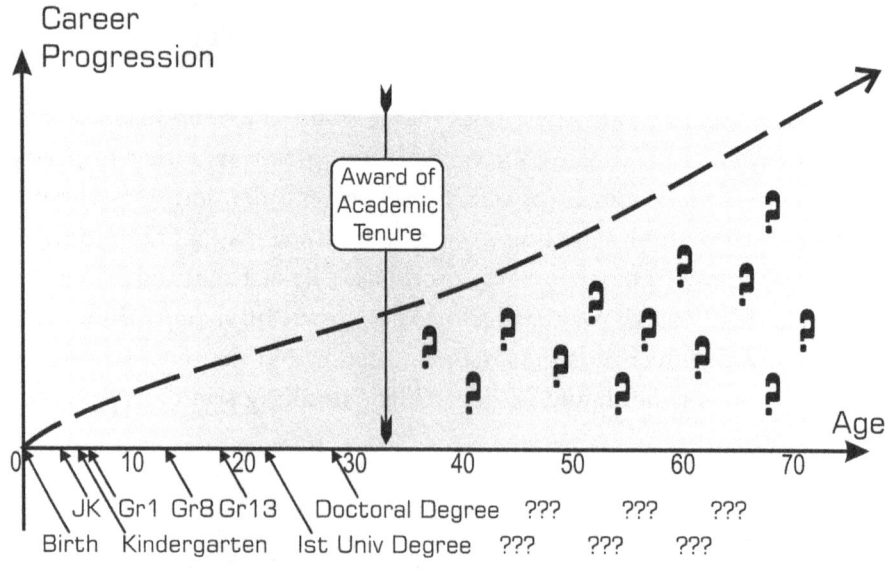

Figure 1.2: Tenure, Clearly Critical, Should be Seen as the Launch of One's Academic Career.

As Fig. 1.2 shows, a great deal has been accomplished by the time tenure arrives. Much more by far, at least academically, than that vast majority of the population. Combined with the high likelihood of job security until retirement, it is certainly understandable that the just-tenured professor can draw a breath of relief and say, in effect, "It is finished." Tenure is high praise indeed for one's accomplishments thus far, but perhaps sight should not be lost of the high price one has paid for this accolade.

Most readers will have known schoolmates, either pre-college or in college, who were thought to be Potentially Big Achievers, yet somehow these schoolmates staggered later under greater performance demands, or faded under the standards expected of higher academic institutions. Others, called Late Bloomers by most academics, seemed to have somewhat pedestrian prospects (at least as judged by their academic performance) and yet they persevered to enjoy admirable careers.[10]

The occurrence of Potentially Big Achievers and Late Bloomers, and indeed many other seemingly anomalous career trajectories, can be easily explained from the following simple principle:

> **The Most Important Principle**
> An academic career is a *journey*, not a *destination*.

This observation, often made about *life* in general, is not original with the authors. However, the stance we propose to take here on *academic careers* in particular is rarely expressed. In particular, tenure is not just an important milestone, it is a vital launching pad. This is because—if the reader will forgive still more swizzling of metaphors—all academics do not progress, post-tenure, through a long one-dimensional tube, from tenure to retirement, but can pursue a rich tapestry of career colors and alternatives. Examining this tapestry will be our enthusiastic occupation in this book.

It is perplexing that many of our academic colleagues seem not to be fully aware of the "journey" principle, especially as regards the conferral of tenure. Are they "there" yet? The clear answer is "No." Moreover, they will *never* be "there." The career journey of an academic is longer, and more complex, than even the most brilliant of young professors suspect. The purpose of this book is to provide a helpful travelogue for that journey.

1.4 Post-Tenure Career Advice in Short Supply

We shall show in the succeeding chapters that an inflexible view of professorial careers is highly inaccurate. There are an immense number of career variations on the academic career theme. One can and should design and pursue a career profile that is ideally suited to one's talents and tastes. This is a subject worthy of the best reflection by all professors, before, at,

---

[10] More likely is the explanation that, while they may have been somewhat average academically, they had many other critical skills that were not taught—or even much valued—in the academy.

and after tenure. This is how one can gain the highest reward for one's career investment. This is the search for the path of maximal happiness.

Academicians and professors have many of the talents and inclinations necessary for long-term planning. They certainly have *intelligence!* Even though that word implies a much broader scope to some than others, it would be difficult to find a group of individuals with more neurons per pound of body mass that a typical high-class university faculty. And they certainly have *focus!* Exhibit A? Nothing less can produce a successful doctoral thesis.

Anyone who wishes to produce the best results from their daily efforts, however, must have more than patience and a fine brain. They also need *information*; they need some *structure* or *theory* to the subject; and they need some model of trial and error. In other words, they need a *scientific approach*, wherein they can make judicious conclusions based on their observations of how well specific initiatives or actions on their part succeeded in stimulating a desired result.

Sources of Academic Career Information

The intelligence and the attention focus are givens. Yet the sources of information and opinion to which this intelligence and attention should be applied are far from ubiquitous. The importance of career issues is great, but the tools for dealing with these issues become fewer as one proceeds further along the academic path.

There are many sources for advice on pre-tenure issues. Choosing colleges; applying to universities; getting scholarships; evaluating curricula; being selected by the best research supervisors; writing effective dissertations; getting on the best university faculties (on probation, but tenure track); how to get research grants; how to teach courses appreciated by students. Generally, there are multiple resources for how to prepare for the award of tenure.

Once an aspiring academic has achieved tenure, however, job security is now assured (except for the sorts of high crimes and misdemeanors mentioned in §1.1) and the demand for career guidance has lessened substantially. Yet, we can make a much stronger statement on this subject: Professors who have attained tenure often seem not to be aware that there are serious career issues on which they need information and reflection. Thus

CHAPTER 1: TENURE (FINALLY!)

newly tenured professors suffer from both of lack of information and lack of demand for information (which is the cause and which the effect is not clear). The authors hope, through this book, to draw attention to this paucity of post-tenure career interest, and also to submit some ideas worthy of consideration by their just-tenured colleagues.

As Darley *et al.* [2004] have noted (p. xi):

> "[In the past], norms and guidelines for academic behavior were passed down from generation to generation, but these were generally discussed behind closed doors and not necessarily explicated in public."

True enough; surely some public explication is warranted.

To this we would add an important question: Can the apprentice trust the advice given? Inadvertently or otherwise, suboptimal advice is often given. For example, if the advisor is a committed and successful teacher, much of his guidance to the advisee may be slanted in that direction, even though the advisee should really be headed along a somewhat different road. Or, if the advisor is strong in research, he may, consciously or otherwise, understate the satisfactions and rewards that flow from teaching activity. Likewise with administration, and so on. In this book, we attempt to be unbiased and to shed fair light on the many career strategies that are available to the recently tenured.

Chapter 2: Professorial Species

Chief Inhabitants of the Academic Ecosystem

Chapter Overview

We begin this chapter by offering some comments on the *academic culture*. Since this way of life is unique, it bears reflection by young professors on why they should wish to spend their entire working life in this fashion.

To gain further insight, we shall next step back to the pre-professorial days of a sampling of those who eventually became successful academics and examine why these young people aspired to become professors. Just saying, "Well, they're clever, at least in school, and they like to read a lot," doesn't quite cover it. There are many clever young people who like to read, yet only a minority of these ever seriously consider an academic career. It is important for each young professor to explore this question honestly. While tenure is a critical milestone, there should be a logical relationship between pre- and post-tenure planning. The latter should be a smooth continuation of the former.

The next topic in this chapter is a brief overview of the post-secondary academic enterprise, with special emphasis on the wide range of roles that professors can play. There are cultural influences in academia that would pressure one into believing that all professors are in exactly the same game,[11] and that all must pass, from hiring to retirement, through some sort of big long one-dimensional tube—rather like the gut of the university. Yet, this is a dangerous myth. Although most professors undeniably share many attributes in common, there are, when examined in more detail,

---

11 For example, they are all called by the same job title: "professors"!

a great many distinct variations within the species, and countless permutations and combinations of academic roles. Understanding these patterns and options are key to making choices and developing plans for one's own career.

In order to give our discussion some structure and to keep the presentation within readable bounds, we next distill the many career possibilities down to four major, and relatively distinct, species of professor.: **Advanced Teachers, Eminent Scholars, Academic Executives, and Entrepreneurial Professors.** These will serve as career paradigms in the four subsequent chapters (Chapters 3 through 6). The recipe for most academic careers can be specified as some combination of these four "species."

2.1 Academic Culture

Describing the academic culture in all its manifestations would take a very large volume (or, more likely, a series of volumes) to explicate. The authors claim neither the training nor the wisdom of sociologists, and are thus not up to this hefty challenge. Fortunately, the thrust of this book is aimed in a somewhat different direction, namely, how to assist young, gifted proto-academics to realize their potential, both as to impact (as judged by others) and also as to personal satisfaction (as judged by themselves).

Still, to write a book inspecting something so fundamental as lifetime careers that transpire within a culture as intense as the academic kind without any recognition of the key influences of that culture, would not be of much use. So we pause for a few pages to portray the cultural framework for these careers.

What Is Culture?

Culture is an abstract concept and a brief definition is not easily come by. Opinions will also vary on the details of its meaning. In this book, the following[12] definition will suffice:

---

12 Used previously by one of the authors (PC Hughes, *Engineers Becoming Managers: From the Classroom to the Boardroom*, Xlibris, 2006). We recognize that other disciplines will differ in their definition of "culture."

CHAPTER 2: PROFESSORIAL SPECIES

> **Definition of "Culture"**
> The culture of a group is the set of all common traits, responses, values, beliefs, priorities, attitudes and behaviors.

In short, a group's culture is *what its members think about, how they think about it, and what these thoughts (and consequent actions) produce.* There will inevitably be some degree of variation among individuals in the group, but significant deviations by group members will lead to dissonances; if a putative member of a culture exhibits cultural traits that are not normative, such a member will be said to be "not really one of us, more like one of them."

A group's culture is plainly of the utmost importance to that group, but a culture's most interesting characteristic is that it is normally not passed on, from older group members to younger ones, by some public or even written declaration of principles, policies, or intentions, or other type of manifesto. It is transmitted instead by a thousand subtle messages, most being nonverbal. It is largely uncodified and intrinsic. One deviates from one's supposed culture at one's peril, although there may often be good reasons for doing so.

Intellectual Strength

By academic culture, we mean the culture of professors. (We include also those professors who move on to academic management but who still think of themselves as professors.) Other stakeholder groups in universities and colleges—students and support staff—also have their important cultures, but these are not focal points here.

The primary foundational element of academic culture is easily identified: virtually all professors have a quite unusual level of intellectual ability. One doesn't have to be able to walk, and one doesn't have to be able to talk, to function quite acceptably as a professor. Arguably the best-known professor in the world can do neither.[13]

---

13 We might ask, rhetorically: Who *is* "the best-known professor in the world"? We would argue that this distinction falls to Professor Stephen William Hawking, born on 8 January 1942 (exactly 300 years after the death of Galileo Galilei) and, since 1979, Lucasian Professor of Mathematics at Cambridge University (the chair given in 1669 to Isaac Newton).

This is certainly not to claim that there are not several other professions and groups in the world with impressive cerebral horsepower, only that university professors must surely be among the highest ranked assemblages in this regard. This brings us to IQ, the infamous *intelligence quotient*, developed originally for youngsters as an aid to predicting their academic performance.

Certainly, the potential of the human mind is far too complex to be captured by a single number. Psychometricians, who specialize in measuring many of the large number of distinguishable mental abilities, have devised tests that home in on, not only the best known abilities, such as verbal IQ, abstract IQ and quantitative IQ, but also more specialized versions, like mechanical IQ and spatial IQ. Woe to the professors of mathematics, mechanical engineering, and architecture, who do not have very high values of, respectively, quantitative IQ, mechanical IQ, and spatial IQ. In fact, it would be helpful if there were measurements of law IQ, medicine IQ, history IQ, and so on, to help younger students ascertain which field was most attuned to their natural aptitude. Still, all these measurements, while helpful if evidence-based, are only indicators, to be used as part of a complete dossier of relevant information in each particular case.

Even with this modest observation—that professors are (in the vernacular) extremely "smart"—we can make some important inferences. The first is that professors are smart enough to know that they are smart. Professors are justly proud of their mental abilities and accomplishments, just as athletes (for example) are proud of their physical attributes and achievements.

One must also observe that there are many other qualities, both mental and personal, that are important to one's quality of life, and that anyone as mentally talented as professors should have no trouble creating high-quality relationships with all university personnel with whom their positions require them to have contact. In particular, one must always be aware of the following advisory, which applies to any career, not just to the professorial variety:

> **Maxim:**
> It is one's **attitude**, not one's **aptitude**, that determines one's **altitude**.

This is never more true than when dealing with one's students.

CHAPTER 2: PROFESSORIAL SPECIES

Scholarly Activity (Deep, but Narrow)

The second primary characteristic of the academic culture is scholarly activity in one's chosen field—usually a very narrow area in the totality of human thought. Great depth in a highly specialized area is the norm, and many renowned professors know more than all but a handful of others in the world about their thin specialty. It is simply not possible to get that deep and also stay broad. This high degree of specialization can often lead to a narrowness of personal outlook generally, which means that not only do academics sometimes find it difficult to interact with many people generally (as discussed above), they also find that they have little in common with academics in other fields. Indeed, it is not unusual for professors to be uninterested in, and thus largely unaware of, the academic activities of some of their professorial colleagues *in their own department*.

Professors are well trained to read and think about issues in their specialties. Each has achieved[14] the highest earned academic degree in his or her field—the doctorate—and has had several years since to further develop knowledge and experience in that field. Teaching and writing about their specialties are activities professors are also expected to engage in, but here the preparation is much less and the aptitude much more variable. In particular, most professors have had essentially no training in teaching, other than their personal observations of the best (and worst) professors they themselves had as students.

Adding to cultural slenderness is the practice of hiring only freshly minted doctoral graduates or professors from other universities. Only rarely does one hear of a hire being made from outside the ivory tower. Those outside are considered to be "not as well suited," or "not as good a fit" as someone from inside—in other words, they come from a somewhat different professional culture. The pure academic species is continually bred using very strict rules.

As a final comment on the phenomenon of having to focus on a highly constricted scholarly area in order to make further progress at its worldwide leading edge, we would note that professors usually spend any professional time they have away from the university again with other professors in

---

14 A generation or two ago, there were professors—including very successful ones—without doctorates, but this would be unusual today. (Bill Buxton will provide us with a study case on this issue a little later in this chapter.)

their own narrow field. If they go to a seminar; if they attend a conference; if they take a sabbatical: all are likely to be further experiences with other like-minded academics. This does improve their understanding of the research problems they're working on and it does have the virtues of cross-fertilization and networking, but alas it also intensifies their insularity.

Other Views

Many others have also offered commentaries on academic careers and culture, most of these being from insiders. For example, Blaxter *et al.* [1998] devote their Chapter 2 to these topics. They write from a U.K. perspective, but the tenor is familiar to North Americans as well. They have several strong criticisms of the present academic culture, which they leaven through the use of humor.[15] Humor adds interest also to Eulau's [1998] descriptions of academic culture, as applied to a political science department.

Darley *et al.* [2004] have a chapter on "Power, Politics, and Survival in Academia," and another on "Managing the Department Chair and Navigating the Department Structure." These headings alone suggest that conducting an academic career can be viewed as a blood sport.

Many of the commentaries emphasize that although academic culture evolved hardly at all for many decades, the current rate of change is relatively dramatic. Bender and Schorske [1998] provide an excellent discussion of this aspect, particularly in the social sciences and humanities, although most in other disciplines would say that they, too, are experiencing rapid change. The entropy associated with bureaucratization continues ever to increase, often in response to external societal changes and concerns. The academy is, every day, less and less independent of the external culture in which it is situated. To be a successful academic nowadays—as with most other interesting careers—requires adaptability to change, or even (as some say) being able to "thrive on chaos."

Miscellaneous Abuses To Be Avoided

There are several uses of the word "academic" that are derogatory (and are intended to be so by the users). The authors' use of this word is largely

---

15 See, for example, their "Myths in Academia" (Box 2.4).

CHAPTER 2: PROFESSORIAL SPECIES

confined to the definition given in the accompanying box. It is felt that this definition is reasonably accurate and complete, and that it will inspire the reader to be enthusiastic about an academic career.

> **Definition of "Academic"**
> Concerned with **learning** and with the **transmission** of this learning to others, through **teaching**, writing, oral presentations, and other media. Academic learning includes gaining familiarity with what is already known, or claimed to be known, but also emphasizes the discovery of **knowledge** that is **new** to the world. This latter learning—a form of **research**—requires, among many other qualities, a thorough understanding of the **fundamentals** of the subject.

There are, however, other usages and nuances of "academic" that are far from flattering. As in "He seems to live in an ivory tower," meaning "He is out of touch with the world at large." Since "insane" or "psychotic" can be defined as being out of touch with reality, this use of "academic" is a clear derogation. A similar usage is exemplified by "She is fascinated by her work but she can't explain what it has to do with anything," meaning that no practical purpose for her scholarly activities can be discerned—even by her! In brief, sometimes "academic" is used as a simple synonym for "irrelevant, impractical." Useless. Similar commentary on what others may do in their private life is more light-hearted, rather as Person A might remark on the philately hobby of Person B. But when this flavor of comment is targeted on academics—persons relatively well paid and who should deserve respect for their professional effort—something has apparently gone wrong.

Over the long term (which for universities means at least one or two generations), the only way to avoid these disparagements is for academics to avoid behaviors and statements that reasonably prompt them. Here we most emphatically do not refer to the normal differences of opinion that arise as well-equipped intellects grapple with the best way forward. As Robert Hutchins (formerly Chancellor of the University of Chicago) observed, "Education is a kind of continuing dialogue, and a dialogue assumes different points of view."

This brings us to the concept of *academic freedom*, another issue that can become vexed. Subject to specific rules of conduct defined by the university's academic governing council, professors often take it as a holy grail that they should not *ever* be interfered with, in either their teaching or their research, by their "administrations," including the Heads or Chairs of their own departments. Just to be very clear, some professors take this protection to be *absolute*. In support of this view, many iconic cases can surely be cited[16] where one would inescapably conclude that, had the protection of academic freedom been absent, major breakthroughs in human knowledge would have been stifled. One can thus readily conclude that academic freedom, defined *somehow*, is of great benefit to society and to humankind.

The only remaining question is this: Should this freedom be absolute? Should society entrust a group of individuals—namely, academics—with the absolute right to say whatever they like, any time they like? The best answer is probably "A very strong right, but not an absolute right." One does not have to be overly creative to cite situations where it is not the barbarians at the university's gate that are dangerous, but the Trojan-horse barbarians inside.

How does one decide which it is? Here we would recommend a methodology that is of relatively recent vintage in the long sweep of human history but that has shown itself to be as objective and truth-seeking as any human process can be: the Scientific Method. In the case of claimed academic malfeasance, and where the misbehavior is judged to have serious effects,[17] a group of external academics could easily be convened, respected and from diverse perspectives in the subject field, to examine the case. In effect, the principle of peer review would be applied, just as it is to research

---

16 Many of the epochal research discoveries mentioned later (Chapter 4) would have been vigorously suppressed were it not for the protective cover of academic freedom. (Note also, however, that not all these discoveries were made by professors in academia.)

17 Sometimes the professor's alleged misbehavior does not involve his or her research papers, but his or her classroom statements or conduct. Here, the treatment should depend on the Teaching Level, as discussed in §3.3. At the youngest extreme, freshmen students should be treated to an exciting and efficient climb up the learning curve in their chosen fields of interest, and do not deserve to become embroiled in the idiosyncrasies (not to say scholastic perversities) of their particular professors. At the more mature extreme, graduate students (who are themselves embryonic professors) may as well get involved in the fray. Only if their research dissertations are also affected should more drastic action be taken. In any case, the normal process of course assignment by departmental chairs should help with this "teaching" version of the problem.

CHAPTER 2: PROFESSORIAL SPECIES

papers, departmental reviews, and other similar situations. This is, to paraphrase Churchill, the worst approach—except for all the others. It is precisely the process (argument from mutual rationality) and corrective action shown to be best by the Scientific Method.

Perhaps the following remarks[18] by Carl Pfluger (German painter) are worthy of reflection, as applied to self-styled but offside intellectuals, whether they operate outside or from within academia:

> Cranks, in defending their mental constructs (and here, curiously, may be their closest approach to psycho-pathology and to serious scholarship), can be formidable logicians, if not exactly sound reasoners. Most cranks, in fact, see themselves as free-lance scientists, scholars, or investigators of mechanical problems, assassination conspiracies, the origins of poetry, the destiny of the universe, the meaning of life, the nature of crankery, the fate of man, or the will of a god. They share with more orthodox scholars both a professional curiosity and a possessive attitude toward whatever domain of knowledge they have chosen to make their province. They differ from them most critically in the soundness of their critical faculties.

Note the emphasis on *reason* as the discriminant characteristic of the more reliable positions.

A similar conflict can arise at a higher institutional level. Just as individual professors should be given wide-ranging freedom to pursue their academic inquiries, so too should universities[19] be given a high degree of autonomy in their advanced teaching and research activities. This is their public[20] trust. However, as with all public trusts, this trust cannot be constantly abused without consequence.

Donald Kennedy [1997], Bing Professor of Environmental Science at Harvard University (and President Emeritus of Stanford University), in his book *Academic Duty*, argues forcefully and eloquently that academic protection also implies academic duty:

---

18 "On Cranks," *Harper's* (Nov 1991).
19 According to the definition of *university* that we are using. See §1.1.
20 For private universities, the details are somewhat different, but the principle still applies.

The phrase "academic freedom" is heard so often around colleges and universities that it has come to resemble a mantra. Though the term has only been in use since the earl twentieth century, it seems as if it has always been with us. As easily understood as it is important, academic freedom refers to the insulation of professors and their institutions from political interference.

At various points in the twentieth century, that kind of protection has proved essential . . . . In practice, such freedom extends further, permitting unusually creative people to lead unusually creative lives . . . .

Academic freedom has a counterpart, academic duty, that is much more seldom used. John Gardner put it well when he said, of the symmetry between individual freedom and communitarian obligation, "Liberty and duty, freedom and responsibility: that's the deal."

Kennedy goes on in his book to explain how this duty manifests itself in teaching, mentoring, researching, publishing, and serving the university.

2.2 Why Choose an Academic Career?

Universities typically expose undergraduates to the vastness of human thought and experience. At one time, a liberal arts education was considered to be an essential foundation for a functioning democracy, encompassing such critical fields as history, economics, philosophy, political science, languages, psychology, music, sociology, fine arts, drama and theatre. These areas of human endeavor were generally considered to be of a 'higher order,' separating high-achieving humanity from the rest of the animal world. More recently (the last two centuries) students learning the 'professional' fields—law, medicine, engineering, for example—are similarly presented with the opportunity to study collective human knowledge in fields that provide a sense of connectedness and community with the larger world. And, as we have seen earlier, there are also the sciences—learning about nature's laws—that affect everyone in myriad ways: from the familiar physics, chemistry and biology, to archaeology, paleontology and geology.

CHAPTER 2: PROFESSORIAL SPECIES

Sometimes, professors have an opportunity to develop (and students at the graduate level students have the opportunity to study) a *cross-disciplinary* or *interdisciplinary* curriculum. For example, epidemiology combines elements of history with elements of medical science. In any case, having dramatically expanded their perspective and their world view, many undergraduates unsurprisingly become enthusiastic about some aspect of their studies, and contemplate going on to graduate school. Whether this enthusiasm is sufficient to lead to a career in academe must be subject to further scrutiny.

The canonical reason for choosing an academic career is that one is strongly interested in a cerebrally challenging subject, and one also possesses the intellect to meet that challenge with a high likelihood of success. By the end of one's undergraduate program, one can normally judge for oneself whether these two requirements are met. If they are, an academic career becomes a possibility.

A Process for Career Selection

For the most successful professors, to say that they are "strongly interested" in their field doesn't cover it. They are, in fact, "passionate," a word they often use themselves. For example, Dr Michael Collins says this:

"The essence of being a good academic is doing something you really love. You find a passion; I think that's the essence of both good research and good teaching. You find something that you obsess about and you're an enthusiast about. We'd like to make a difference in life. You get a sense of accomplishment by knowing 'I've done this; I'm leaving this; this is my legacy'"

This recipe, of course, is not restricted to academics. Finding something that (a) one loves, and that (b) one is very good at, is the long-standing formula for success. By "loves," we mean enough that two thousand hours (minimum) can be spent at it quite contentedly every year for forty years. Each potential career is a point in the "four box" shown in Fig. 2.1. The southwest box contains careers that can quickly be dispensed with. In the southeast box are careers that may lead to a good living[21] economically,

---

21 People tend to be paid for how well they do what they do, not for how much they enjoy it.

and that might garner approval from one's co-workers, but that will wear one down in the longer term.

By contrast, the northwest region comprises careers that are less well-paying but that lead to a contented lifestyle nonetheless. (One thinks perhaps of many of those in the fine arts here.) Finally, one finds one's best-suited careers in the northeast box; these offer the best chances of both happiness and success. If one can't think of any careers that can honestly be put in this northeast box—and given that it is extremely difficult to change one's natural inclinations—one must either get further training and experience to migrate to such careers, or face a degree of failure and economic frailty.

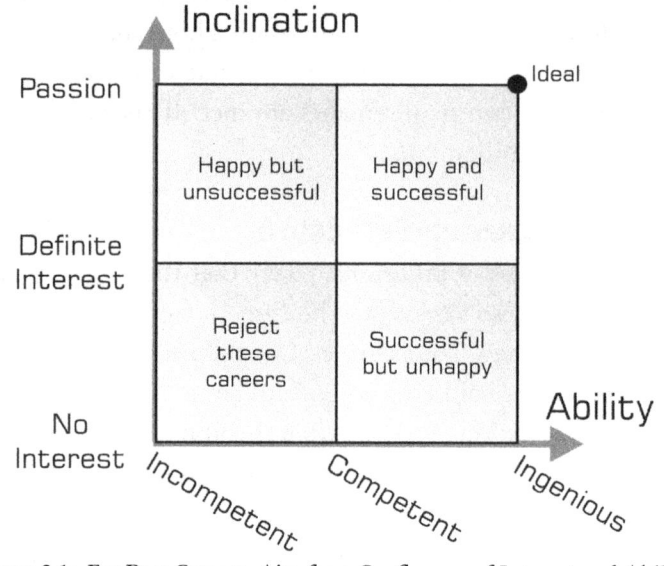

Figure 2.1: For Best Careers, Aim for a Confluence of Interest and Ability.

Most readers of this book will presumably be young professors, near or just past the tenure point, and they will thus have already chosen an academic career. So that bridge has been crossed, though not irreversibly, because many young professors can also find excellent positions in the private or nonacademic public sector. (This tends to be more the case in the departments connected to the professions than in those tied to, say, the arts.) However, the case is made in this book that all professors need not be cut from the same cloth; some may emphasize certain kinds of contributions more than others. (See next section, §2.3, on the "basic types of professor.") Many decisions, even after tenure, are yet to be made, and these can benefit from the process suggested by Fig. 2.1 just as much as the decisions made by undergraduate or graduate students.

Some may deride the process implied by Fig. 2.1; certainly most spend very little time engaged in that process. And Goethe (genius German poet) famously said, "How can one learn to know oneself? Never by introspection, rather by action. Try to do your duty, and you will know right away what you are like." There is much truth to this view, and in fact we generally endorse it. However, our special readers, just-post-tenure academics, have completed about 25 years of formal education; have spent another half-decade working hard toward tenure by performing teaching and research duties; have likely had some administrative involvement (and possibly other activities as well). Time, surely, to pause in the continual and frenzied "action" recommended by Goethe. Time for a little introspection!

Reflections from Successful Professors

The views of successful academics can also be plumbed for further wisdom. Most, if asked why they chose to become academics, would answer as succinctly as Dr Donald Mackay:

> "I decided that doing research was enjoyable and that the university was where I would go."

This would seem almost a non-answer were it not for the fact that, for many professors, likely a large majority, that's all there is. In the framework of Fig. 2.1, they were in love with one or more academic subjects and they were getting sky-high marks in those (and probably some other) subjects. No process really required. Just keep doing it. In Don's case, after establishing himself as an excellent researcher, he later became Director of an important environmental research center. But this latter appointment did not come as the result of strategic career planning; it was just a natural outgrowth of his stature as a researcher.

For others, the path is less direct, usually a sign of great versatility. Dr Molly Shoichet's trajectory included an exciting interlude in an entrepreneurial business, which makes her story somewhat more detailed:

> "I've taken a non-traditional path. Honestly, I had a great job in industry. I was working in a biotech company and we

were doing cell therapy. Very high-tech, on-the-edge research. It was really exciting stuff. But when I looked at what was going on at the [university], I was really excited about what was going on there also, because I grew up here. I wanted to come back here.

"But I've been involved in a couple of spin-off companies, so part of my motivation is to grow bio-tech [closer to home]. That's really my motivation for trying to spin off technology. There's nothing more satisfying, I think, than to have worked on something . . . and for it to be translated into a product, either through a spin-off or through licensing. That's incredible."

Molly exhibits not only the excitement associated with academic research; she also clearly demonstrates an avocation for *entrepreneurial behavior*—an academic preference that has not previously been adequately portrayed in the hardcover literature on academic careers. (We shall attempt to remedy this omission in Chapter 6.)

Dr Barry French is another example of how some academic researchers (and entrepreneurs) feel about the utility of their findings:

"I was misguided by a high school teacher. My marks in mathematics were only average, but I liked chemistry and physics. He said, 'Well, if your mathematics is only average, take engineering, don't go into arts and science.' So I took chemical engineering.

[Eventually] I home-built a gas chromatograph from glass tubes and charcoal and it worked. Next I went to England to study gas dynamics further. [A senior colleague] then suggested graduate work. That was fun—plasmas expanding into rarefied gases. . . . The first time I seriously thought about being an academic was when [my graduate department head] offered me a chance to join the staff. I literally had never considered it before."

Apparently, one does not have to have a precise long-term plan in order to end up in the right place. Barry went on to found Sciex[22] Ltd., bringing

---

22 Sciex has since been acquired by a larger company; now a division, it has continued to grow and flourish.

CHAPTER 2: PROFESSORIAL SPECIES

to market trace-gas analyzing instrumentation that got its academic start on the Viking mission to Mars. However, as Barry's detailed interview also makes plain, there can be some unnecessary twists and turns if a strategic vision has not been put in place.

Wm (Bill) Buxton went on an even more extensive journey before finding the right combination of academic elements for his career. Eventually, he successfully straddled the continental divide between arts and technology:

> "I was working in Holland, doing concerts, making my living teaching and playing/composing music. I came back to Canada as an artist in residence. In the art history library I saw a catalogue for what was in fact the world's first curated show here of computer graphics—computer-generated art. One of the exhibitors was doing something graphically that was very similar to what I had been thinking about musically, compositionally."

Bill went on to take further training,[23] this time as a graduate computer scientist, eventually developing a computer-based tool for music composition, which was well received by other musicians.

Our next case study involves Dr Tom Brzustowski, who has mastered two of the three "solitudes" (academia and government) and thoroughly understands the third (the private sector). It would be difficult to find anyone in Canada who was involved in science and engineering at a senior level who was not familiar with Tom.[24] Yet, he says that he never foresaw (much

---

23 Bill never did pursue a PhD. What was the point? He was already highly proficient, both as a musician and as a computer graphics developer. He was already active in teaching and research, and was helping to bring his new devices to market. He preferred the cross-disciplinary nature of his work to the narrowness of a PhD. Unfortunately, because his culture did not fit perfectly the narrow mould expected by a university, he was not treated well, and was denied tenure-track status. Despite this, he was able to find an alternative path, balancing corporate research (Xerox PARC, SGI, Microsoft Research), academic involvement (supervising or co-supervising 10 PhD and 19 MSc theses), and his diverse creative interests. Cumulatively, despite having left formal academic life, he is the third most cited research in his field (Human-Computer Interaction), has received 3 honorary doctorates, and has status at a number of universities in the world. The lesson here is that there are other paths to success for determined researchers.

24 For details, see Appendix.

37

less planned) the exemplary career he must realistically admit that he has had:

> "In my case, opportunities arose. I have gone so far beyond any hopes or dreams that I ever had for myself and in such different directions that the (planning) question becomes irrelevant. My father was an engineer; I wanted to be a good engineer. Interested in aircraft, I got a job with Orenda after [Bachelor's graduation]. I then went to Princeton to get a Master's degree and while there, the Arrow [a fighter aircraft program] was chopped, so I stayed for a PhD. Clearly, that was not thought out in advance.
>
> "[Thanks to a great mentor,] I joined the faculty at the University of Waterloo—then a very new university, a very small place whose future was not at all certain. It was on the verge of receiving full approval from the province for development of a faculty of engineering with guaranteed funding. I was faced with an empty space that was supposed to be a research lab, with no resources to create it. That focuses one's ambitions. I became Chairman of mechanical engineering five years after I arrived as a wet-behind-the-ears junior faculty member.
>
> "I took only one term, because I needed to get away. I needed to go on sabbatical. But the sabbatical I chose was not to go to a university, to sit in somebody else's lab and do some research. Instead, I went into industry in the USA as a Ford Foundation Resident in engineering practice."

Tom eventually became Vice-President (Academic) at Waterloo, then Deputy Minister[25] (Colleges and Universities) for Ontario, then President of the Natural Sciences and Engineering Research Council (responsible for all academic grants to scientists and engineers in Canada). Tom has now "retired" to two university posts: he is the Royal Bank of Canada Professor in the Commercialization of Innovation at the University of Ottawa's Telfer School of Management, and he is Senior Advisor to the Institute for Quantum Computing at the University of Waterloo. All in all, not a bad career for one that, he says, was "unplanned." (More on this paradox below.)

---

25   Undersecretary, in U.S. terminology.

CHAPTER 2: PROFESSORIAL SPECIES

Last, but certainly not least, let's enjoy the reflections of three university presidents. The first is Dr David Naylor, currently President of the University of Toronto. His comments on his early plans:

"I had a longstanding interest in research, and by the middle of medical school had already decided that I would pursue an academic career. By late 1978, I had formulated some ideas about a career path, and followed through on these as a graduate student at Oxford and thereafter during clinical residency and post-residency Fellowship training. Before the end of my residency at the University of Western Ontario, I concluded that my eventual interest was likely to be in some form of academic administration. However, I certainly did not have any pre-specified timeline or endpoint. My first goal was to find a rewarding and engaging line of research that could be coupled to a part-time clinical career."

Here, one can clearly discern some careful *career planning*—not the whole career at one shot, of course, but always looking at least two steps ahead. David solved the "problem" of doctoral-level narrowness by achieving not only a MD (Toronto) but also a DPhil (Oxford), by serving on national and international boards and committees, and by working closely with hospitals and other universities.[26] With a rocket-powered career like this, being Dean of Medicine was not a destination, merely an important stop on the way.

Our second President—although at McGill University they call her "Principal and Vice-Chancellor"—is Dr Heather Monroe-Blum. She recollects this:

"It was happenstance that I developed an academic career because I initially began as a psychiatric social worker at McMaster University. But I was very interested in whether the treatments we were engaging had a positive effect. And I had a mentor who saw academic potential in me and who nominated me for a faculty appointment in the faculty of health sciences and wrote a letter about my intellectual strengths and academic

---

26   These brief comments do not do justice to Dr Naylor's resume, and the Appendix must be consulted for the full details.

promise. He had a trajectory for me that didn't immediately resonate for me (go into medicine) but the notion that I could study more and actually do research sounded very good."

Taken at face value, this is a startling statement. Heather says it was "happenstance" that she had an academic career at all, much less a Vice Presidency at one of Canada's leading universities, and then the Presidency of another, all at a relatively early age. Does this mean that career planning—and this book—are worthless? That where one goes is a mere roll of the dice? Well, not quite, in the authors' opinion. We shall conclude these interview excerpts shortly with some commentary on this paradox.

Finally some reminiscences from our third President in this section, Dr Peter Likins. Actually, Peter could be called our third and fourth presidents because he was for 15 years President of Lehigh University before his current[27] position as President of The University of Arizona. His comments are, like many of those above, simply stated but complex in their interpretation:

"I didn't start out with any grand plans. In fact, my background expectations educationally were quite modest. In the sixth grade, I read an inspiring book about the engineer who finished the Panama Canal, but I didn't really know what education was required to realize this ambition.

"I began my professional life as a development engineer at the Jet Propulsion Laboratory of the California Institute of Technology, involved in the very early years of spacecraft development. (Graduating with a Master's degree from MIT at about the same time as Sputnik I made this a very exciting time!) My advisor at MIT had urged me to consider a faculty career, although that had not been an earlier plan in my life."

Sounds like no planning is no loss. Well, not quite. We shall return to this issue before closing this chapter.

---

27   Since this interview took place (03Apr2006), Dr Peter Likins retired as President Emeritus from the University of Arizona Presidency in Jul2006, after nine years of service. This capped a career devoted to learning, teaching, research, entrepreneurship, acting as the world's foremost consultant in his field, and eventually to academic administration and leadership at several top universities.

CHAPTER 2: PROFESSORIAL SPECIES

Factors that Underlie Career Planning

What can we learn from the comments above from highly successful academics? No two cases are the same—and one suspects that, had another dozen successful interviews been logged, each new case would still have significant differences from all the others. Does this mean that it's all a crapshoot? In particular, does this mean that academic career planning is at best a waste of time and at worst meaningless? The authors would claim not. Let's look again at the evidence and try to discern some patterns in the diversity.

1. **Natural Ability.** Everyone who does this well in careers this demanding has to be, as an absolute minimum, not just *bright*; they have to be *scintillating*. Whether this is nature (genetics) or nurture (upbringing and other early influences)—or a combination thereof (the truth)—may be an interesting question but is not the subject here because, for the target ages under discussion, both nature and nurture are complete and neither is controllable or fixable. This means that one must look forward and make the best of one's natural ability.

2. **Hard Work.** Everyone quoted above regarded their "work" as a passion, perhaps almost an obsession. This is a largely controllable factor and one can decide how much personal effort and sacrifice one wishes to expend to achieve career goals. Thus, though some will not work as hard as others, the former must realize that, among those "others" there will be some who have the identical natural ability. If one is talented and works hard, one will always do better than someone who just works as hard; and if one is talented and works hard, one will always do better than someone who is just as talented. These self-evident constraints should always guide one's career expectations.

3. **Mentoring.** Several interview excerpts above made mention of one or more key persons who had a definitive influence on one's career, often through something as minor as a brief conversation. This is akin to nurturing; but at this late stage of one's basic development (though at an early stage of one's career development), it is called mentoring.[28]

---

28 This is plainly a push-pull situation. As academics, we all have a multitude of opportunities (if we are alert to identifying them) to make a major impact on a

4. **Broadening One's Skill-Set.** The academic learning process always tends toward greater and greater depth, with a concomitant sacrifice in bettering one's breath.[29] This is another personal policy decision, one that can have a huge impact on one's career. It is possible to have an exceptional career as an academic while staying very narrow—assuming, of course, that in one's narrow research field one eventually reaches at least national (possibly international) stature. That is a perfectly rational decision—but it must be a *decision*, not just a state of being into which one drifts. The rest of this book could be described as a tour of how your career could in principle be broadened.

5. **Choosing a Life Style.** Current demographic data indicate that "academic families" tend to have fewer children, with reduced incentives or opportunities for mobility. Since academic careers start later in life than do most other occupations, when to have children becomes a serious concern. Most faculties have rules for "stopping the clock" for maternity and paternity leaves which can adversely affect career progression.

All these factors become part of one's career planning. You have the brain you have. You have the childhood and adolescent background you have. Now it's up to you to plan what's next—that is, to make career policy choices, some of which are complex. We have mentioned just above three basic policy decisions that all contribute toward career planning:

(*a*) How hard do I intend to work? This is about work-life balance, a very personal decision, but also about time-management, which can provide more time for both "work" and "life," by making more efficient use of one's available time. For example, many faculty find it difficult to balance both professional and personal

---

young person's life through such mentoring. Exercise for the reader: The next time a student comes to your office and asks advice on some hyper-minute point about the course he or she is taking from you, take advantage of the opportunity to ask, "I'm glad you dropped by. What are your career plans and how are they going so far?" That conversation might be recalled by a university president thirty years later. It is unlikely that your answer to the "hyper-minute point" in your course will be.

29 Here is the primary symptom of terminal narrowness: The patient doesn't know what breadth vs. depth *means* in an academic setting and has never thought about it.

obligations, such as raising a family. Potential conflicts can also arise in a two-career family. Whether to have children prior to or after tenure is also a major career issue for women in terms of delayed tenure and research interruption. The fact that in the USA and Canada, women constitute 41% and 32% respectively of the national faculties obliges universities and colleges to provide a supportive environment to retain this growing segment of the faculty population.

(b) Can I get good advice nearby? Seek mentors. Without a proactive policy, most of these opportunities will go unnoticed much less exploited. An older professor. A trusted school chum. One's life partner. One's old boss. Finding someone who has advice to give is easy, and finding someone who has *good* advice to give is not all that difficult. The trick is to find someone who can give good advice and who also knows *you*—well.

(c) How do I handle the depth vs. breadth issue? Some careers, like leading-edge research, seem to demand great depth to really make an impact. Others, like entrepreneurship and academic leadership, seem to require much more breadth than can be learned in school (at any level). Again, this is a personal decision, but better a *decision* than listlessly sleepwalking.

The Role of Competitiveness

There is another vital personality trait of which one must be aware. Though often maligned, in the real world one's degree of competitiveness can make the difference between winning and losing. Let us recount more of the interview with Dr Likins:

[Likins]: "I don't think I thought in terms of a 'career' as I think you are using that term, and I don't feel quite comfortable with it. As a professor at UCLA, I concentrated on good teaching, high-quality research, and an active consulting activity with both American and European aerospace companies and government agencies. To me, my teaching, my research, and my consulting projects were all mutually supportive. Each of the three supported and was fed by the other two.

[Author]: By this time, were you developing a career strategy? By now were you thinking about your long-term future?

[Likins]: No, not really. My fixation was not with a pre-planned series of "career moves." Instead, I would say that my obsession was really a "competitive" one.

[Author]: Meaning . . .?

[Likins]: I just wanted to do the best darned job I possibly could—whatever my job was; you know, teaching, research, consulting, and some administration—and I wanted to do it better than anybody else doing similar things.

[Author]: I see your "Likins" college wrestling trophy up on the wall there, with many of your other awards and achievements. Would you say that the same personal qualities that made you a champion wrestler were similar to those that made you excel at academic pursuits?

[Likins]: Yes, there are many similarities.

Likins correctly stands aside from the "movie making" interpretation of career planning. Then he goes on to make several key related points. In the formative stages of his post-tenure career, he says, he did not choose any one of teaching, research, consulting, or administration, at the expense of all the others. Instead, he managed to develop all in unison, and to accomplish this difficult feat he found ways to create a mutually beneficial relationship among and between them all. (Where else would all the needed time come from?)

The pre-existing requirements of great natural ability and sustained hard work need scarcely be mentioned for careers like this. Thus, one begins to form general *strategic goals* quite early on, while the gradual achievement of these goals requires many mini-decisions every week for many years, as new information and opportunities present themselves (closed-loop feedback). A similar pattern can be discerned in the reminiscences of both Dr Naylor and Dr Monroe-Blum.

Finally, Dr Likins mentions the aspect of competitiveness. This may not, by some, be thought something one should openly discuss, but why not? The finest competitions in the world are openly called competitions.

There is, of course, no hint here of shady behavior, or of "winning at all costs," or of "trampling one's colleagues" on the way up to winning. Indeed, only the solitary researcher can sometimes do well without benefit of an attractive personality. No one can win teaching awards without having (in the view of one's students, at least) an apparent charisma; no one can ascend the ladder of academic leadership without the skills needed to cope with coteries of demanding, egocentric professors; and no one can successfully create a new business without having a wide-ranging appeal to a broad assortment of professional stakeholders.

Like hard work, competitiveness is a personal characteristic that one can decide how much to employ as one develops one's career. In fact, these two share much in common. Competitiveness relies more on working smart and less on working hard. In the following four chapters, we will see the true range of academic career goals and how to achieve these goals.

All the above points, with occasional minor modifications, are valid for *any* career, academic or otherwise, and all should be treated with Fig. 2.1 in mind—the balance between ability and inclination. Now we turn to career decisions, stances and objectives that are targeted specifically on academic careers.

2.3 Approaches to Career Planning

After tenure, the situation is changed markedly. As explained in Chapter 1, the probationary period is over, and one has the right—indeed, one has *earned* the right—to make, within the wide bounds of academic variation, whatever contribution one wishes. What *are* these bounds? There is no one-sentence answer. Indeed, the rest of this book is about just this answer. One thing is for certain, however: The permissible bounds of "academic variation," while rather tight *before* tenure, are much less so *after* tenure. They are not so constricting that every professor must contribute in an identical way. In truth, if professors are creative, intelligent people, perhaps the first thing they should be creative and intelligent about is their long-term evolving role, both within their own institution and in society at large.

One Possible Career Plan: Keep On Keeping On

Some may say that career planning in an academic setting is really a contradiction in terms. After all (they may say), having found one's true love, what further introspection is necessary? It must be admitted that for many academics, there is some truth to this position, and perhaps nothing in this book triggers even a moment's interest. On the other hand, how can *any* group say that, for them, there are no questions of career interest over, say, four decades?

Even if they are at the forefront of teaching and research, could it be that all these energetic, high-powered minds are now and always satisfied with their current academic style because they are continually renewed and refreshed by the ever-changing challenges out on the creative fringes of their chosen (narrow) fields of interest? Perhaps so, for many. Perhaps not, for others.

With the "Keep On Keeping On" non-plan, one's professorial *functions* (usually, teaching and research) are constant. Some people, by contrast, do like an eventual change of scene.[30] Blaxter *et al.* [1998] have expressed it in this manner:

> "Remaining in the same position and doing much the same job for the whole of one's career can be stultifying and unchallenging."

Besides, the "We're all right, Jack" mentality does smell somewhat of the "Long One-Dimensional Tube" approach mentioned in the Overview at this Chapter's outset. This model may be appropriate for underground waste water systems, but it is not the best for a cohort of highly trained young potential leaders. Universities and colleges have many modalities for societal contribution and the idea that all their best people must make their contributions in exactly the same way, and in precisely the same proportions, seems somewhat silly.

---

30 As is said of the *Iditarod*, that sparkling race in the far north—from Anchorage, in south central Alaska, to Nome on the western Bering Sea coast—where each team of 12 to 16 Husky dogs and their musher cover over 1,150 miles in about two weeks, "only the lead dog gets a change of scene." Sarah Palin has recently widened considerably the range of awareness of this type of High North competition.

CHAPTER 2: PROFESSORIAL SPECIES

Boy Scout Planning

Next, we examine another misunderstanding that may arise about academic career planning. Here's a candidate plan: teach until Year 5; do research until Year 10; move to the west coast and become a Dean at Year 15; then find a university presidency on the east coast at Year 20. Perhaps this plan is more impressive than the "Keeping On Keeping On" plan or the "Big Long Tube" plan, but unless changed many, many times, this so-called "plan" is pretty much useless. For one thing, no experienced person will believe any *detailed* plan—that is, a plan with numbers—that extends beyond five (or perhaps ten) years. More important, this is an *open-loop* plan,[31] meaning that the planner will continually attempt to implement it regardless of any new relevant information that is encountered in the meantime.

If planning is still recommended, how do we explain those professors who have had very successful careers, but who say (in effect) that they had no plans? In fact, they sound, at least superficially, like their whole progression of career moves and improvements were some sort of sequential stochastic process. Not likely. For one thing, people who are (truly) highly successful always come across as being modest, because they *are* modest. This is not only an artifact of their superior people skills—tooting one's own horn is rarely thought desirable—they have met so many highly gifted people that after a while they have realized that, even in the largest fishponds, there are a lot of big fish. For a second thing, many have career plans that are, while not written down, nevertheless guiding their life. When the only person involved is oneself, one doesn't have to be as formal.

Look again at the remarks earlier by Dr Brzustowski. He says, point-blank, "In my case, opportunities arose. I have gone so far beyond any hopes or dreams that I ever had for myself and in such different directions that the (planning) question becomes irrelevant." One must agree, if by "planning" one means a detailed career trajectory, worked out years earlier, methodically and unerringly executed. But consider a different interpretation of

---

31 The terms *open-loop control* and *closed-loop control* are from Control Systems 101. The former implies that the plan will continue to be executed blindly, regardless of any new, relevant information available *en route*, while the latter implies that new information will be exploited in the continual decision-making process.

"planning," one that can perhaps be traced to a concept that it is taught with ease to those as young as Boy Scouts:

> **Academic Career Planning Maxim**
> *Version 1: (Boy Scout Version)*
> **Be Prepared.**

This is definitely not a passive approach; it is an active one. It goes well beyond the "Keeping On Keeping On," the "Big Long Tube," and the "Just Lurching Along" schools of academic career non-planning. It is clearly in the *closed-loop* category (responsiveness to new information), since it is precisely on the basis of this new information that one promises to be prepared to adapt one's actions and plans!

There is a second version of this same maxim, very similar to the Boy Scout version, but somewhat more prescriptive:

> **Academic Career Planning Maxim:**
> *Version 2: (Luck is Rarely Luck)*
> **"Good Luck" Happens When Preparation Meets Opportunity**

This latter form of the maxim, rather like the chess maxim[32] that one should "accumulate a series of small positional advantages until one has achieved a position strong enough to launch a winning combination" is true, but hard to apply, unless one has some ancillary guidance. How does one know that one has achieved a "small positional advantage"? Even more, how does one go about achieving such an advantage? Finally, having somehow achieved all these small positional advantages, and having recognized that the "winning combination" can now be "launched," how does one find, launch and execute this winning combination?

Or, in the case of academic career planning, how does one prepare? And how does one recognize—or even encourage—such opportunities? Answers like these will flow from the discussion in the next several chapters, but for now we emphasize that planning is not like making a movie about one's future career. It is more like building and tending a garden; choosing those blossoms that one wishes to see flourish; encouraging and working

---

32 This chess maxim has been associated with both Steinitz and Lasker, both of whom were World Champions.

CHAPTER 2: PROFESSORIAL SPECIES

to provide elements that nourish; being aware of and working to surmount elements that are injurious.

In encouraging this development of diversity in professorial styles, we must be forthright and disclose a degree of variation with some of our interviewees. For example, Dr Collins said, in his interview:

> "The ideal for which we should strive is that every professor should teach and every professor should do research, and if they can do one of those things superbly but not the other, they're in the wrong place."

The authors choose respectfully to disagree. Although it is understandable how Dr Collins has come to this opinion—he is, himself, both a superb teacher and an outstanding researcher[33]—this and similar definitions of "professor" should not prevent academics from contributing in modalities that do not conform to the classical definition.

If all professors are singing from the same song-sheet, this book has no purpose. Perhaps it is exactly because of the culturally-accepted norm in academia that all professors are functionally identical that the present authors have collaborated to write this book. How, speaking of a large university, can all professors have the same job[34] description? Surely it requires only a brushing acquaintance with the broader theory of human employment (or some experience with the properties of multivariate optimization) to realize that, if some large organization has, a large number of key individuals performing a few critical functions, the policy of having every one of the key individuals spending exactly the same fraction of their time on each of the critical functions, this policy is far too simplistic. It flies in the face of everything learned over the last 500 years about creating effective organizational structures and about fitting each employee's responsibilities to that employee's skill-set and aptitudes.

---

33 At Dr Collins's university (being also the university best known to the authors) extraordinary performance in teaching and particularly in research are recognized by the promotion to the position of Distinguished Professor, a position that Collins has held since 1999. Collins was also a finalist in the province-wide public-television (TVO) contest for "best (teaching) professor."

34 Some professors may not know what their JD (job description) is. They should ask to see it. How can an intelligent person work for an organization (sometimes for 40 years or more) without knowing what they are legally expected to do? (That question answers itself.) Accept no flimsy excuses. Demand to see it!

Refinements on the Notion of Career Planning

The word "plan" is used in many contexts and (as academics tend to know better than anyone else) getting this word's meaning more precise now will save much misunderstanding and argumentation later.

First, all meanings of "plan" have this in common. The "Keeping On Keeping On" plan is not a plan. It is the avoidance of a plan, and it is probably meant to avoid change as well.

Second, the "Big Long Tube" plan, where all professors, rather like robots, are supposed to proceed in some sort of lockstep manner, is not a personal career plan either. Some changes may occasionally be incorporated, over time, if everyone else is changing that way also, but there is no allowance for individual variations, nor for personal differences in aptitudes and inclinations.

Third, the "Just Lurching Along" plan, wherein the professor (one is asked to suppose) is not averse to change, but where no real effort is made to think beyond next week's lectures or next year's grant application, cannot be associated with the word "strategy" or designated as a form of "plan," as meant here.

Fourth, planning is about the *future*. This would seem obvious, but a surprising number of planning exercises, both within academia and without, seem to get bogged down in rear-view-mirror gazing. One doesn't drive well that way. To use a specific example, the last section (§2.2) started with natural ability—both from genetics and from early childhood influences—as a given. Perhaps there may be regrets; perhaps there may be wishful thinking; but these are not part of the planning process. More specific examples include what degree one has, and from where, and under whom, and where one works now, etc., etc., but one cannot change the past. These facts are highly relevant as a basis for planning, but no time should be wasted on second-guessing their reality.

Fifth, one frequently hears that all planning is a waste of time because plans usually have to be changed.[35] Of course plans will have to be changed,

---

35 Scratch someone of this view a little and they will be revealed as one who is very averse to change. To plan is to admit that change is inevitable. Change-averse individuals want to resist change at all costs, and when change comes (as it always will), they like to think of themselves as victims of change rather than as poor planners.

since no planner can predict the future. Does that mean that one should not plan? Of course not. It just means that planning is part of a never-ending process. One should be willing (determined, actually) to change one's plans when important new facts come to light. Planning is ever on-going and requires updating at key intervals. Theoretically, this could lead to too much career planning, but such a disorder is very much an orphan disease in practice.

The Four Main Paradigms

If the reader is a general reader, the authors hope that the book to this point has been salutary, and we welcome him or her to stay aboard. If the reader is a young academic (or a potential young academic), this is where matters get really interesting. The remainder of our discussion herein will be sited squarely on the many flavors of academic career available; on the necessary first step of identifying them; and on the tradeoffs between these various alternatives. Indeed, four fundamental alternatives will provide the framework for discussion in the remainder of this book:

1. **Advanced Teachers.** Mentors Who Inspire.
2. **Eminent Scholars.** A Noble (Perhaps a Nobel) Profession.
3. **Academic Executives.** From Bureaucratic Administrators to Inspiring Leaders.
4. **Entrepreneurial Professors.** Reaching outside the Cloister.

These four rather distinct species will be discussed in Chapters 3, 4, 5 and 6, respectively. They can be distinguished more clearly as professors leave the safe port of tenure and begin to navigate their careers on the worldwide academic oceans.

Chapter 3: The Advanced Teacher

Mentors Who Inspire

Chapter Overview

We begin this chapter with a broad vision of a university as a community of scholars engaged in learning and teaching. The many members of this community vary in experience from the newest freshmen to the most seasoned and distinguished scholars. In defiance of all prevailing ideology, this book makes the claim that, once tenure requirements have been met, it is (and should be) possible to develop one's career as a "teaching professor," without all the heavy commitment to research (beyond the modest research required to support fundamental teaching). However, to make this enterprise a success, one should be a truly outstanding teacher; one should expect to spend more time teaching than colleagues who also carry a heavy research load; and one may have to change schools to find a niche where outstanding teaching is truly valued.

Then, in §3.2, we treat the simplest form of this learning-teaching duality—classroom learning and teaching. Students pay to learn and professors get paid to teach, and this transactional model can, the authors maintain, form the basis for a rewarding professorial career. (In succeeding chapters, other career paradigms are also examined.) Teaching as a primary career is examined more closely in §3.3 and the subtleties of dealing with several student maturity levels are discussed.

Some of the many skills necessary for effective teaching are briefly mentioned in §3.4, the most important message being this: Startlingly, most post-secondary teachers arrive behind the lecture podium *with no formal training at all to do the job*, so unless they are naturally gifted teachers—and in fact even if they are—they should set aside some time to study and learn that profession. Some basic behaviors to avoid are then explicated by counterexample. From the more positive side, §3.5 discusses how to get a university course off on the right footing through **(a)** course selection, **(b)** getting important procedural issues straight on the first day of class, and **(c)** being aware of the key do's and don'ts of successful post-secondary teaching.

The information technologies that have recently stood the world on its head have barely been heard of in some areas of the academy, despite the fact that, properly used, they can greatly increase both the effectiveness and productivity of teaching. Some of these ideas are introduced in §3.6 and once again an all-too-realistic scenario is employed as a counterexample to drive home some vital themes. Further, the unpretty landscape of much of post-secondary teaching is further charged with being almost totally unresponsive to all the modern trends in communication (and their supporting theories and technologies) over the past fifty years.

This is all good news for young professors with a serious ability and a consuming interest in teaching: They can take their eyes off the classical university teaching targets—proving how smart and knowledgeable they are, and the banal transmission of largely trivial facts in a soporific fashion—and focus instead on the latest understanding of the theory and practice of teaching, and the technologies that support these objectives, so as to make university courses a life-changing experience for the students in their courses. Finally, as a suitable dessert on the menu, we end this chapter, in §3.7, with some thoughts on teaching from some of those who have granted interviews for this book.

3.1 Learning and Teaching

In Chapter 2 (more specifically, in §2.1, on the subject of academic culture) it was stated that "the primary foundational element of academic

CHAPTER 3: THE ADVANCED TEACHER

culture is easily identified: virtually all professors have a quite unusual level of intellectual ability." Surely this is true. How could anyone familiar with academic personnel demur? There are of course many other professions, besides academic ones, whose members are also characterized by strong intellectual requirements, but these are not as directly concerned with learning and teaching.

It has also been prominently acknowledged in the foregoing that intellectual ability is not well defined; that it has many worthy definitions; and that, most importantly, it must be combined with a large set of added personal characteristics[36] in order to portray a person of truly high value in an academic culture.

The Input-Output Balance

One learns to use certain conceptual tools to help grasp complexity. One such tool is the input-output diagram. This approach is particularly facilitative when the concept is portrayed as a block diagram. These diagrams become the lego™ from which very complicated situations can be analyzed and discussed.

Embarking as we are on a discussion of learning and teaching, the block diagram in Fig. 3.1 will be helpful in showing the key ideas. It shows that the academic mind craves to be fed by a continual flow of inputs. To be economically productive, that same mind must concomitantly generate a variety of outputs. Thus, the academic mind must be intelligent enough to understand and integrate the inputs, and organized and creative enough to create meaningful outputs based on them.

Figure 3.1 shows the most generic definitions of teaching and learning, emphasizing the many inputs (learning) and the many outputs (teaching). Such a figure can never be complete, but does represent the general approach under discussion—much more general than the normal, highly specialized use of the word "teaching." Most of the key inputs and outputs for academics are in the respective lists shown, but some professors will have important sources and/or receptors for their

---

[36] As one example, *integrity* is an amalgam of several such attractive characteristics. Integrity is not measured by IQ tests, but its absence can be quickly detected.

professorial activity that are more specialized and therefore unremarked upon in Fig. 3.1.

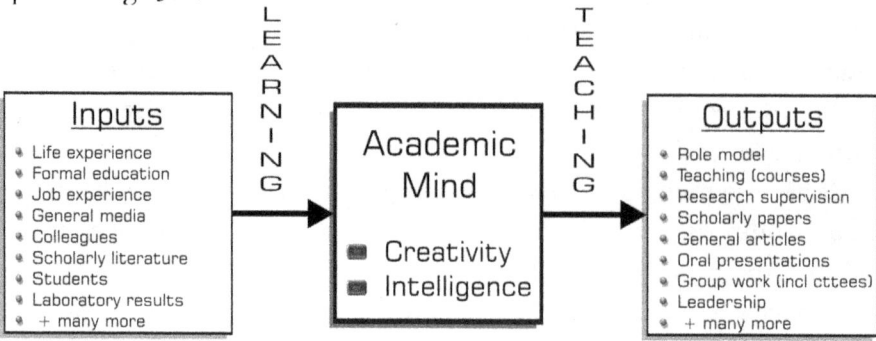

```
                    LEARNING                           TEACHING
┌──────────────────┐          ┌──────────────┐          ┌──────────────────────────┐
│ Inputs           │          │  Academic    │          │ Outputs                  │
│ • Life experience│          │    Mind      │          │ • Role model             │
│ • Formal education│   ──▶   │              │   ──▶    │ • Teaching (courses)     │
│ • Job experience │          │              │          │ • Research supervision   │
│ • General media  │          │ ■ Creativity │          │ • Scholarly papers       │
│ • Colleagues     │          │ ■ Intelligence│         │ • General articles       │
│ • Scholarly literature│     │              │          │ • Oral presentations     │
│ • Students       │          │              │          │ • Group work (incl cttees)│
│ • Laboratory results│       │              │          │ • Leadership             │
│ • + many more    │          │              │          │ • + many more            │
└──────────────────┘          └──────────────┘          └──────────────────────────┘
```

Figure 3.1: Intellectual Inputs and Outputs for Professors.

It has been noted in the figure that two absolute requirements are intelligence and creativity. Yet, although each of these mental gifts is endlessly multifaceted, they are still insufficient for a highly successful career *in academe*. The lists of inputs and outputs are not in any canonical order, although "life experience" and "role model" were consciously chosen to head their respective lists. Thus, in brief, Fig. 3.1 should be helpful but cannot be encyclopedic.

Input (or Output) out of Balance

Figure 3.1 already demonstrates two primary mechanisms for input-output disorders among professors; these are shown in the accompanying two boxes. Either disorder will (or should) adversely affect one's career.

Input Overbalance Disorder might be expected in a context where a hungry mind must be fed, while tenure protects from the consequences of no productivity. A professor thus afflicted, though often very bright, and though rightly prized by his or her colleagues for these intellectual endowments, is actually largely useless. The university can correctly brag about the putative enormity of this faculty member's knowledge, but unless this knowledge benefits others, all this frenzied learning is just a private hobby and should not attract compensation derived from student fees or taxpayer dollars. The disorder arises, in brief, when it's all input and no output.[37]

---

37 There is, however, a happy state when this "disorder" is quite normal and not objectionable: unsalaried professorial retirement.

CHAPTER 3: THE ADVANCED TEACHER

> **Input Overbalance Disorder**
> The professor constantly feeds on sources of information, but rarely takes the trouble to create any outputs. The most common form of this disorder has the primary symptom of **constant reading**, with no discernable benefit to anyone else.

The mirror-image disorder is Output Overbalance Disorder. High-powered minds are usually thought of in terms of their outputs, and reasonably so. We have just observed that, in a rational system, only productive outputs should be admired and only useful contributions should be financially rewarded.

> **Output Overbalance Disorder**
> The professor constantly teaches, gives talks, writes papers and generally pontificates to all in sight, but eventually the lack of timely information and mental stimulation take their toll. The most common forms of this disorder are of two (related) kinds: The primary symptom is either **(a)** writing increasingly **banal** or increasingly **fewer scholarly papers**, or **(b)** teaching increasingly **outdated course material**.

Of *course* the need for the intellectual nourishment of appropriate inputs should be allowed for in the time budget. But when these outputs, perhaps spurred by the peer recognition or financial rewards that rightly accompany quality outputs, become an obsession, while at the same time the background of supporting inputs is permitted to become arid, one is creating an ever-increasing deficit in one's intellectual stock. The pretense that this deficit can be sustained indefinitely will eventually collapse.

Teaching as Output

Everything about the university is (or should be) fundamentally driven by the twin obsessions of learning and teaching, and sustained by other activities essential to the support of learning and teaching. We have just seen that learning and teaching (in their most general sense, Fig. 3.1) are two sides of the same coin,[38] and that either in the absence of the other over

---

[38] For academics, teaching and learning are also connected in another, nonsemantical way, one whose truth is captured by this old proverb: "To learn, teach." It

an extended period creates some sort of intellectual pathology, at least from the career (productivity) point of view. For a professor, the pressure is on output,[39] and teaching is one such output.

Strictly from the viewpoint of feeding hungry intellects, this picture might suffice. However, when one realizes that there is a wider society outside the academic cloister; that a throng of students will leave every year to join that wider society; that a throng of new students will arrive to replace the throng of old ones; and that everyone involved has work-life-balance issues to consider—*then* we must add a number of broader issues, foremost among them being practical economics.

The "university community" is not just a collection of abstract minds in communication; they are real people with real sets of complex objectives. For professors in particular, this means that a shared global intelligence among disembodied minds is not enough. They must realize that they can't actually do in practice everything that they might like to do in theory. They must organize and prioritize their academic activities to meet conflicting goals. This requires having long-term vision, strategic planning, and discipline. The result of this long-term plan—if they are smart enough to construct it—is their *academic career plan*.

With this practical tension between intellectual inputs and intellectual outputs in mind—together with the practical verity that one is paid directly for one's output and only indirectly for one's input—we turn now to one highly important output: Teaching.

3.2 Post-Secondary Teaching — Could This Be a Career?

If one is to have a satisfying career, one must take care to furnish valued outputs. We have just discussed, briefly, what some of the scholarly

---

is not unusual for a professor to hear a colleague say something like this: "I think Subject X is becoming more important every day and I've never really studied it properly. I'm thinking about offering a course on it this fall." Though seemingly paradoxical, such a new course, in the hands of a skilled academic and a talented teacher, will be not only a great and timely new course, it will also be delivered with the contagious excitement and the enthusiasm of an instructor who is still in love with the material.

39 Students, who pay fees, have a right to emphasize their intellectual *input* (learning). Professors, who are paid salaries, must emphasize *outputs*.

CHAPTER 3: THE ADVANCED TEACHER

outputs in the academic context are, and what some of the intellectual inputs needed to sustain those outputs also are, over a career-long period. The most fundamental scholarly output, it is argued here, is that of *teaching*. Although we used a quite general meaning for "teaching" in Fig. 3.1, to prepare the foundation for several possible professorial career flavors, we shall for the remainder of this chapter devolve this general meaning to a narrower one—essentially to the meaning of the word "teaching" as would be used by students.

Is Teaching Even Desirable?

There are not a few in society who have had quite successful careers without ever graduating from college. These folks, who must be admired for their achievements, sometimes make statements that say, in effect, "Formal advanced teaching is not necessary, and is likely a waste of time. I graduated from the School of Hard Knocks and am not sorry for it." Here are some examples, with varying degrees of sternness:

Viola Spolin [U.S. theatrical director]: "We learn through experience and experiencing, and no one teaches anyone anything." Perhaps, in theatre, this is quite correct. As another example, the authors have had some experience in business and neither of them would hire a salesman strictly on having four years of lecture courses on salesmanship.

Ralph Waldo Emerson [U.S. essayist and philosopher]: "We learn geology the morning after the earthquake, on ghastly diagrams of cloven mountains, upheaved plains, and the dry bed of the sea." It seems one might wish for a less traumatic way to learn, however.

Still, this from Samuel Butler [British author]: "Don't learn to do, but learn in doing. Let your falls not be on a prepared ground, but let them be bona fide falls in the rough and tumble of the world." Again, they seem to say, "No pain, no gain."

Vernon Law [baseball pitcher, Pittsburg Pirates] summarized the problem succinctly, and with humor: "Experience is a hard teacher because she gives the test first, the lesson afterward."

It seems to depend strongly on the subject being taught. For subjects that are primarily rational, that have a strong logical and historical foundation, and that do not involve a great deal of human interaction: classroom time and the reading of books can be an efficient (and relatively painless) way to stand on the shoulders of giants. We leave the final word here to Albert Einstein: "It is the supreme art of the teacher to awaken joy in creative expression and knowledge."

Teaching vis-à-vis Research

From the standpoint of Fig. 3.1, teaching is the totality of all useful academic output. According to this view, research is a complex activity that includes both learning (by the professor) *and* teaching (to graduate students, to colleagues at seminars, to readers of scholarly journals through one's papers, to attendees at conferences, etc.). Thus, for Fig. 3.1, teaching and research are not opposites; they are two ambipolar names for the same process. Still, though teaching and research may often blend in our cerebral development, they often compete for institutional attention and resources. And they contend for time and attention within most academic careers. We may as well recognize these competing priorities, up front.

In practice (meaning, how one apportions one's time priorities), there are important models other than the "intellectual" block diagrams typified by Fig. 3.1. There are also the "economics" block diagrams that a business major or an economist would draw. One of these is shown in Fig. 3.2:

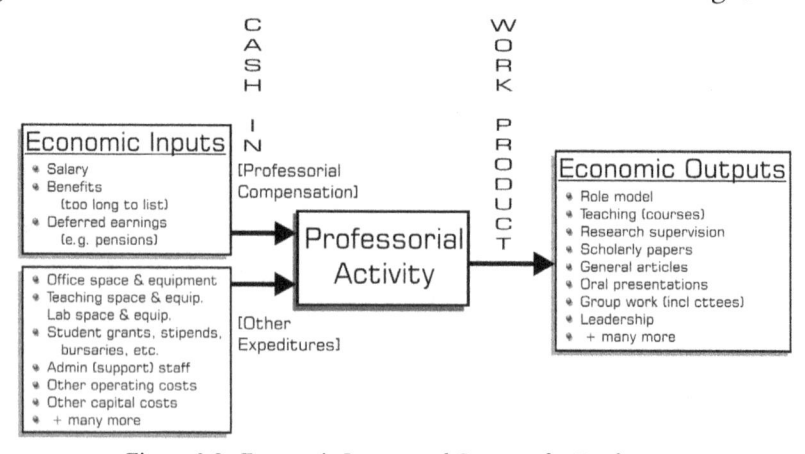

Figure 3.2: Economic Inputs and Outputs for Professors.

CHAPTER 3: THE ADVANCED TEACHER

Note that those items called "intellectual outputs" in Fig. 3.1 are now called "economic outputs" in Fig. 3.2. The position has been taken that, by definition, intellectual outputs with no conceivable benefit to the institution that pays one's salary are not under consideration.[40] The "inputs" for Fig. 3.2 are not intellectual, as in Fig. 3.1, but are economic. Some of these flow directly to the professorial staff, while others are of a more indirect variety. To neglect these latter expenditures is to follow Narcissist Rule III in the accompanying box.

Three Rules for Narcissists

Rule I: Nothing happened before I got here. No achievements before mine were truly worthy; no ideas before mine were transformative; no decisions before those in which I participated could possibly have pointed matters in a helpful direction.

Rule II: Everyone above me in the organizational hierarchy is basically expendable and not really needed. Accordingly, in my penetrating analysis of organizational finance, I shall ignore any money spent on the salaries and expenses associated with higher-ups, since this is probably a waste of money.

Rule III: My salary is the most important—indeed, the only—worthy expense of my university. Although the buildings in which I work are practically falling down, that is a lesser issue.

Post-Tenure Career Planning

While preparing for tenure, the context of being in a probationary period must remain paramount in the near-term thinking of tenure-track professors. To obtain tenure, one must demonstrate competency[41] in both of the fundamental activities viewed as primary for professors, namely: **(a)** teaching (in the narrow, student-usage sense), and **(b)** research. Other

---

40   All the chess games played in the common rooms on weekends may have mammoth intellectual content but are of no economic interest to the university.

41   Some academic institutions, who value highly the teaching prowess of their faculty members, will demand more at tenure hearings than mere competency in the teaching dimension. Similarly, universities who are (or seek to become) "research intensive" will require more than mere competency of the research expertise of their tenured staff. We shall speak of the research dimension more fully in the next chapter.

activities and characteristics, such as demonstrations of leadership, becoming well known (positively) by the media, or any of dozens of other positive predictors and attributes, may or may not be taken into account, either consciously or unconsciously.

Post tenure, professors may (indeed, *must*) decide for themselves, at least to a large extent, which academic outputs they wish to stress. It is in this context that "research" and "teaching" compete for the scholar's time. Many academic institutions claim that their professors must continue to split their time, energy and enthusiasm more-or-less equally between both teaching and research. It is difficult to see what the basis can be for such a claim. No other profession, no other organization, requires all its members to have the identical job description, to be all things to all people. Why should this be true of academics? Despite four decades of looking, no satisfactory answer has been found by the authors.

It seems to be largely just "received wisdom," almost *ex cathedra* and thus to be taken on faith, that all world-beating researchers are expected also to spend a lot of their time in the first-year classroom, and that all first-year teachers and lecturers should be judged primarily by their international research reputation. This paradox is self-evidently nonsense to all but the True Believers in academia.

Many professors—those who are (or could be) much better at teaching than at research, or vice versa—can be more productive and make a larger contribution by focusing primarily on what they are good at and on what they enjoy doing. No other business, public or private, would manage its affairs in such a bizarre manner as to make everyone a jack of all trades, master of none.

Can We Justify Teaching as a Post-Secondary Career?

The authors firmly believe that post-secondary teachers (whether called lecturers, teachers, professors, or any other label) can develop for themselves a strong, viable career. We now make several arguments for this bold assertion.

Argument 1. Fundamentality. If, for the sake of simplicity, we say that in practice the two most fundamental activities of professors are teaching and research, which is the most fundamental for the academic institution? We would argue that the correct answer is: teaching! Not just in the empty, hypocritical sense, where an institution claims to value "teaching and research," while never reversing the order and saying "research and teaching," but in the serious belief that teaching does have priority.

Argument 2. Uniqueness. Certainly there are many non-academic organizations that have *research* as their *raison d'être*. There are major governmental research centers; there are significant research laboratories in the private sector; and there are many think-tanks (and similar institutions) in the not-for-profit sector. Research is hardly unique to universities. In fact, especially given that most of the research conducted at universities is government funded, it could be argued that the research needs of advanced modern society could still be reasonably well met even if universities ceased to exist!

Argument 3. Support of Research. One of the best arguments for conducting research within the walls of modern universities is probably this: The effects of involving students in the fundamental, intellectually stimulating activity of research are so beneficial to society that it would be a strategic communal blunder over the long term to deny students such an exposure. The only place to find such a large population of bright, young, promising individuals is, of course, in the universities and colleges.

In connection with Argument 3, it might also be candidly observed that university graduate students provide a ready reservoir of apprentice academics, who welcome the opportunity to assist in teaching and research activities. Without a graduate education program, this ready source of cheap labor would not exist.

And, speaking of finances, it has been stated[42] that

---

42 Elliot Eisner, professor, Stanford School of Education, in the *NY Times*, 3 Sep 85.

> "We have inadvertently designed a system in which being good at what you do as a teacher is not formally rewarded, while being poor at what you do is seldom corrected or penalized."

The reward system, including professorial salaries, seems more tied to research success than teaching success, especially at research-intensive universities. This is closely related to the phenomenon wherein (in most institutions) all researchers must teach and all teachers must conduct research. In what other sophisticated profession are the many diverse contributions so mixed up? On Detroit's assembly line, must painters also weld, with the missing painting hours filled in by welders? Must respirologists also give anesthetics, while anesthesiologists provide treatments for lung disease? Teaching, especially in the early undergraduate years, should be done by great teachers, who should be rewarded accordingly. If great *researchers* have the talent and desire[43] to teach freshmen courses, that also can be arranged, but to say they *must*, absent either talent or desire, is a perverse use of human resources. It is assumed in this book that one can pursue a successful and rewarding career as an outstanding post-secondary teacher.

Historically, Research Was Meant to Support Teaching

If one reads the histories of the faculties and schools that are now spires of excellence on modern university campuses, one finds that there was initially the need to teach advanced courses to students who were *en route* to enter the disciplines and professions underlying these selfsame faculties and schools. Teachers, perhaps not yet called "professors," wished to offer the most erudite, modern courses they could, from the body of knowledge for which they were responsible. They accordingly undertook to research their subjects—with "research" having its original meaning of *finding out what knowledge is available in codified form*—so that they could offer a coherent course of study with well-organized lectures.

Over the past many decades, and in sundry institutions with varying relative commitments to teaching and research, teaching has always led to research as a support activity. Unfortunately, in many cases the pendulum

---

43 Margaret E. Sangster, in her autobiography, said "No one should teach who is not in love with teaching."

CHAPTER 3: THE ADVANCED TEACHER

has swung, not just toward the other direction, but (in some cases) in direct opposition to the original intent. To modern university administrators, this research-first precedence seems to be the best strategic stance. It leads to the most income from external[44] sources; it leads to the best publicity, sometimes nationwide or even internationally; and these two factors, combined, lend a sense of pride in graduates and jurisdictional taxpayers that attracts still further donations and contributions. Everyone wants to fund a winner.

It is likely that no scrupulously audited investigation has ever been conducted to determine whether, in general, all the university resources allegedly devoted to teaching (i.e., to the benefit of students as customers) are actually expended in support of that activity. Anyone who has had any experience at higher levels in a modern university knows that research is much more expensive that teaching. The natural inclination of senior administrators to want to move their college or university "a notch up" cannot be faulted, but the question of whether a first-rate teaching college or trade school should be "elevated" to a third-rate research university by subtly diverting financial and other resources towards research is more problematical. Certainly, for those who have chosen to dedicate their professional lives to teaching at such institutions,[45] this strategy is not very conducive.

In any case, the viewpoint herein is that there are no such disorders as Teaching Overbalance Disorder or Research Overbalance Disorder.[46]

---

44   Apparently not obvious to some senior university administrators is the fact that much of their external research income comes without any allowance for indirect costs. What are these indirect costs? In the private sector, where costs tend to be accounted for accurately (5% of sales as a normal profit margin focuses the mind wonderfully), organizations of similar size, but operated much more tightly, can often have "overhead + G&A" rates in excess of 100% of direct costs. Yet universities often say (with a straight face) that their indirect load rate, on research costs, is 40% or 60% of direct research costs. If they get this much, they are ecstatic. Sometimes they get 0% —and celebrate that they have gotten "research funding." In such cases, teaching is obviously subsidizing research to a high degree.
45   Any reader who thinks that the authors are biased in favor of teaching over research should recall that this chapter is about teaching as a career. Research (and other) careers will be discussed in subsequent chapters.
46   We should stress once more that we are not speaking of the *pre*-tenure climate here, but of the *post*-tenure one. In the former (probationary) period, it is understandable that one must show proficiency at both of the two bedrock academic output activities: teaching and research.

Indeed, it is argued that, for most professors, stressing primarily one of the two to optimize their productivity and value, is a wise course.[47]

3.3 Teaching as a Career — A Closer Examination

Returning for a moment to the context of §3.1 we have seen that, in the most general sense, teaching occurs when the intellectual output from one sentient being becomes the intellectual input to another sentient being (see Fig. 3.1). In the academic context, knowledge and/or skills are transmitted from Scholar A to Scholar B by one of a large number of modalities, many of which were suggested by Fig. 3.1. In an academic (or any other) context, "A teaches B" and "B learns from A" are in tended to have identical meaning.

Teaching in a University

The idea that all one's learning happens within educational institutions (in general), or within universities and colleges (in particular), is preposterous. Much happens in one's upbringing and the benefits of early intellectual stimulation last a lifetime, as recent results in pediatric neurology make clear. One also learns life skills from one's friends, relatives and peers, both inside and outside school, and work experience is especially salutary in developing skills for the workplace. Nevertheless, there are certain subjects (or disciplines) which are so complex, yet sufficiently codified, that a focused, organized study of them is needed to absorb the material. These are ideally suited to the university academic approach.

In fact, the current sociological data are incontrovertible: Members of society who have successfully pursued and completed an advanced education in colleges and universities are (statistically speaking) far better off than those who have not.[48] The benefits of advanced education are surely

---

47 If one is currently at an academic institution that requires strict equality of effort between teaching and research for all its professors, it is comforting to realize that there are hundreds of colleges and universities out there. One's skills may find a better fit elsewhere.

48 University administrators are quick to seize on such statistics as proof of the great benefits of post-secondary education, thereby making one of the cardinal errors in statistical analysis—that correlation implies causation (in the direction that favors the speaker). Could it not be equally valid to claim that, since these students were highly competent (as judged by their later success), they naturally did well in university? It is likely that both mechanisms are at work: strong performers do well

CHAPTER 3: THE ADVANCED TEACHER

one-to-one with their sources—effective teaching, within suitable curricula, through courses well taught, by committed teachers and professors. These "success data" prove that universities and colleges have much to be proud of, and that they have rendered an enormous benefit to society, being responsible for nothing less than the preparation of the next generation for its productive role in professional society.

Given the definition of "teaching" used just above (or the more general definition implied by Fig. 3.1), and given this book's aim of helping teachers and professors employed by universities and colleges with their careers, the discussion now centers on the much more constricted meaning of "teaching" used in the parlance of universities and colleges. The accompanying box sets out a sequence of four scenarios in terms of which the discussion can proceed constructively.

Teaching Levels in Universities and Colleges (simplified)

1. **Early undergraduates:** Being weaned from secondary school.
2. **Late undergraduates:** Becoming broadly proficient and perhaps preparing for graduate school.
3. **Early graduate students:** Focusing on learning about a chosen specialty.
4. **Late graduate students:** Becoming experts in, and contributors to, their chosen specialty.

The best academic teachers always keep foremost in mind, not just the view of the forest from behind their favorite tree, but the forest as observed from 20,000 feet—an inspiring view long after their special tree no longer obscures. Outstanding mentors also are keenly aware that their strategic function is not primarily to inculcate the minutiae of a narrow subject, but to instill also these three virtues:

1. The love of learning.
2. The skills of critical thinking (including, without exception, initial skepticism).
3. The bone-deep knowledge that learning as a lifelong commitment, a long journey in which one's formal education is but the first tentative step.

---

wherever they are, and their university experience does help to prepare them for their intellectual needs later in life.

Teaching Early Undergraduate Students

The immediately-post-secondary teaching segment is considered by many to be the most challenging of teaching assignments. Class sizes tend to be large; the course material seems (to the professor) to be rather elementary; the students are generally immature and difficult to manage; and their expectations, conditioned through grade inflation by grades in the 90s in high school, are often unrealistic when placed in a group of students many of whom are quite a bit sharper than they are.

The teaching challenges include the need to establish a higher academic standard and many students find the step up more difficult than others. Some students—normally the brighter ones—are enthusiastic about being instructed by professors who know so much more than their secondary-school teachers did; others, used as they were to the kind of "spoon-feeding" that cannot be afforded in university (and that is, in any case, antithetical to the energetic skepticism that characterizes intellectual rigor) are uncomfortable with the new, higher expectations placed upon them.

Often, early undergraduate courses are, by university standards, so basic that quite drastic measures are taken by the administration to accommodate their numbers without expending serious dollars or professorial hours to meet the challenge. Class sizes of 400 students or more—one is afraid to consult the Guinness Book of Records—are not unusual, which is really just an indication of how incompetent universities can be at meeting these teaching challenges with innovative approaches. (None of this is really necessary, as we shall discuss later in this chapter.)

Teaching Late Undergraduate Students

Late undergraduates are, by comparison, a pleasure to teach. The students who were not really suited for a university experience have fallen through the cracks (sometimes almost literally); class sizes are more manageable; and the subject matter taught is more interesting, to both teachers and students, because it more closely represents the real academic interests of all concerned.

More sophisticated teaching structures can also be employed. Some courses can include certain integrative aspects—because there is, by now, some earlier material to integrate. Students find exciting the mention of

CHAPTER 3: THE ADVANCED TEACHER

incidents that happened and ideas that were developed after they were born, a more likely occurrence at this level. Class participation now begins to be more practical.

Some teamwork can now be inserted, always good experience for the real world, and laboratory work and field trips are pleasant experiences (or should be) for some kinds of courses. If the professor is also active in research,[49] he or she can use examples from his or her recent experience, and the accompanying *excitement*—not always present in academic lectures, will be palpable. More serious "projects" can now be defined and worked on, where the student role is more creative and less regurgitative. Even a bachelor's thesis, or some similar nontrivial academic opus, is often on the agenda as the grand finale.

Teaching Early Graduate Students

Here, pedagogical practice tends to be more variable as between one academic field and another, and as between one country and another. In some universities—the UK is typical—the general climate of study is that students are by now expected to know how to find information of relevance to their studies. From this stance, the university's responsibility is to provide excellent libraries, modern laboratories, computer facilities, and a teaching staff to stimulate, organize and be the resource of last resort for early graduate study. In one sense or another, the student is considered to be in "research mode" for graduate studies, although the research results are not required to be ground-breaking or publishable; a thesis, however, may be required.

A somewhat different viewpoint, more typical in the USA, is that early graduate study is essentially a continuation of previous study toward the first degree. The courses are more specialized, but the basic approach does not change.

Both approaches have their advantages and the authors do not take an advocacy position on either. The point here is that to select an emphasis on teaching should not be an extraordinary career strategy in a university. As

---

49   If professors can draw on their own research experience—such as new insights on the subject from leading edge, contemporary articles that they have read, or some new examples that have arisen from their own research studies—this will be a turn-on, especially for those students who are contemplating graduate studies.

the students become more mature and the material becomes more specialized, the meaning of "teaching" becomes fuzzier and a broader range of teaching modalities becomes appropriate.

Teaching Late Graduate Students

The emphasis is now almost entirely on research and the grand aspiration is a doctoral degree. There may still be some courses, depending on the pedagogical philosophy of the institution, but these "courses" have an almost unrecognizable character when compared to the undergraduate courses of a few years earlier. These may be "seminar" courses—student presentations of research topics related to their dissertations and excellent practice for a potential academic career just around the corner—or "reading" courses, given to as few as one student to fill in some blind-spots related to the dissertation, and satisfy the institutional mandate for some courses, but they do not imply any academic breadth. (In connection with "reading courses," see also the eye-opening discussion in "Help from New Technology" in §3.6.) In the nearer term, an internet reading course can be effective with proper technique.[50]

Advanced research supervision is an ineluctable combination of teaching and research components. This is the one place where this book's analytical stratagem of breaking down career options into four paradigms (teaching, research, leadership, and entrepreneurship) doesn't quite work.[51] Not only are teaching and research inseparable in this handoff of the spark of research creativity from an older to a younger generation; the meaning of "teaching" is itself unusually subtle.

Ostensibly, the supervisor (professor) is passing his or her profound knowledge of a highly specialized academic area on to a younger research apprentice. There can be no argument that this is "teaching." But far more important is that the supervisor is coaching the student into the art of how

---

50   For example, by scheduling 'live' internet sessions where students, having read prescribed material, are questioned by the professor; students interact; attendance is taken and students are graded on the questions and the discussion.
51   One factor that makes this book's "stratagem" still work is that many tenured academics pass through two or more of the paradigms in the course of their careers. This is especially true of the most talented professors. Moving from one paradigm to another usually involves being bi-modal (two or more paradigms at once) for a transitional period.

to do research itself; as the decades pass, and the specifics of the graduate research topic fall by the wayside, the research skills[52] learned across the desk from a master will linger all career long. This is teaching that lasts!

Still, the teaching doesn't end, even there. The relationship between a graduate student and his research professor is one of the most meaningful—assuming they are both compatible and of high quality—that any student can experience in his life. Family influences are more visceral and lifelong; relationships with a professional superior later in life may last more years; but a graduate student, sitting hour after hour, one on one, with his or her research professor, over a period of several years, learns much more than the technical niceties of the dissertation topic, and much more than the procedural methodologies of how to conduct research. One learns how to think as a professor; how to be dispassionate, unbiased and rational; how to comport oneself with one's colleagues; how to be enthusiastic about the quest for truth.[53] Most graduate students, ten years out, if asked to rank the important things they learned from their research professors in graduate school, would rank technicalities third, research prowess second, and overarching professional life skills first. It is difficult to think of a more awesome teaching responsibility.

3.4 Teaching — A Career that Requires Skill

Choosing post-secondary teaching as an emphasis (or even an exclusive activity) is an honorable profession, and can be very rewarding, but is not without significant obstacles. Most formidable among these is to find oneself at one of the research intensive universities that simply do not permit their professors to take such a path. Despite the fact that most of these institutions claim teaching as their most important function, perish the professor who wishes exclusively to pursue this function! This is the perverse effect of the "everybody must do everything" ideology. Paradoxically, many of their research colleagues would love them to do more teaching, so that these research colleagues could focus more time on their research!

---

52 More will be said about research in the next chapter.
53 Unfortunately, one cannot always learn these days, how to dress, how to speak with erudition, or how to respect civil authorities, from one's professors. Perhaps the pendulum will swing back.

Alas, these colleagues are compelled to teach, while those willing to teach more courses are forced to do research. The monastery is loath to amend its ancient doctrines!

In this situation, the would-be teaching academic must make a conscious choice: either **(a)** forsake the normal potential for promotion, **(b)** possibly be demoted to some position[54] such as "lecturer," or **(c)** move to an institution that values his or her contribution. The last seems clearly the best theoretical option, but other personal considerations may make this a difficult choice.

Other Obstacles

Charles Colton (a British clergyman) opined that "It is always safe to learn, even from our enemies; seldom safe to venture to instruct, even our friends." While Colton was likely thinking of a social context, one can also infer that a classroom full of bright young students is a domain where angels should fear to tread.

Another major obstacle to post-secondary teaching as a profession is shown in the accompanying box. This astonishing state of affairs belies the claim that teaching is as important (or even more important) than research in a university.

Formal Skills Development Levels at Doctoral Graduation	
For Research:	From three to ten years.
For Teaching:	From three to ten hours.

Clearly, post-secondary teachers enter the fray essentially unarmed, with only the good and bad examples from among their own professors they have personally observed—and with, one hopes, some common sense—to guide them. By the time tenure is reached, one presumes that the teaching component is at least not disastrous; otherwise, tenure would not likely be granted.

Still, if one chooses to base one's professorial career on teaching, "not disastrous" does not mean "acceptable." One should aim for the top decile of all professors who teach. Not all will make this grade, even with dili-

---

54 "Lecturer," is referred to here, is from the North American lexicon; in the UK, "lecturer" is a more prestigious post.

gent study and hard work, but all should aspire to it. Many professors find that, by the time they prepare their class notes, travel to class and deliver lectures and tutorials, attend to course administration including all the necessary grading, there is little time left for professional (i.e., teaching) development. (Sadly, many professors may never even *consider* that some of their time should be allocated to their teaching *development*.) For those who are not attempting to be frequently published researchers, however, there should be the time available to hone the skills necessary to achieve greatness in the chosen academic paradigm—teaching.

First Principles

Many tomes have been devoted to pedagogy, although this book is not one of them. We are, instead, trying to cover a much broader range of academic career possibilities. Still, perhaps some mention can be made of the basics, so that the reader my gain some insight whether this teaching career paradigm is for her (or him).

As one of many possible examples, The Ohio State University has an Office responsible[55] for the teaching development of its faculty members and their teaching assistants. This Office issues a handbook covering all[56] aspects of teaching. For example, the following is an excerpt[57] from the handbook's Chapter 2, on the subject of "How Students Learn":

> . . . "How Can I Teach You If I Don't Know How You Learn?" . . .
>
> "Amazingly, colleges and universities have traditionally had no formal requirements for the study of learning theory [from] the people they hire to teach. The long-standing assumption has been that if one knows a body of knowledge, one can teach it. Recently, this assumption has been questioned . . . Knowing

---

55 If you are planning to emphasize teaching in your career and your university does not have such an Office, that would be a bad sign. On the other hand, if you are also entrepreneurial, you might be able to develop such an Office by making the appropriate representations to the central administration—with yourself as Director, of course. That would signify that you were emphasizing teaching in your career—but also entrepreneurship and leadership.
56 At least at the undergraduate levels; see the four levels discussed earlier, in §3.3.
57 For the entire handbook, consult http://ftad.osu.edu/Publications/TeachingHandbook.

how students learn involves exploring theories of cognition and motivation, knowing the backgrounds of the students one will teach, and being aware of the differences in learning styles and stages of development among one's students."

A Profession with a Long Past . . .

Once again, cultural influences are quintessentially important. For many of the older professors, the following scenario[58] is almost sacrosanct, although we use it here as an anti-example:

An elderly gentleman, one who has obviously lived his entire life in the cloister of the university, enters the lecture room. He is relatively well dressed, although his suit has not seen a store hanger for several decades. He carries in his left hand a rolled-up set of 8½" x 11" paper sheets; one learns, by long observation, that these are his course notes. He rarely consults them. He walks to the front of the blackboard [a whiteboard with varicolored markers available would likely cause him serious psychological trauma], without any salutation or recognition of the collection of young human beings in front of him, and begins to deliver his lecture.

He speaks with little modulation and his vocal volume is essentially inaudible in the back row.[59] Those students (if any) who are already excited (for extraneous reasons) about the subject being taught give the learnèd gentleman the benefit of the many doubts, but no one else finds his enthusiasm contagious, since no such enthusiasm is transmitted. His scribbles on the blackboard are legible only to those with natural ability in

---

58 This scenario has been contrived entirely by the authors as a counterexample to the more modern thinking advocated here. (It does, however, have considerable authenticity, based on the authors' conversations with colleagues, and based on two lifetimes of observation.)
59 In a slightly more humane (and more humorous) version of this story, the gentleman lecturer, just as he is beginning to hold forth, asks no one in particular, "Can you hear me all right?" Three students *in the front row* mutter something to the effect that they can. Thus reassured (and not realizing that the opinions he has just received contain zero useful information), he continues, possibly at a slightly lower volume so as not to exert himself unduly.

CHAPTER 3: THE ADVANCED TEACHER

ancient languages, but most of the students who have bothered to show up nevertheless diligently scribble some approximation in their own notes. No text book has been assigned.

The elderly professor, who can boast of having "taught" many generations of students, largely avoids eye contact with the class. Some students claim extravagant psychiatric diagnoses for this behavior (such as mild autism), while others more pragmatically interpret his conduct as natural for one who doesn't much care for questions (or answering them).

At almost precisely the instant appointed for the lecture to end—meaning that there is now about ten minutes for students to leave, find their next classroom, make a quick phone call, or grab a quick bite—the gentleman glances at his package of notes and announces in his most studied muttering voice, and with a wry smile, that he would "just like to finish the section," and begins to scribble even more feverishly (and illegibly) on the blackboard. Students start to leave . . .

This performance should not be sacrosanct; in modern times, it should be swept aside. The elderly gentleman should either be given remedial teaching classes or he should not be allowed in the classroom.

Lest the reader wonder whether the authors should be accused of ageism, here's an actual vignette from a recently hired mathematics professor to a first year calculus class:

> "I'm sorry to have to tell you this, but I can't stand teaching. I came here to do research, but the department Chair said I had to teach this class. Good luck to all of you!"

This provides one more argument for one being permitted (nay, encouraged) to do what one is best suited to do—unless this "recently hired professor" was not an exemplary researcher either, in which case his (distant) destination should be even more obvious.

. . . And a Challenging Future

The Ohio State handbook referred to earlier goes into much more detail on the scientific basis for teaching and learning. Primarily explored by psychologists, such bases included the behavior-association approach, which has dominated the thinking in much of modern college teaching, to the even more recent cognitive approach, which seems most relevant to post-secondary teaching, where the focus is more naturally on memory, reasoning, critical thinking and problem solving. The point at issue is not that we should sort out all this pedagogical theory here, but to emphasize that a great body of wisdom now exists on post-secondary teaching and that it should be consulted. Sadly, very little of this is even of interest—much less the object of study—by most professors who teach.

Such professional incompetence should not be tolerated in a professor who aspires to be primarily a great teacher. In addition to many sources of formal education on the subject, there are also numerous websites with quality information available. Two examples are The Teaching Professor, at

http://www.magnapubs.com/subscribe/magnapubs_tp.html

and the Chronicle of Higher Education, at

http://chronicle.com/

which has much on teaching and many other topics as well.

Virtually all modern universities have realized that the old ways are no longer the best ways (if they ever were) when it comes to teaching, and provide various types of remedial training, from informal coaching to quite extensive instruction. However, these are rarely mandatory and, as Murphy's Law would predict, those who need this help the most do not deem it necessary to expose themselves to it.

Measuring Success

Measurements of teaching quality are not easily made and this is sometimes used as an excuse for not making them. Truly outstanding teachers (on either tail of the distribution) usually become known relatively quickly: the outstandingly great ones should be feted and promoted; the outstandingly poor ones should be removed from the classroom. More refined determinations, though badly needed, are not as straightforward.

It would certainly seem reasonable that a small staff at central administration be tasked to occasionally visit classrooms throughout the university—unscheduled and unannounced, of course—to assess the teaching quality of lecturers and to offer constructive advice later as needed. For

CHAPTER 3: THE ADVANCED TEACHER

all its self-evident merit, this seems rarely to be done. Instead, student evaluations are typically used, although this is better than no information at all.[60]

Still, as pointed out[61] by Sullivan,

"Apart from the fact that an appropriate training in experimental psychology is required to fully understand the results of the experiments [in the literature], teaching evaluation research is prone to the vagueness, controversy and dogmatism that is endemic to the social sciences...

"How is a professor to divide his time and effort? ... [P]ersonal preferences will influence the distribution of his time. But perhaps most influential will be the extent to which each type of activity is rewarded—in terms of rank, salary, and professional recognition."

It is clearly in the interests of professors who wish to emphasize teaching that they understand thoroughly how teaching quality is measured and rewarded at their institution. This will enable them to develop an optimal strategy—except to the extent that such optimizing requires a compromise of principles or unethical behavior. Such professors may wish to become active in improving the measurement process, which will require leadership abilities. The recent appearance of ubiquitous student evaluations on the internet is problematical in that it is unsupervised and somewhat arbitrary, but others might claim that it has a claim to populism.[62]

Additional suggestions on how to became a better teacher have been given by, for example, Darley *et al.* [2004, Ch. 5] and Blaxter *et al.* [1998, Ch 5]. Some additional concrete suggestions are proffered in the following discussion.

---

60 Letters from students, pre-selected to give only glowing praise, such as are often tabled at promotion and tenure committee deliberations, are of course completely useless as a scientific assessment of teaching.
61 P A Sullivan, "Essay on Student Evaluation of Teaching," [internal document for the Teaching Methods and Resources Committee, 21 pp] Faculty of Applied Science and Engineering, University of Toronto, 1975.
62 A proper study of the relationship between internet data on teaching effectiveness and institutional measures of same has not, to the authors' knowledge been made, although it would be of great interest.

3.5 Getting Off on the Right Foot

It is dangerous to launch a discussion of "how to teach" unless the reader clearly understands the attending limitations on the discussion. The honorable profession of teaching merits much more space! There are whole departments and faculties devoted to the creation and dispersal of better methods of teaching, but this devotion is not our primary motivation here. Still, some guidance on these matters is a reasonable expectation from this book's readers, and thus we elaborate at least somewhat with some suggestions for the classical undergraduate teaching scenarios (i.e., Levels 1 and 2 in §3.3). With relatively obvious modifications, these principles can also be applied to graduate teaching as well (Levels 3 and 4 in §3.3).

Consider Teaching an Existing Course (at least initially)

Bernstein and Lucas[63] describe a picture consistent with the one we have stated above:

> Many new professors enter their first classrooms after having spent years as apprentices to expert mentors in research and scholarship but with little or no formal preparation for their role as a teacher. They are forced to rely on their wits and their guts.

One of the first issues is this: Are you just to teach the course, or are you required to develop (prepare) the course as well? The first impulse of young professors is often to prefer the one they can really make their own, by developing it from scratch. After many years of taking courses from others, it is understandable that they wish finally to give a course "entirely," including detailed preparation. However, this may not be the wisest choice. Choice of material alone will consume a great deal of additional time, as will detailed notes, not to mention visual aids (if any). There will be no time left over for even the scantest consideration of teaching technique.

Now, compare that approach with a strategy based on the facts. The students in the class do not care a fig about who developed the course;

---

63   D A Bernstein and S G Lucas, writing in Darley *et al.* [2004].

CHAPTER 3: THE ADVANCED TEACHER

they are impressed (or otherwise) only by the professor's performance in the classroom. They also are essentially neutral on the details of what is or isn't on the course; they just want it to be relevant and to get a good grade. So why spend hundreds of hours on matters that are unimportant to the students, while ignoring what they passionately care about? Yet this is paradox is a common occurrence for young professors, who are often saddened by weak teaching evaluations at the end of term, especially after they have "spent so much time on the course."

Wouldn't it be better to teach a course that has a fine reputation, that has been well-prepared, including a good set of notes, and to give it as well as you can? The authors' experience is that the professorial course notes of others can range from splendid to vexatious, but don't embark on a brand new course if there is a chance to teach a good existing one.[64]

A more senior professor who has previously developed an excellent course broadly related to your field may also be a good candidate to become one of your *mentors*. Every younger staff member can benefit from being mentored and the important strategy of finding a mentor (see accompanying box) applies not just to teaching but also to all the other career patterns profiled herein.

Strategic Hint: Find one or more *mentors*.
Mentor (definition): Wise and trusted counselor.

It would certainly not be surprising to find senior professors inclined to act in this way.[65] Not only are you in their field, but you have paid them a great compliment: You have chosen their course as an excellent model for your young teaching career. Professors respond positively to compliments no less than members of other professions. At the very least, you will have a mentor for your new course!

---

64 These opportunities are not rare. Professors who have developed excellent courses take sabbaticals, retire, die, or just move on to other things. In spite of these facts, sometimes, no such courses are available. But surely they should be considered, and such opportunities are usually easy to find when available.
65 From a legalistic standpoint, this is hardly plagiarism. The course was developed under departmental funding and thus the intellectual property rights should belong to the university. Better, of course, to avoid all this hassle by getting the original course developer on your side..

SO YOU WANT TO BE A PROFESSOR?

The First Day

Many universities specify how a lecture course should begin; others leave it to the wisdom of the lecturer. Here is a minimal checklist for the start of Lecture 1 (*handed out*, not scribbled on the blackboard) based on the experience of the authors:

1. Course title, course number, name and contact coordinates of the lecturer.
2. Short CV of the lecturer (optional).
3. Short description of course motivation, goals and content (in that order)
4. List of Lecturer's Responsibilities. This could be a long list, but must include items like **(a)** define course responsibilities and goals; **(b)** select course material that is useful, accurate, timely, and important; **(c)** prepare teaching aids that will convey course material to students in a clear, efficient, and enjoyable manner; **(d)** start and stop lectures and tutorials punctually; **(e)** attempt to answer all questions raised in class; **(f)** give ample time in tutorials for special needs and questions (preferable to office visits because more will benefit); **(g)** hire Teaching Assistants who are competent to answer questions and who will grade fairly; **(h)** keep course schedule up to date (separate document).
5. List of Students' Responsibilities. This could also be a long list, but typical entries are **(a)** understand course responsibilities and goals; **(b)** attend lectures and tutorial periods faithfully (otherwise, does not request special tutoring for the material missed, or blame the lecturer for not imparting the material missed); **(c)** is responsible to make personal notes during the lectures and tutorials as necessary to augment and amplify any handouts and projected material; **(d)** keep current in the course material presented; **(e)** study the course material outside classroom time to a degree necessary to perform well on mid-term exams, class projects, and the final examination; **(f)** participate in classroom discussions and debates (particularly in tutorial classes); **(g)** act ethically and in good faith with respect to mid-terms and the final exam.
6. List of textbook(s) and other reference material.

7. Some Disclaimers. Items such as (a) not every molecule of course material is in the class handouts; (b) if the lecturer says something in class that is not in the class handouts, this is not "going off on a tangent"; (c) there will be material disclosed and/or discussed in lectures and in the tutorials that is not in the class handouts—such material is, nevertheless, on the course and is completely legitimate for examination.
8. For those students for whom the course is compulsory, the lecturer undertakes to make the proceedings as helpful and relevant as possible; for those students for whom the course is optional, the lecturer pledges likewise, but if the student comes to feel that the course is not of interest, he or she is encouraged to leave, with no hard feelings on either side.
9. Grading Scheme. For example,

MidTerm 1	MidTerm 2	MidTerm 3	Case Study	Final Exam	Raw Grade
10%	10%	10%	15%	55%	100%

One of the authors has another rule: With respect to midterm tests, quizzes, etc., unless an answer has been completely overlooked or an obvious arithmetic error has been made in adding points, there will be no discussion, whatever, with any student, on the grading of these minor evaluations. Two or three points on such a test are negligible (less than 1% in the final result). Such messing around with students whose approach to success is to try to claw their way up by 0.1% is not a good use of your time[66] and is a poor preparation for how things actually work in the real world.

Some Suggested Do's and Don'ts

We now present a list of issues that are not meant to be philosophically deep but that can cause the teaching boat to capsize if one is not aware of them. They are all well known to mature practitioners of the professorial vocation.

---

66 Better to spend it with another student on course material, for example.

SO YOU WANT TO BE A PROFESSOR?

1. Beware of grade inflation, particularly in the early undergraduate years. In secondary schools, where teacher success is judged on the pass rate and where these selfsame teachers grade the final examinations in their subjects, there is every reason to use the last decade of the 100% range almost exclusively for college-bound students. The threat to post-secondary teachers is formidable: The students say, "I never got less than an A before, so what is this B-minus about?" and the parents say, "I paid several tens of thousands of dollars to send my son/daughter to this prestigious ivy-league school, so is this what I can expect to get for my money?"

2. You are always being compared (implicitly) to TV, movies, and other state-of-the-art media. This means that you must be *very* well prepared for your classes—and in many ways, not least of these being your "production values." Video, movie and TV images flash past at one-second intervals, compared to which the energy-free drones of a bottom-tier professor can produce only slumber and dissatisfaction from young students.

3. Students do not take kindly to your opinion that you are the only expert in your field and that they should have no course material other than your notes, your lectures, and you. Let them learn every day the same way *you* learn every day—from a variety of trusted resources, not from a sole expert. You already have enormous leverage in the pedagogical sweepstakes—you are the one who sets (and is responsible for grading) the course submissions and examinations—so there is no need to claim uniqueness or infallibility. Give them several reference books to consult that are really relevant, and, these days especially, *give them suitable websites*.

4. Have some form of class handout. There are many varieties of this practice, and the choice will depend on the type of material taught and the preferences of the teacher, but the practice of *no* handouts seems beyond any pale. The days when professors typically had a set of scribbled lecture notes, which they then scribbled on the blackboard, which the students then scribbled in their

CHAPTER 3: THE ADVANCED TEACHER

notebooks, should be all gone; these procedures are incompetent and unacceptable on their face. Hand out at least *something*, and the more the better. Class time should not be spent with everyone involved pretending to be human photocopying machines. It should be spent on guided discussion among a spectrum of scholars who have read the same material in advance (text, handouts, etc.) and who are now excited to parse the intellectual structure of the material. Since most students have laptops, course material and handouts can also be posted on the course web site; these can be accessed during the lecture and easily updated.

5. Never, *ever*, go overtime. Nothing is more annoying to students who have to go perhaps some distance to their next class than to be held up by yet more of the same stuff. Note, carefully, that *no one has ever been resented for finishing a few minutes early*. Just once, try stopping five minutes early and invite students who to come up to make comments and ask questions. The results may be dazzling.

6. Always keep in mind that the importance of your lectures in the education of your students is *almost never about impressing them with your knowledge*. Except for some brief regurgitation on tests and exams, the real long-term benefit is always *learning how to think* and *how to analyze issues*.

7. Have clearly understood office hours for additional course help. The two extremes—(i) unavailability outside class, and (ii) availability 24/7—are unreasonable. In some cases, competent teaching assistants can be used for this purpose. One hour outside class for every hour inside seems more than fair. The professor must be careful and professional, however. Set a time-limit per student visit (five minutes seems about right for an undergraduate course). Be aware of students whose opening gambit is, "I didn't understand the last lecture." (Why not? Were they talking? Were they absent?) No professor can reasonably be expected to give a lecture first to the class and then to all its members individually. Confine office time to reasonable and difficult questions about the course content. Avoid re-hashing grades, the most voluminous

black hole for time in the entire teaching process. Explain all these policies at the first lecture, and stick rigorously to them all year.

8. Have a course website, if possible, but the bleeding heart approach to this technology is even more dangerous than for course office hours. Explain the carefully restricted use of your time through this medium. Course results and announcements are helpful applications but detailed typing contests between a professor and his or her 100 students will lead to a time-management catastrophe for the former. Encourage the students to e-talk to, and help, each other.

9. Don't just *lecture* to the class; *interact* with its members. One very effective technique is to pause every 20 minutes or so and ask them *their* opinion[67] on some related issue! Done with dexterity, these open discussions can be the highlight of the class period.

Many items in the above list take skill to execute successfully. Of course! Being a highly successful post-secondary teacher requires skill. One's reaction should not be to shirk these dimensions to teaching but instead to learn the skills needed to make you a potential teaching awardee.

3.6 University Teaching Needs Innovation

Professors are becoming aware that the classical approaches to teaching in academia are no longer adequate. In all of human history, there have been only a few revolutionary transformations in human communication: the invention of alphabets and writing; the invention of the printing press; and, currently, the flowering of computers, information technology, and the internet. Professors also know that the demographic group most aware of these technological eruptions is precisely the one they have to teach, namely, young, bright, post-teen adults. The penalty for an inadequate

---

67 This is admittedly more applicable to some types of course material than others. One should not entertain opinions on, say, the date of the signing of the Treaty of Versailles, but opportunities in all courses are available to teachers who look for them. An informal debate can often be constructed. Limit strictly any one person's speech time. Ask for comments from those reluctant to participate. Explain that this is a university and that, in your class at least, everything is open for discussion.

CHAPTER 3: THE ADVANCED TEACHER

response to these changes (and opportunities)—both as institutions and as individual professors—will be slow but enormous.

Help from New Technology

If we define *technology* as "any man-made thing that helps us do what we want to do" then we should enquire as to what technologies are available to aid lecturers to teach. (We have already commented that a chalkboard and chalk have their limitations.) Indeed, it is astounding how some of great intelligence, who apply admirable creativity every day in their chosen fields, seem quite paralyzed to change and improvise when it comes to teaching.

Technology, of course, is not the place to start, as the above little definition makes clear. The place to start is to know what it is you want to do, and how, ideally, to do it well. If one possesses the charisma of a fencepost, technology will not convert one into a stimulating communicator.

Having set appropriate goals, only then will some technology be of assistance. Paul Edwards[68] describes the following scenario:

> "The speaker approaches the head of the room, sits down at the table (but can't be seen through the heads in front of you), and begins to *read* [emphasis added] from a paper, in a soft monotone. (Soon you're nodding off.) Sentences are long, complex and filled with jargon. The speaker emphasizes complicated details. (You rapidly lose the thread of the talk.) With five minutes left, the speaker suddenly consults the time, then announces—in apparent surprise—that the most important points will have to be omitted because time is running out. Now flustered and confused, the speaker drones on. Fifteen minutes after the scheduled end of the talk, and for the third time, the host reminds the speaker to quickly conclude. The speaker trails off inconclusively and asks for questions . . ."

Although intended as a parable regarding lectures to peers, this dreadful (but common) story can also illuminate some no-no's about ordinary teaching as well. (Fortunately, Edwards goes on for several pages about how to do it *right*.)

---

68   School of Information, University of Michigan, www.si.umich.edu/~pne/.

For quite some time, slides and overhead transparencies made highly useful visual aids—when properly used—but they and much else have now been incorporated in the ubiquitous platform technology typified by PowerPoint. It is a conundrum why this technology is used so widely and so frequently, yet is associated with derogatory remarks so extensively that "death by PowerPoint" has now become part of the standard business vocabulary. The visualization of Edwards just above explains how bad things can be.

But these trials by technology need not happen; they are the fault of practitioners who have never been good speakers and never will be good speakers (unless, possibly, they somehow take remedial measures). PowerPoint in the hands of one who instinctively knows how to communicate effectively is very helpful, and a beautiful thing to watch; PowerPoint in the hands of a "kommunications klutz" just affords a further demonstration of ineptitude.

The authors are neutral[69] on whether to use PowerPoint for university school lectures. If it *is* used, hand out these aids—why waste time turning students into mindless scribes?—while emphasizing that what is being said by the teacher (including material not mentioned in the PowerPoint aids) is also course material! It is the teacher, the teacher's personality, the teacher's message, and the teacher's human way of transmitting that message that is the focus of the class. PowerPoint presentations, alone, can just be e-mailed.

Death by PowerPoint—NOT

1. Start off with a (strong) motivation.
2. How does this presentation "fit in"?
3. Keep the number of bullets on one slide to as few as possible.
4. Don't mention unimportant details.
5. Relieve "bullet boredom" with photos, simple diagrams, or even cartoons.
6. Don't get too fancy. (E.g., showing one bullet at a time may be helpful, but too much razzmatazz is distracting.)

Remember: YOU, not PowerPoint, are responsible for giving a memorable presentation!

---

69 One of the authors has used PowerPoint in every class since 2000; the other author does not use PowerPoint in class. Both authors have, for several years, used PowerPoint for presentations to peers.

CHAPTER 3: THE ADVANCED TEACHER

Technology can also be used to generate greater productivity. (In fact, this is the normal function of technology and the usual reason for adopting it.) The classical approaches to increasing post-secondary teaching productivity seem to be these three:
1. Professors should work harder for the same pay.
2. Professors should be replaced wherever possible by lower-paid teachers (teaching assistants).
3. Professors should teach class sizes that are larger than they are now.

Note that *not one of these three strategies involves technology*, and that *every one involves an inferior educational experience for the student.*

Since this subject leads somewhat far afield from the careers of professors, a detailed discussion is beyond the scope of this book. The Ohio State University's exemplary handbook on teaching is again commended to the reader, particularly (in the present context) to Chapter 6, titled "Incorporating Instructional Technology." There are also a number of useful websites, of which

http://www.educause.edu/

is a prime example, its (nonprofit) mission being "to advance higher education by promoting the intelligent use of information technology." The excellent overview by Ayers[70] is an example of the kind of thoughtful help that can be accessed at this site.

This discussion cannot end without acknowledging also the didactic tsunami about to overwhelm all of teaching: the internet. Perhaps one's first reaction might be that an intimate classroom situation cannot be bettered by an impersonal internet site. However, more reflection indicates that a room of 150 freshman students is hardly an "intimate classroom situation."

Still further reflection considers that surgeons in the leading teaching hospitals are about to perform lifesaving cardiac procedures in the Far North, remotely, through the best of internet technology[71] combined with advanced robotics, which permits the surgeon to carry out intricate pro-

---
70   EL Ayers, "The Academic Culture and the IT Culture: Their Effect on Teaching and Scholarship," *Education Review*, Nov/Dec 2004.
71   Specifically *telepresence*, where all non-corporeal human characteristics are transmitted over vast distances.

cesses that were until recently confined to the best-situated medical environments. If this is possible, can one really say that a university lecture, or tutorial, or laboratory, cannot successfully take place over the internet? The primitive "reading course," alluded to briefly in the §3.3 discussion of "Teaching Late Graduate Students," for as few as one senior graduate student, now becomes an intimate learning experience for an unlimited number of students at any level.

It also seems likely that, once this technology model reaches its peak, students will demand the best lectures from the best (teaching) professors. There will no longer be any reason to make compromises based on propinquity. Young professors who are the best teachers and who realize the extraordinary possibilities of this disruptive technology will be the stars of this revolution.

Career Opportunities in Teaching

Many who have examined post-secondary teaching both knowledgably and dispassionately have come to view the approach to teaching, of even the best universities, as deserving of a failing grade. New technologies have provided some glitz—when used—and major didactical benefits as well, but these are not enough. Every other service-oriented organization in the developed world has undergone tsunami change over the past quarter century. Has university[72] teaching done so? Most who have thought deeply about this issue would say no.

In spite of the positive changes now under way in some quarters, many established professors have never optimized their teaching skills, and—worse still—remain comfortably unaware of their degree of ignorance in this area. This may not be good news for students; but for young professors considering a career that features primarily teaching, this provides a wealth of golden opportunities. They are in a position not only to become outstanding teachers themselves (worthy enough) but also to pioneer "dis-

---

72 Universities offer not one, but several, kinds of service. Professors and most administrators like to smear all these kinds together as one grand service, but to an undergraduate student there is but one service on offer: post-secondary teaching. A confusion of goals (and customers) helps temporarily with the general state of chaos about how well services are being delivered, but clarity eventually asserts itself and those institutions who are perennially out of step with best practices with respect to one of their key service types (teaching) will eventually pay a high price.

ruptive" technologies[73] and processes with respect to teaching within their institutions.

Teaching-focused professors can become the pedagogic leaders and alpha-teachers at their colleges, driving the uncomfortable but absolutely necessary changes in how the services of teaching are delivered to their customers (students). Not an easy task, admittedly—but since when is any great, rewarding career supposed to be easy?

3.7 Insights on Teaching from Our Interviewees

We conclude this chapter with some thoughts on teaching from our interviewees. Naturally, they may not always agree 100% with each other (nor, for that matter, with the authors) but their opinions are always worthy of reflection.

Molly Shoichet echoes the tension between high-quality teaching and the desire to carry out high-quality research:

> "I do like teaching, both grad and undergrad. What I don't like is too much teaching because you spend three to five hours in front of the class and it takes probably 20 hours to prepare for that and then marking . . . so it can take a significant amount of time to do. I have taught two courses in one semester, and it just kills research productivity."

This tension is not necessary (as we point out repeatedly in this book) if the doctrine that "everyone must do everything" can be cast aside.

Still, the strong connection between teaching and research, for many professors, is not just ideology; they truly love doing both. Consider Bill Buxton:

> "To me the only reason to be at a university is if you really love teaching. I loved supervising students; I loved one-on-ones; I loved small seminars. But no, I wasn't a great *teacher*, and I'm not being falsely modest; I'm a very good lecturer. I give a

---

[73] It is well known that humans are generally averse to change, and that the intensity of that aversion intensifies as one gets older and more comfortable in one's daily activities. Over five centuries ago, Machiavelli said, "There is nothing more difficult to carry out, nor more doubtful of success, than to initiate a new order of things." This is particularly true when the change is *disruptive*, i.e., is not a simple flourish on existing praxis but requires *discontinuous* attitudes and tools.

great talk, but in terms of the day-to-day grind, twice a week going in and talking on a course, no I don't think I'm very good because it's hard to stay motivated."

Michael Collins says this:

"University is about teaching, in my opinion. Until you try and teach something, you don't really understand it. Rutherford[74] once said, 'Unless I can explain what I'm doing to the charlady that cleans the laboratory, I don't understand it.' If you really understand what you're doing, it doesn't matter how complex it is; you can explain it at every level."

Tom Brzustowski had a very personal recollection of his early start in teaching:

"I had to develop all my course material—teach myself the stuff that I was supposed to teach. In fact, I had a sort of epiphany on the drive up from Princeton. My worldly possessions were mainly books and papers, a really run-down old Chev, and maybe about $25–30. On that drive in early September of 1962, I realized I was supposed to turn from somebody who had questions to somebody who had answers. It was a rather sobering thought."

Apparently, a little modesty never hurts.

---

74 Ernest, Lord Rutherford is one of the most illustrious scientists of all time. Of Rutherford it has been said, "He is to the atom what Darwin is to evolution, Newton to mechanics, Faraday to electricity, and Einstein to relativity."

Chapter 4: The Eminent Scholar

A Noble (Perhaps a Nobel) Profession

Chapter Overview

In Chapter 3 we viewed an academic institution ideally, as a community of scholars—all bright, curious and learning rapidly. We then focused especially on those activities where the learning is primarily being done by the youngest members (students) as they are being taught by the older members (professors). We claimed that nothing is more fundamental to an academic institution than teaching. We endeavored further to point out the many exciting career opportunities that teaching offers, especially if one considers teaching as one's primary career in academia rather than as merely a responsibility secondary to other, more "elevated" duties. One can define contributions of enormous potential, not just in the classroom, but relating to the overall framework of how the teaching function is conducted at one's institution. In this chapter, we move on to discuss activities in which it is primarily the professors who are doing the learning.

Professors also learn from students, of course, and the farther up the hierarchy of the "teaching levels" discussed in §3.3 one goes, the more teaching of professors the students do and the more learning from students the professors do. At the highest level (senior graduate students) the teaching and learning are flowing both ways to the point where much of what seasoned professors know about their fields of expertise they learned from their graduate students.

Is the supervision of graduate students "teaching" or "research"? Why, both, of course. Clearly the student is learning much from his or her supervisor (and, one trusts, from many other sources as well) but by the time their doctoral research dissertations are written, solid students often know more about their narrow research topics than their professors. The interaction between professors and their graduate students is at the very nexus of both teaching (previous chapter) and research (this chapter).

Unless the sole function of the institution is to *teach*, and to teach primarily *undergraduates*, one must spend at least some of one's time conducting research, and this itself can become a central focus of one's career. Such researchers must learn a great deal from their graduate students. Similarly, they must teach not just their students, but many others as well.

The first section below (§4.1) expands the meaning of *research* to encompass a great many subspecies and nuances, all of them important for academics. Then in §4.2 we ask, "When is a research career desirable?" There are many forces that tend to push the young professor in this direction, but there are also certain characteristics that must be possessed if one is to shine as a researcher at the highest levels. Most universities require that *all* their professors, including those who are great researchers but mediocre teachers, also teach, based on the *Normative Paradigm*. One hopes that this will change in future so that outstanding researchers need only conduct research (and outstanding teachers need only teach) in order to best serve their institutions.

Section 4.3 examines more closely research as a career. Again, there are many types and styles, some more suited to some fields than others, and some more appropriate for some professors than others. The goal is always to enable the professor to make the most important contribution he or she can. Section 4.4 introduces two habits of thought that are essential to outstanding research, though rarely mentioned. Without these, the results may be pedestrian. Several historical examples are given.

Up to this point, the discussion will be rather philosophical and general, but in §4.5 more detailed strategies and tactics (and the differences between them) are suggested. Finally, in §4.6, the insights of our interviewees are added to the mix, as the icing on the cake.

4.1 Research: A Theme with Many Variations

The idea of a career in which one attempts to do everything mentioned in this book (teaching, research, academic leadership, entrepreneurship,

CHAPTER 4: THE EMINENT SCHOLAR

and more), *all at the same time,* seems (to the authors) to be passionate but fanatical; it is suboptimal at best and likely impossible to achieve effectively. Best, surely, to focus on one or two of these modalities at a time. However, and this must be noted with equal force, there have been many brilliant academic careers in which, at *various times and as part of an evolving career,* one made contributions in all or nearly all of the primary modalities. (More on this subject in Chapter 7.)

Certainly the reader, even if he or she has just attained tenure, is already familiar with important research activities, in at least three ways:

1. **Graduate Student.** Modern colleges and universities, especially those who regard research as one of their main activities, will hire only new staff members with a doctoral degree,[75] signifying an ability to produce original, meaningful research results that are well-reasoned and well-presented, and that are acknowledged to be such by external assessors in the field.

2. **Pre-Tenure Research.** Since the pre-tenure period is a *probationary* period (as explained in §1.1) designed to test all the primary skills needed to perform as a tenured professor, the ability to produce publishable research results[76] must be demonstrated for all universities and colleges that feature research as an organizational goal—and especially for the *research intensive* universities.

3. **Research Ancillary to Teaching.** One cannot teach effectively, especially at the higher post-secondary levels (see §3.3) without some research-like activity in support of the classroom presentation, and it was historically this fact that led to the specification

---

[75] More senior individuals are hired less often, especially if they did not go the purely academic route, on the grounds that they "don't have a doctoral degree," and that they "are more expensive than new graduates." For the best of such candidates, this view is parochial and short-sighted, since real-world experience beyond the academic cloister is much needed in many university departments. The real reason they are not hired is that they are not of the purely academic culture.

[76] It is to this requirement that the phrase *publish or perish* refers. Nevertheless, this research requirement, though often loathed by those who must meet it, is merely a measurement to ensure high ability at research. We all know of secondary schools where the effectiveness of teachers is based on the grades attained by their students—as measured, of course, by these teachers' own grading of their own students! If research performance is to be taken seriously, it cannot be assessed via such conflicted criteria. It must be based on peer review.

of research as part of the necessary duties of a teacher of advanced subjects.

A much deeper understanding of the meaning of "research" is, however, necessary if the young academic is to make wise career decisions over the longer term.

Research—A Many-Textured Word

Once again, we have a word that is used frequently and ubiquitously, leading to the presumptions that its meaning is (a) important, and (b) understood by all. The first presumption is self-evidently true: any word used so profusely must be important. Certainly a comprehension of the meaning of "research" is important to *this* chapter, which intends to discuss an academic career devoted primarily to research. However, the second presumption—that all users of the word "research" are referring to precisely the same thing—is to walk through a minefield of error.

Many feel that semantic clarifications are at best boring and at worst a waste of time. We choose to disagree. More boring by far are discussions, debates and disagreements—whether casual or formal, whether learnèd or lay—in which, unknown to the participants, the only issues are the dissonant meanings of the words used. A penny of semantics is worth a pound of disputation. Thus we choose to pause for a page or two and add some clarifying structure to the keystone word of this chapter.

What one means by "research" tends to reflect the 'professorial culture' in which one resides. Generally speaking, scientists and engineers focus on physical processes, while social scientists and humanists, among others in academe, study sociological issues and examine (for example) culture, ethics and history. In any research undertaking that can result in a potential 'commercial product', another phrase crops up when academics mingle with the commercial world: 'research and development'. Confusion can arise, as illustrated by the following example:

> When academics use the phrase "research and development" they tend to mean the discovery of new results in applied science and (if pressed) some potential practical applications for their work. When business leaders, by contrast, use the phrase "research and development" they often mean *market*

CHAPTER 4: THE EMINENT SCHOLAR

research and *product* development. There is clearly an enormous difference between these two interpretations. Note that both "research" and "development," as individual words, suffer from a critical diversity of meanings and that the two meanings for "research" in this vignette are almost completely disconnected. To listen to conversations about R&D between academics and business leaders can be either highly amusing or highly confusing, depending on one's familiarity with their idiomatic eccentricities.

"Well," some self-assured academics may say, "there may be these sorts of dichotomies between academics and non-academics when they speak of 'research.' This is actually to be expected, and is in fact altogether welcome, since non-academics cannot be expected to understand the true meaning of 'research.' But surely all *academics* have a consistent meaning for this concept?"

Research Varies Greatly Within Académe

Complete consistency? Actually, no. Especially for universities. If they are universities in fact and not just in name, meaning that if they cover a very wide range (almost the *universe*) of established advanced human knowledge, their use of the word "research" will have distinct variations as between faculty and faculty, department and department (within the same faculty), and (especially for large departments) even subtle nuances within the same department.

This fussing about the meaning of "research" is not just a desire internal to this book, aimed at assisting the reader to understand what is being written. It is, instead, crucial to an understanding of a career in research. Surely the reader would not wish to spend 80,000 hours (40 hours x 50 weeks x 40 years) of his or her life in the pursuit of something called 'research' without spending, say, two or three hours reflecting on what, quite precisely, the meaning of this word is.

The idea that a person, young by the normal pattern of academic research involvement, should think of research as a "career" at all is foreign (and even heretical) to some academics. Fish swim. Birds fly. Academics do research! Not so fast. We have already agreed that academics who teach senior students, especially senior graduate students, must conduct some "research" that is relevant to those teaching duties. The question at issue here is this: Are these academics primarily teachers (who must do some research in order to make their courses lively and relevant) or are they primarily researchers? Some may say, "Just be mellow. What's the difference?"

Well, this is not a social event; it is one's career! Hence we offer no apology for trying to help young academics identify critical issues and to make wise decisions. If one is psychologically driven, to the point of obsession, at every stage in one's working life, to do what one is driven to do, it is unlikely that this book will provide much of burning interest. The intent of the authors is, instead, to stimulate some sober second thought about (and the means for dealing with) the many-splendored range of options for those academics who are willing to think of their future career as a future career, not just a mad love affair with the subjects that greatly interest them at the moment.

4.2 High-Quality Research—Could This Be a Career?

Now that the idea of "research" has been explored from several viewpoints, we enter a discussion of whether it makes sense for the reader to make research—and here we are referring to *outstanding* research—the focus of his or her career.

One must first admit that there is often great pressure to do so. Having spent several years and hundreds of thousands of dollars in opportunity costs earning a doctorate—which is almost exclusively an apprenticeship in academic research—and having spent several more years earning tenure at least partially through additional efforts in independent research, some may say that this ship has sailed. For better or worse, it would seem, one is already committed to a career of academic research, trying, ultimately, to become one of the best in the world in one's field. Your department likely wants that; and, to a considerable extent, you yourself want that.

Is an Academic Research Career Desirable?

However, we caution some pause for reflection. One of the great benefits of attaining tenure (other than not having been fired!) is that one now

CHAPTER 4: THE EMINENT SCHOLAR

has the security (and hopefully the maturity) to step briefly out of the rat race in which one has been scampering for the past decade, to reflect for a few moments on the *next three or four decades*.

Here are some factors that may lead to a choice of high-octane research as one's academic career of choice:

External Pressure 1. Obsession. Earlier (Fig. 2.1, to be exact), we mentioned that two of the critical factors in choosing one's career are ability and inclination. All tenured university staff must surely have some impressive research credentials, since they have been awarded a doctorate in research and then subsequently given the academic stamp of confidence—tenure. However, the range of research ability, even for tenured academics, is still quite spacious. So *ability* must still be an open issue to be examined in making future academic career decisions at this point.

However, as to *inclination*, some researchers have one that could be described as *passion*, even *obsession*. They would not go through the process recommended here (or, if they did, the outcome could be foretold without danger of error). They are so wrapped up in their research activity that they simply cannot *not* do it. Not all obsessions are sane, and in fact "obsession" means that one cannot control one's thoughts. For university researchers, however this single-mindedness is often a primary virtue, a career-long source of unlimited intellectual vigor. Together with their mental acuity and their demonstrated ability at research, some of these "obsessed" academics will produce the most remarkable results in their field.

External Pressure 2. Status. Of all the professorial activities at a research-intensive university, being a research star (meaning winning grants and contracts that are numerous and sizable, publishing papers that are many and significant, being invited to give keynote addresses at professional conferences, being extolled by colleagues elsewhere as leaders in the field, etc.) are accorded the highest status. Not everyone is equally needful of status, but most humans are fond of their colleagues' admiration and professors are certainly no exception.

External Pressure 3. Career Progression. Academics are keen to have their professional exploits recognized by their employers and colleagues. (Who isn't?) The primary concrete devices for accomplishing this recognition are promotions and the remunerational increments discussed below. We shall point out in Chapter 5 that these academic "promotions" would not qualify as real promotions to most people outside the academic world, but academics devoutly believe in them, so that is what matters here.

The issue, to be more precise, is not *whether* one gets promoted, but *how early*. For example, someone who is a *competent teacher* and an *effective researcher* might, in a particular university, be expected to attain "full" professorship by age forty-five. He or she can then sign themselves as Professor (capital P) without those bothersome qualifiers, Assistant or Associate. However, at this same university, someone who is a *competent teacher* and a *star researcher* might attain Professorship by age thirty-eight, or even earlier. It is difficult to imagine how one could achieve this internal honor based largely on teaching performance, however excellent.

External Pressure 4. Financial Rewards. Financial rewards have been left for last, intentionally. Some professors claim not to care all that much about money, and there is at least some truth to this, especially in comparison with a number of other professions. Still, professors are subject to the same financial pressures as are other highly educated persons, and less is definitely not more where salaries are concerned.

For one thing, professorial pensions are typically based on final salaries and professors are also living longer, meaning that there is an enormous effect of final salary on the cumulative pension received. If younger (just post tenure) professors had it explained to them, in clear terms, the hundreds of thousands of dollars difference that are at issue, they might look up with the penetrating look of intense interest that they normally reserve for their work.

Second, academics are, as mentioned above, also concerned with status and career progression issues, and it is a tough sell, for example, for a department Chair to tell Professor A that he or she is, with respect to Professor B, more valuable to the department, more revered by his or her colleagues, and more appreciated by the administration—although for [fill in your own empty excuses here] reasons, he or she is paid less[77] than Professor B. Other things being equal, being considered an outstanding researcher will make such conversations highly unlikely.

Still, it comes down to one's personal characteristics. If the Normative Paradigm (discussed just below) were accepted as absolute truth by all academics, this book would be meaningless and—much more important—there would be no variation between academic careers. All academics would pass through the same Career Tube.

The Normative Paradigm

A brief aside is first in order on how modern organizations are *organized*. The strategic direction is set by top management, which also oversees the process of breaking this mission into goals and sub-goals. So far, all readers would presumably agree with the wisdom of such a process (although many chapters in a strategy or management textbook have been condensed into only two or three sentences). Now comes the part that would be equally sensible to any reader—except possibly for the academic readers of this book! That part relates to *staffing*. In plain terms, who, exactly, are the human beings who are going to execute the tasks implied by the strategic goals? What should their qualifications be? What personal emphases and objectives are appropriate?

---

77 Salary comparisons with peers from similar universities and colleges constitute a detailed topic not considered here. Suffice it to say that the internet, government disclosure rules, and one's personal network of colleagues, are primary tools in this quest.

The critical function here is to match, as precisely a possible, the abilities, aptitudes and experience of the individual employee[78] with the particular needs of the position he or she is expected to fill. Even within small companies or partnerships, this can be a serious problem: If the role of even one person is not finely tuned to the requirements of their responsibilities, the consequences can be threatening (or even fatal) to the organization. If this relatively self-evident principle is true of a small company or partnership, how much more must it be true for a larger, more complex organization? Surely it is proper for a college or university.

In fact, this principle is largely honored by colleges and universities, as it should be, for all labor categories *except when it comes to professors and similar academics*. The senior management. The support administration. The plant and operational units. All are based largely on the principle that strains to find the best fit between the worker and his or her work.

But there is another theory, one that cannot be understood by most people in most vocations, one that flies in the face of all advice by management and human resources gurus—indeed, one that would tend to baffle most reasonable people. That theory is the *Normative Paradigm*.

According to this paradigm, all academics are expected during their careers to pass through a sort of organizational tube. They enter at tenure (or earlier) and they move through The Tube together, eventually exiting at retirement (assuming they retire). There is little or no room for any material variation between the many and various Tube-crawlers in how their contributions are defined or evaluated. More prescriptively, according to the Normative Paradigm it is the ineluctable duty of every professor, on being granted tenure, to spend $X\%$ of his or her time teaching, $Y\%$ of his or her time doing research, $Z\%$ of his or her time doing {the next thing on the list}, and so on, where of course $X + Y + Z + \cdots = 100\%$. The critical point is that, within any one university, faculty or department, the weightings $\{X, Y, Z, \ldots\}$ are essentially *identical for all professors*.

However, this book creates important career formulas by forthright deviation from the constraints of the Paradigm. As we shall see later, there

---

78 Some professors may bridle at the idea of being referred to as an employee. In law, they certainly are, even if in their minds they are something more special.

CHAPTER 4: THE EMINENT SCHOLAR

are ways of breaking free from these constraints,[79] although they do require proactive forethought by the academic in question. Indeed, the previous chapter has described a Teaching Paradigm, wherein teaching is emphasized to the exclusion of almost everything else—including research (except for the much more restricted type of research needed to support course development).

Similarly, this chapter explicates a Research Paradigm, where most effort is spent on research and no apology is made for not teaching undergraduate courses (unless, of course, the professor, the department *and the students* all are strongly in favor). Academic executives and entrepreneurial professors (Chapters 5 and 6, respectively) are two further ways to think (and eventually arrive) outside the Normative Paradigm. Thus, although the NP may be the career path leading up to tenure, and just after tenure, and will remain the career-long path for those who don't realize they're in it, or who want to stay in it, or who can't figure out how to extricate themselves from it, escape is possible for those who wish to do so, provided they have sufficient talent and determination.

Here are a few sample scenarios that may help one to diagnose some of the disorders that can arise when the prevailing culture or policy insists that the Normative Paradigm be applied to everyone:

Example 1. Jane has a great research program, but . . . . "Great" program meaning that Jane's research is producing a steady flow of interesting and useful results—but she is below the departmental average as to weekly hours spent teaching. Her colleagues are distressed by this state of affairs. Some are probably envious of her successful research, but here we concentrate on her alleged contravention of the NP. Some of her colleagues murmur thus: "Nice for Jane, but if I weren't loaded down with all this teaching I'm doing, I could also have a better research program."

Example 2. Frank loves to teach, but . . . . Not only does Frank love to teach; much more important, his students love him to

---

[79] One is often advised to think "outside the box," although the advisor almost never defines the "box" whose escape is advised. Here, it quite clear: the "box" is the Normative Paradigm!

teach them, as measured by student teaching evaluations and by the glowing retrospective comments of students who have been graduated for a year or two. So, one may reasonably ask, "What's the problem?"

Apparently, Frank is teaching so many courses and spending so much time with his students that his research is (in the opinion of not only his departmental Chair but also most of his departmental colleagues) "not up to expectations." The department is under pressure to increase its overall revenue from research grants and contracts, and Frank is simply not pulling his weight. He doesn't seem to be interested in having senior graduate students, and, although the departmental personnel files are supposed to be confidential, there is a well-founded rumor to the effect that Frank hasn't published a research "paper" in almost three years. Everyone realizes that Frank is doing exceptionally well at what he is doing, and there is some admiration for that, but the bottom line (the NP speaks!) is that he is falling short is a key performance area—research! He's not really one of us.

Samir is a solid performer at both teaching and research, but . . . . Samir is a faculty member at a relatively large university. His winning of tenure and recent promotion to Associate Professor testify to his demonstrated ability to teach effectively. His graduate students and his undergraduates seem equally enthusiastic. Moreover, his research program is well-funded. Once again, one may reasonably ask, "What's the problem?"

It turns out that Samir has an alleged defect, a professional behavior syndrome that is not NP-consistent: for one thing, he tends to think like an engineer. He voraciously reads the trade magazines related to his engineering specialty, although he tends to neglect the "research journals" published by the "learnèd societies." He has many contacts in the business world, and in fact he is often consulted by companies who value not only his sage advice and research, but are also impressed that **(a)** he does what he says he is going to do, **(b)**

CHAPTER 4: THE EMINENT SCHOLAR

that he delivers what he has agreed to deliver, and (c) that he does so on time.

In fact, most of his research is funded, not by the usual government agencies, but as adjuncts to the research programs of the companies whose company he keeps. Very strangely to True-NP-Believers is this fact: Samir has had only one sabbatical thus far, and he chose to spend it at the corporate research lab of a *Fortune 500* company. Some readers may still be saying, "Yes, Samir is a bit strange, acts quite like an outside professional, not really one of us, but he seems to be doing great things. I still don't see the problem."

More information will reveal all. Apparently, the Normative Paradigm has many shades of influence, many more than implied by the brief description given earlier.

New Fact 1: Samir tends to teach his students as though they will become professionals, not university professors; he's a bit light on the calculus, replacing its claim to class time with material on other subjects (design, public safety, quality assurance, marketing, best practices, the list is long). Although his students tend to find stimulating positions on their first interview, his colleagues continue to be suspicious that, in some subtle way, "He's not really one of us."

New Fact 2: Because Samir's research is funded primarily by corporations, many of his colleagues are disturbed by what they see as a "corporate sellout" on his part. Samir's responds to them as follows: his research contracts have reasonable provisions for publication of non-proprietary data; the university gets reimbursement of many of the indirect (overhead) costs of his research (unlike most of the governments grants awarded to his colleagues); his students tend to get high-power jobs fresh from graduation; his classes excite his students with their emphasis on real-world issues; and one of his most important corporate clients is thinking about a major financial contribution to the university. And finally, Samir says, the taxpayers and general public will surely be favorably impressed by his direct contributions to society; this will have a long-term positive effect on societal impressions of the university.

New Fact 3: Not mentioned in formal discussions of the somewhat strange case of Samir, but mooted in a more clandestine manner among his inner circle of departmental detractors, is the perception that Samir is doing rather too well financially, thanks to all his "consulting jobs." This view became especially inflamed when Samir invited all his departmental colleagues and many of his key high-tech company contacts to a dinner at his home, with the intent that, among other things, new contacts could be developed between his fellow professors and the corporate technology leaders invited.

"Gawd," said a colleague, "I wonder how much that swimming pool cost poor old Samir." Another colleague led a group speculation on the value of Samir's home. The steaks were well-marbled. The wines were consumed with pleasure but remarks on their vintage and cost were common. When one colleague's wife who was known for her direct approach to personal conversation broached this general subject to Samir, he gently explained that, while he had the largest research budget in the department and was generally well-regarded as a teacher, he had indeed benefited from his consulting fees, and that absent those fees he would probably have left the university quite a while ago.

Departmental hall conversations the following week: "Samir is a great guy. He is very successful at everything he does. He even throws a great party. But I'd feel better if he were more like us."

Such are the injurious and debilitating effects of the Normative Paradigm. This book advocates that the reader regard the NP as a strange and possibly dangerous anomaly.[80] It is admittedly difficult for an indi-

---

80 Thinking about the cohabitation of research and teaching activities is not of recent vintage. Czar Peter I of Russia (1682–1725), a.k.a. Peter the Great, founded the Russian Academy of Science with the express purpose of doing research. His view was that scholars in universities do the teaching and scholars in the "academy"

CHAPTER 4: THE EMINENT SCHOLAR

vidual (one reader) to change the cultural norms in which he or she is immersed, however pathological and outdated they may be. They have, after all, been in place for many decades, and are a primary influence on most of one's colleagues. But one does have a controlling influence on one's career.

Once a substantial fraction of the academic community realizes that the NP is more a religion than a management principle, it will surely change. Everyone's career is involved—and the health of universities and colleges are also at stake.

4.3 Research as a Career—A Closer Examination

The preceding two sections have explored, respectively, (i) how "research" generally fits in a post-secondary academic context, and (ii) some aspects of how one's research activities interact with one's other academic duties.[81] In this section we focus more closely on the many types of research among which an individual academic may choose to emphasize. The aim is twofold: (a) to furnish further information that will prove helpful in deciding whether and to what extent "research" should be the principle component of one's academic activity at any given stage of one's career, and (b) to provide career advice on how to navigate the many types of research available.

Of course, not all types of research are appropriate in all the many departments of a large modern university. To a major extent, having already chosen one's general academic interest (sociology, medicine, history, forestry, computer science, law, anthropology, engineering, etc.) natural constraints are already placed on the degree to which one can participate in the full range of research modalities that are practiced university-wide. Still, a

---

would do the research. Thus, back in the 1700's, advanced teaching and advanced research were regarded as equal—but separate—professions.
81 From this point on, it will be assumed that readers understand the Normative Paradigm culture, as well as this book's objections thereto (as explained in the latter half of §4.2). We shall henceforth in this chapter ignore the NP's requirements and demands. In particular, it will be assumed that one is free to choose the type and amount of research activity one wishes to pursue, within the specifications of an intelligent senior university management that wishes to optimize the fit between the talents and interests of its academic employees and the needs of the institution.

quick examination of such modalities is likely to benefit everyone, even if some more than others.

Many Variations and Textures

Unlike the two remaining paradigmatic academic careers considered later—the Academic Executive (Chapter 5) and the Entrepreneurial Professor (Chapter 6)—the teaching and research careers (considered in the last chapter and this) are so normal and so interconnected that it is only through the filters discussed in this book that one can contemplate the finer points of career optimization.

A careful examination of the many research species within academia will lead to further refinements in one's detailed career choices. For example, which kind of research do you most enjoy? Which seems most likely to produce significant results? Which has the best external financial support (assuming you want or need such funding)?

> ### The Main Message
> Before embarking on a career in academic **research**, spend 0.005% of your cumulative career time at the outset examining not only
> (a) **whether** academic research is your best career, but also (if yes)
> (b) precisely what **type** of research career you wish to pursue.

These and many other questions will be addressed more fully below, but ultimately the key message is the same for research in this chapter as it was for teaching in the last chapter (see accompanying box): Don't be dragged along, unthinkingly, into a lifelong commitment to research, or, even more amazingly, into one specific type of research, without a thorough inspection of your options. In other words, if you consider yourself a hotshot researcher, you should not find it difficult to *do a little research on your career!*

Re-Search (Searching Again) vs. Original Research

If one looks at the word "re-search" with fresh eyes, it clearly means "to search again"—that is, to find, organize and assimilate what is already known in a field or subject of interest, following in the footsteps, one pre-

CHAPTER 4: THE EMINENT SCHOLAR

sumes, of many others who have searched and learned before.[82] In the middle ages, there wasn't much being done that would be thought of as the intentional development of new knowledge.[83] *Scholarship* comprised primarily the searching of existing learnèd texts, much of it either theological in nature or at least studied and taught with the tacit approval of ecclesiastical authorities.

Zooming ahead to modern times, our university libraries fairly burst with textbooks and monographs, most written quite recently. Surely, it would be quite consistent with a university's most central activity—learning—if all this knowledge were well read and familiar to most scholars in their chosen topics of expertise. Copious quantities of new research results also appear monthly in an ever widening plethora of archive scholarly journals. But is all this material being absorbed as well as it deserves to be?

Passing on that which *is known*, to others who *do not know*—and especially passing on that which is known at any epoch in the development of a civilization *to the next generation*—is a grandiose task all on its own, quite apart from whether anything at all is added to the inventory of "what is known." If, echoing Plato, one believes that the success of society depends on the most effective learning by the best minds, this process—which is clearly the *teaching* process—equally requires that the teachers who shoulder this undertaking, and who are merely the previous generation of learners, also themselves learn at a level that permits them to discharge their awesome responsibility.

One group of individuals who should be familiar with the relevant body of written material (and who should also be allocating significant time each week to keeping up-to-date with important additions to their fields) are the teachers responsible for energizing the rapid ascent of *undergraduate* students up the learning curve. This corresponds to the teaching levels called "early undergraduates" and "late undergraduates" (and to some extent "early graduate students" as well) in §3.3. Pity that so many of these students' teachers are so busy pursuing their own personal "original"

---

82 One is reminded of the witticism of Wilson Mizner, U.S. raconteur: "If you steal from one author, it's plagiarism; if you steal from many, it's research."
83 Thinking here of what is now Europe.

research that they are often unfamiliar with the broader currents of thought of most interest and greatest use to their undergraduate students.

Better, surely, that these students, most of whom will never be engaged in academic research, receive a broad, balanced view of the main subjects in their major field, presented by professional teachers who are aware of the most salient issues to stress and the best ways to present these issues. Some academics enthuse about the rare cases of career academic researchers who are in a position to cite to their freshman class some little result they reached earlier in the day in their own research program. Perhaps such vicarious eureka teaching moments can be relevant to their undergraduate students—especially the tiny minority who are going on to graduate work and hope to become academics some day—but most students would trade such exceptional hypotheticals for plain old outstanding teaching, day in and day out, by professional academics who love to teach and inspire.

Lastly, in §3.2, in the subsection labeled "Historically, Research Was Meant to Support Teaching," it was remarked that "Over the past many decades, and in sundry institutions with varying relative commitments to teaching and research, teaching has always led to research as a support activity." Now we see with greater clarity the nature of the "research" that these teaching institutions were "always led to." It is, in fact, the type of scholarly research just discussed above—the abundant and up-to-date familiarity with the existing state-of-the-art.[84] It is a plain error of logic to try to extract an argument here for a full court press on some kind of *original* research results on the part of these (largely undergraduate) teachers. If one is focusing one's career on undergraduate teaching (as assumed in Chapter 3), one will simply not have the time that all the efforts major original research programs require (not to mention inclination and ability). The only way to do credit to one's "original research programs" is to do harm to one's "undergraduate teaching." Unless one is a genius—we've

---

84 Once again we see the pathology of the Input Overbalance Disorder, mentioned in §3.1, with reference to professors who spend virtually all their time reading. From the standpoint of knowing their fields, assuming they are reading in their alleged fields, they are ideally placed to pass on all their perspectives thus gained to the next generation. But they don't. Clearly the inclination to teach (and perhaps the ability) is absent.

all met some but there are only a precious few—one shouldn't try to do everything superbly well. And universities and colleges should not base core policy on the assumption that everyone on the academic staff is a genius.

Fundamental Research vs. Applied Research

There are, as we shall see, many dimensions along which we can spread the varieties of academic research. None of these coordinates is more elemental than the spectrum book-ended by *fundamental* vs. *applied*. These two appellations seem generally self-evident to anyone with experience with the various species of research, but to be perfectly clear, "applied" research seeks answers to questions that are prompted by some need outside the research area itself (sometimes indirectly so), while "fundamental" research cannot make any such association.[85]

There are several alleged synonyms[86] for "fundamental" research. One of these is "pure" research. What does "pure" mean? Might it mean that academics who spend their careers in other departments and faculties are engaging in impure research? Why make the veiled implication?

Or, alternatively, does the modifier "pure" mean that research without any identifiable utility is intellectually or morally superior to research that will, in contrast, uncover knowledge of interest to the world outside the academic cloister? Again, one would hope not—unless the researchers are working on their own dime and refusing to accept any component of their personal paychecks from the world outside (not normal in academia). This position is an ideological wasteland. Much more exciting, for both academic and nonacademic researchers, is the truth: fundamental and applied research play mutually supportive roles, for academic institutions and for society.

So, unsurprisingly, we shall not use the somewhat arrogant term "pure research." Another self-serving term, sometimes used in serious discussion, is "curiosity-based research." Whose curiosity? Paid for by whom?

---

85 Nothing is more transparently obvious to an experienced reviewer of an academic request for research funding than a phony claim for various ghostly "applications."
86 "Basic" research is a full synonym, meaning that no distinction will be made as between "fundamental" research and "basic" research.

While intense curiosity is quite necessary to *any* kind of research, it is, as the mathematicians say, a necessary condition but not a sufficient one. If no one else, *anywhere*, is curious about the results of this research, it should become simply a hobby for the individual involved, not a paid career activity.

Some professors feel most comfortable doing fundamental research, while others feel most incented by producing results that are of immediate interest to an external community of application. (And one should never let "fundamental" slide into "useless.") The position on the fundamental-applied research spectrum one eventually inhabits, which tends to depend heavily on the faculty or department in which one resides, is thus a consequence of much earlier career choices (including one's undergraduate specialization).[87]

Another key attribute of research, whether performed in academia or elsewhere, is the degree to which it is intended to be a general exploration of an intellectual domain as distinct from the focus on results of a more specific kind. It is the "general exploration" that leads to the nomenclature of the Doctor of *Philosophy* degree, even though many PhD graduates have no familiarity with philosophy. The authors need search no further than their own suburb of academia to find these strange goings on.

Young academics considering their future careers must weigh the low probability of a large, possibly paradigm-shifting, long-term appreciation of their *fundamental* research vs. the higher probability of a substantial short-term appreciation of their more *applied* research.

Theoretical vs. Analytical Research

It is also useful to distinguish between *theoretical* research and *analytical* research. Much so-called "theoretical" research is so labeled either because it is unsubstantiated by any experimental evidence, or because it is a collection of (perhaps important) calculations based on a (perhaps real) theory

---

[87] This fact also implies that one should, ideally, give intense scrutiny to one's undergraduate program from a career standpoint. Once ensconced in the intensely defined pipeline of a particular faculty or department, it is difficult to re-define one's personal research goals if they vary in even the slightest degree from those valued by that faculty or department.

CHAPTER 4: THE EMINENT SCHOLAR

of the subject, *the theory being attributable to someone else*. As an example, Einstein was, as everyone knows, primarily responsible for the Theory of Relativity; once promulgated, *calculations* based on this Theory are oversold if labeled "theoretical," unless, of course, they truly extend the Theory itself. They simply analyze, based on the best available Theory, what this Theory implies for their chosen situation.[88]

Still, there is admittedly no neon-bright line between theory and analysis in research. One should at least avoid the most egregious nonsense in claiming that a calculation or assertion is a contribution to theory. The graybeards at your student's dissertation defense will know the difference: Even for research that is Theory-based (meaning that the research uses the apparatus of a particular accepted Theory), the mere use of some equations or logic implies "analysis" or "analytical," not "theoretical. Only the top decile (at most) of researchers in a given field is capable of making substantive contributions to the Theory itself. The rest make useful calculations (analyses) based on the Theory.

Young academics having an introspective trance focused on their future research careers must consider whether their chosen research specialty even *has* a Theory in the scientific sense. If *not*, then they might ask this question: might they be the one first to lay at least some of the foundations[89] for such a Theory? If *so*, they might ponder whether they might use this Theory in a new, creative and useful way; their work will then be noticed by colleagues in their field—and appreciated by those who find the work useful.

---

88 It should be emphasized that the word *Theory*, as used in this context, refers to the usage of that term in science, the most reliable process for the determination of truth yet developed. As in *Electromagnetic Theory*, the *Theory of Evolution*, the *Theory of Gravitation*, etc., it often involves the quantitative precision of mathematical form (hence the many follow-on analyses for specific situations), but *must* be established by corroborating data together with rational inferences. Such Theories, when first confirmed beyond reasonable doubt, often lead to a paradigm shift, not only among researchers in the field but among educated people generally. However, not all scientific Theories are expressed primarily in mathematical terms—for example, Darwin's Theory of Evolution.

89 Or is their subject forever immune to such progress? It is encouraging to realize that all the subjects now based on solid theories were not, back when shamans alone ruled the world of thought.

Library/E-Research vs. Laboratory (Experimental) Research

By library/e-research, we mean re-search (acquainting oneself with what is already known), or theoretical research, or analytical research, or (more recently) computer simulation research, using existing documents in libraries and information from data bases and the internet. As distinct from these, another significant item in the research glossary of discrimination involves *experimental* research. This is not just a matter of furniture; the distinction goes far beyond that.

Granted, there are many important areas of academic research where this plain adjective is not applicable. In the history department, for example, what does "experimental" research mean? At best it may mean an interdisciplinary examination of what the recent experience has been under circumstances similar to the historical context under consideration. Although historians generally consider themselves humanists, many of them have social science training and use social science methodology in their research. For example, many of them work in social history such as analyzing census data and other sources, putting together large data collections, which they would run through computer models and enable them to offer certain conclusions. The emergence of e-research, which allows academics to access large data bases of relevant information, is transforming humanities and social science research applications.

What does experimental research mean to an astrophysicist? It can't mean the ideal of designing an ideal series of experiments, wherein certain parameters are held constant while certain others are varied in a known way, with all the data collected by next Friday. But at least there is a present tense to what is going on and being studied.[90]

In the so-called "hard" sciences, when the field gets ahead of the supporting evidence, it often goes off in some direction that eventually proves[91]

---

90 Indeed, most of the categories in this section (§4.3) would need some subtle revision in wording depending on the research field in question. The whole array of university research is a daunting panoply on which to attempt generic comments. But we try.

91 The authors could cite many examples, critical to the development of some aspect or another of modern science, where well-conducted experimental evidence—which is nothing less than looking directly at the truth from which one aspires to build a higher truth—has either splendidly confirmed or roundly

CHAPTER 4: THE EMINENT SCHOLAR

to have been somewhat silly. Researchers tend to take the easy path,[92] or the fun path, or the elegant path—rather than the path dictated by the facts. There seem to be many equally instructive instances in other (soft science) research fields as well, but readers in those fields will be aware of such instances with a clearer view than the authors. Here's an example closer to the authors' own home-base, applied science:

> How can we predict how fluids behave? There were, as of a half-century ago, two respectable disciplines in this field: *hydrodynamics* and *hydraulics*. The former, more academically based, used advanced mathematics to make predictions, while the latter, unashamedly concerned with what was going on in pipes, had its eye on practical results but lacked any general theory. Books were written in both fields, of course, but the experts on hydrodynamics regarded the books on hydraulics as crass and inelegant, while the experts on hydraulics, whatever else they thought about the books on hydrodynamics, couldn't read them. A divergence was in full flower, as usually happens when supposedly elegant material is written about a subject without any real, substantive data.
>
> Hydrodynamicists liked to ignore the internal friction that all fluids actually have. They found that it tended to screw up the mathematics they loved so much. Fluid friction (viscosity) tended to adversely influence both the mathematics (certain symmetry relationships) and the limited physics they permitted (certain energy conservation principles), so viscosity was (forever and unrealistically) set to zero. This meant that two of the most important issues for hydrologists—How large must be the pipe? and How powerful must be the pump?—were eliminated at line one.
>
> At about this time, flying vehicles, from aircraft to airships and dirigibles, were coming on the scene and this seemed, to the hydrodynamicists, to provide a ready strategy to address

---

disconfirmed the general theory under scrutiny. Often, however, the verdict is ambiguous, and further empirical evidence is required.
92 The great British immunologist Sir Peter Medawar (1915–1987) once observed, "If politics is the art of the possible, research is surely the art of the soluble."

the weaknesses of their theory. "Look," they said (at least implicitly) to the hydrologists, "pipes are old news. They've been around since at least the Romans. Besides, who wants to think about what flows in pipes? Not much sizzle there. We'll concede the *internal flow* questions to you hydrologists, who should have solved all this by now. We'll concentrate on the new age of flying vehicles, with its many questions involving *external flow*."

But the change was not just from internal flow to external flow. It was also from liquids to gases, usually air. And this raised another critical point that many had wished would stay under the rug: compressibility. Air is more compressible than water, and to make things even worse, airplanes were moving faster through air than the liquids were moving through pipes, which alone made compressibility more important. Both these realities—higher speeds, and air rather than liquids—heightened the importance of compressibility. Still, there was the omnipresent need to simplify mathematical models,

The extended example above was not intended to be a history of fluid dynamics, so how theoreticians (the hydrodynamicists) were forced eventually to talk to the practical people with real problems that needed solving (the hydrologists and the aeronautical engineers) will not be recounted in detail. Suffice it to say, there now exists a quite complete theory of fluid dynamics, well-supported by experimental evidence, and with mature computer software to support all needed calculations. Viscosity is included, as is compressibility and several other realistic nasties as well. Supersonic flight, with its shock waves and aeroelastic structural vibrations, have now become commonplace calculations in the aerospace industry.

CHAPTER 4: THE EMINENT SCHOLAR

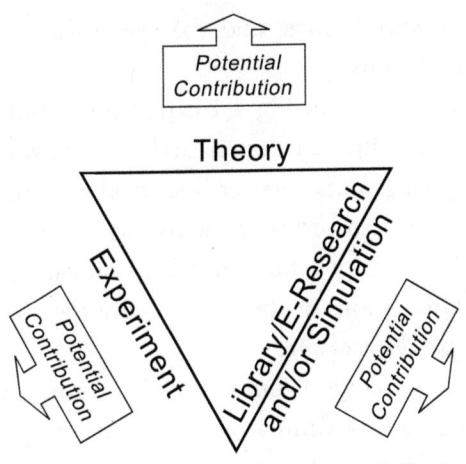

Figure 4.1: Three Legs of the Research Stool.

At the risk of oversimplification, the general situation may be visualized as shown in Fig. 4.1. Shown are the "three legs of the research stool" that ideally support any subject that claims to be "evidence based," or that is, in other words, based on the scientific method. The 'hard' sciences – in which 'hard' does not refer to the level of difficulty but rather to the scientific or technological subject matter – make use of this construct as the basis for beginning research. As soon as too much attention is placed on only two (or even just one) leg of the stool, the truthfulness of the area becomes suspect.

These subjects have a Theory, meaning the existence of some agreed *laws* that are solidly based on evidence (repeatable by well-trained others in other places and times) and sometimes expressed in mathematical form. This leads to the treatment of particular applications of interest via *analysis* (possibly using mathematical tools such as calculus or rigorous statistical analysis). Although such analyses were, until relatively recently, performed using paper analyses and rudimentary calculational aids, the advent of the modern computer has revolutionized both the armamentarium of simulational techniques that can be applied and also the breath and depth of the applications that are quantitatively accessible. However, as the fluid dynamics example above shows, if either the theory or its subsidiary analyses and simulations get out too much in front of the observational data, fissures or even chasms can develop between **(a)** the predictions of the calculations and the simulations, and (b) the realities actually observed under controlled conditions.

The construct illustrated in Fig.4.1 can also be applied to—and operates in—many aspects of humanities research. Some examples:

- Analyzing large data sets, or historical documents, or economic trends can lead to certain conclusions, or theories, about future trends and outcomes. Such information can also be used to formulate explanations or theories on why specific events or societal behavior patterns occur.
- In social psychology, a common and extremely useful experiment is the conduct of a simulated society utilizing a large number of students isolated within a particular area for a set period of time and required to operate under varying experimental conditions.
- An analytical approach in political science, to cite another example, examines precursor commonalities existing in various societies which directly or indirectly contribute to specific outcomes.
- In the legal arena, the operation of 'moot court' provides aspiring lawyers with an experimental environment in which to exercise their increasing legal expertise.
- In the study of English literature, theses most often present a theoretical premise of a particular piece of literature that is subsequently proven or disproven in the text.
- Philosophy formalizes this kind of analysis with a structure of 'thesis, antithesis, synthesis' as one foundation for exploring philosophical doctrine.
- Anthropology examines ancient civilizations and postulates the organization of those societies based upon physical evidence as the foundation of proposed social structure and or hierarchy.
- History often depends, for its point of view, on analysis of historical physical evidence and written documents, as the starting point for an historical theory subsequently proven or disproven according to evidence.

CHAPTER 4: THE EMINENT SCHOLAR

Platform Research vs. Incremental Research

We are using this terminology to distinguish between research that is transformative in its field and research that is essentially just "more of the same." The implications of the former are much more profound than those of the latter: As the name suggests, much future research and important further developments can be built on *platform* research. True, incremental research can also be published (assuming the reviewers and editors find that the work is basically correct), but fewer will use it or refer to it. Leading researchers will likely not even read it.

Incrementalism can have some benefits over the short term. One can score a few quick papers. However, as one's career matures and senior promotions are being considered, world-class researchers in your field will be asked for their opinion of your work. They will claim never to have heard of you, and be telling the truth. Not a good sign.

High-Risk Research vs. Low-Risk Research

Research is an investment, in the conventional sense of financial resources from the university and the various funding sources; more important to readers, it also demands an investment of the professor's time and effort. It is therefore helpful to distinguish between high-risk research paths and those whose outcomes are more predictable.

This is illustrated in Fig. 4.2, which shows a plot of available research projects (or programs) on a diagram that indicates both the risk and the reward associated with each. Two such specific projects are shown, "A" and "B." Note that Project B is expected to have a slightly greater reward that Project A, but is considerably more risky. Also shown in the diagram is a notional boundary indicating that the ideal projects from this standpoint (very large reward for essentially no risk) are not realistic (do not exist). Any such projects have been done long ago. The diagram indicates the general principle that to achieve greater rewards entails being willing to take larger risks. Also shown is the "best outcome" boundary which minimizes the risk for a given reward (or, equivalently, maximizes the reward for a given risk).

Research Reward

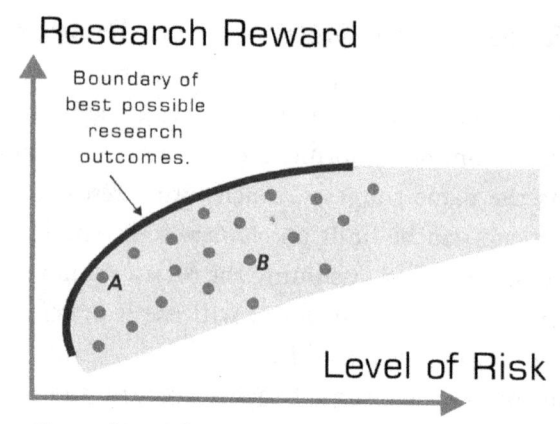

Boundary of best possible research outcomes.

A B

Level of Risk

Figure 4.2: Risk vs. Reward for Research Projects.

One last observation on Fig. 4.2: There are no projects with zero risk. For one thing, a zero-risk research project is a contradiction in terms. (The only way there could be zero risk would be if the researcher knew the answer before he or she started!) Less philosophically and more to the point, an example of a risk faced by all research projects is that one of the hundreds of researchers in the same field throughout the world will (unbeknownst to you) be working on the same project and will publish before you do.

4.4 Extraordinary Research Requires Two More Special Skills

"Research" is a word with which all academics feel very familiar: If *they* are not knowledgeable about research, who, pray, *is*? Yet, as we have just seen, this deceptively simple word connotes a startling number of distinguishable activities. While sharing some important common attributes, these still span a surprisingly broad spectrum of pursuits. The primary question at issue in §4.2—whether to choose an academic research career—has just been shown in §4.3 to devolve into a whirlwind of subsidiary questions. The present section, §4.4, attempts to answer these questions. It is not about research vs. teaching, or vs. administration, or vs. any other academic or scholarly activity. Instead, it provides a mental checkup for the reader to see whether he or she really possesses the necessary attitudes for the best research, and suggests how to tune up one's philosophical stance to foster "extraordinary" research.

CHAPTER 4: THE EMINENT SCHOLAR

Good Questions Precede Good Answers

Before discussing the career corollaries implied by the many research distinctions suggested in the last section, perhaps we should pause and remark on one of the seminal ideas behind all outstanding research. (This idea is encapsulated in the accompanying box.) Most of one's own education is focused on the art of supplying the "right answer." Test after test. Exam after exam. This emphasis begins, early in one's education, with the elementary art of regurgitation: writing or saying exactly what one has been told to write or say, reproducing what one perceives that one's teacher wants to read or hear, aiming always to gain acceptance or higher grades.

> **The Secret of Extraordinary Research**
> - To perform **excellent** research, one must know how to find excellent **answers**.
> - To perform **extraordinary** research, one must know how to ask extraordinary **questions**.

Many thoughtful educators realize that this process is extremely dangerous to civic vitality and informed democracy. If citizens are reduced, from their earliest years, to becoming mere receptors of received truth, they are hardly in a position collectively to make the wise decisions required to ensure the health of the nation. History is replete with examples of the catastrophic failure of political and social ideologies. Large parts of the population sought refuge in the accepted dogma, which permitted them to avoid the discomfort of thinking about . . . . But of course it doesn't matter what it was "about." The point is: They were not weighted down with the intellectual load of original thought. This point may seem like a diversion from the main topic at issue, but there are two important connections.

First, all academic researchers are academic teachers. Not just teachers because they are caught in the trap of the Normative Paradigm ideology of university administrative structure (see §4.2), but teachers because researchers always have juniors for whom they act as mentors (graduate students, post-doctoral fellows, junior research managers) even if they do not teach undergraduate courses. They cannot mentor their juniors regarding how to conduct earth-shaking research if they themselves do not know the basis for such contributions. Second, and more selfishly, one cannot hope to become be a successful researcher unless one is willing intellectually to dwell well above the din of the simple understanding, the effortless response, the easy answer. Only then will one become recognized as possessing the royal jelly that elevates them to the position where all other serious researchers—not just juniors, but peers and wise seniors as well—regard them as someone whose most recent contributions are required reading.

One of the authors had an interesting experience with a graduate student whom we'll call Hank Razor. Hank had the kind of undergraduate record that made his acceptance into graduate work a no-brainer: He was well into the 90's in one of the most challenging, unforgiving undergraduate programs in North America. Accepting Hank into the research group was not a decision; it was an honor.

Specifying Hank's initial list of research activities was not unusual. He was given a list of topics that he should read up on, including some journals and library sources where such topics were readily available. Things went well at first, as one would expect from such a star student. Then some strangeness began to emerge.

"How is your research going?" he was asked. Meaning, at this early stage, the search for existing knowledge.

"I'm learning a lot," Hank said wistfully, "but reading all the references cited in the main references is quite time-consuming. I know it doesn't look like I'm making much progress, but actually I'm working quite hard at this."

As the weeks (and then months) rolled by, the piles of books, reports and photocopied papers grew ever higher on Hank's desk. He seemed to be working harder but enjoying it less.

"How's it going?" Hank's supervisor again asked him.

"Actually," confessed Hank, "I think I've hit a wall. I had a bad experience last week. I was reading a paper, making notes as usual, and then, suddenly, near the end of the paper

CHAPTER 4: THE EMINENT SCHOLAR

I realized that I'd read it before. I checked my notes and, sure enough, I had read it with great care earlier this year. What's going on?"

What was going on with Hank was that he had been trained to find the answers. He always knew the answers. On quizzes. On final exams. Hank was an outstanding student (and his personal and social traits were also of the highest quality). But Hank was never destined to be a successful researcher, much less a brilliant one. No aspiring researcher, brimming with talent and fuming with original ideas, could ever have put him- or herself through the reading wringer that Hank did. Somewhere around Paper #3, he or she would have pounded the learnèd paper down on the desk, grabbed a pad of paper, and started scribbling down something—it matters not precisely what—that would have been the *germ*, not long afterward the *kernel*, and eventually the full flowering, of an *original idea*, perhaps a *seminal idea in the field*. This original idea would have emerged by asking an *original question*, something that people who know all the answers have great difficulty doing, but that grand researchers do all the time.

Extraordinary Research Requires Free Inquiry, Creativity, and Skepticism

If extraordinary original questions are necessary to making extraordinary original research contributions, where do such questions come from? It would be easy to say no one knows, and this wouldn't be far from the truth, but we can do a little better than that. Certainly there is a more than a mere spark of creativity involved, but unfortunately there is no Theory of Creativity. The needed dexterity of thought is often depicted using geometrical metaphors—thinking "outside the box," "lateral" thinking, etc. The "box" frequently means the conventional thinking in one's own research area, and thus one general process for being more creative is to interact with experts in areas contiguous to, or even more distant from, your own. Instances of success from such interactions can be found in the comments of our Interviewees. Einstein once remarked that "Imagination is far more important than knowledge." A more colloquial adage meaning much the same thing is this: "Smart people are a dime a dozen; what really matters is creativity."

Here are four things we do know about creativity:
1. Some people have this ability more than others.
2. Some environments are more conducive to it than others.
3. Creativity is very difficult to teach, but great mentoring can produce more creative students.
4. Creativity is essential to asking the extraordinary questions that can produce extraordinary research results.

An extraordinary researcher must have a free, innovative, and somewhat nonconformist stance with respect to the current state of knowledge, and must especially have a healthy *skepticism* of generally accepted truth. Persons with no training in, or feeling for, the concepts in probability and statistics tend to translate "generally accepted truth" to mean The Truth. No wiggle room. No room for improvement. The Final Word. No Research Needed.

A skeptical stance is often not appreciated in social situations. After all, when friends and associates make statements that they believe to be pretty much true, they don't appreciate someone with a skeptical stance saying, "That's interesting, Fred, although I'd like to hear more views on this complicated situation." Or, "I haven't seen very much data on this and I guess I need some of that before becoming convinced." Or, "Part of me wants to agree with you, Louise, but I gather there are other possible explanations that seem to fit the facts equally well." Thus, one may wish to keep one's skepticism to oneself in non-truth-seeking social situations. Full-blown skepticism should, however, be purring on all cylinders when one is engaged in research contemplation.

When to Question

One must be **skeptical**, which does not mean "to be negative." On the contrary, it means provisionally to accept information or a theory that have been obtained under proper protocols or from authorities in the field, and possibly accept them even more willingly as they become replicated by independent researchers or accepted by other independent researchers. As these reliable data and/or references become ever more plentiful, and as the potential inferences therefrom are rationally interpreted by more researchers in the field, only then does the level of confidence in their truth become great.

Never to 100%. But often to a very high degree of confidence.

CHAPTER 4: THE EMINENT SCHOLAR

Skepticism vs. Cynicism

Skepticism—the necessary intellectual sorting system that permits a researcher to distinguish between claims that are presented largely on emotional grounds, or with scant or distorted data, or with flawed or self-serving arguments—is different from *cynicism*, a philosophical stance that is neither life-affirming nor truth-seeking.

If one is *skeptical*, one says to oneself, "Freda really seems convinced of what she's saying. I really doubt that Freda would knowingly lie to me. Moreover, I respect Freda's powers of analysis and have, indeed, learned a lot from her in the past; nevertheless, I have to keep open the possibility that what Freda is saying may not be the final word on this subject. She has whetted my appetite here but perhaps there is more to this than meets Freda's eye."

To be *cynical*, in contrast, is to ascribe negative intentions to those who make assertions. The cynic, listening to Freda's remarks, would say something like this: "Obviously, what Freda is saying is bunkum. But what I really resent is that she *knows* it's bunkum and that, for some nefarious reason, she insists on trying to fool me about this."

It need hardly be said that, if skepticism (despite its lofty goals) is usually unwelcome, cynicism is the kiss of death in a social situation. Nevertheless cynicism has its place—in responding to the ubiquitous onslaught of advertising, for example, and likely in many other spheres as well.

For greater clarity, it should be stated that skepticism is definitely not *nihilism*. The latter is a quasi-psychosis in which the sufferer believes in nothing: not (at all) in the government; not (at all) in the social structure; not (at all) in any scientific results. Everything must be torn down as mistaken and menacing. This is the ultimate negativity; it will produce no research results and will, more profoundly, produce a sad and depressed life for the so afflicted.

Skepticism is often portrayed as "being negative," especially by those whose convictions and opinions are viewed skeptically. They may say, "Okay, we know you like to be negative and skeptical, but come on now for a minute, put your positive hat on and tell us what you think." Surely, this is an enticing (and irrational and mildly insulting) appeal from one's friends and colleagues, requesting that one shut down one's critical faculties—in some cases, almost to lose one's mind—and join with friends in the bond of common belief or viewpoint. This is not a book on social behavior by Miss Manners, so advice on the best response to such social temptations will not be given; but when it comes to research, one's powers of skepticism and one powers of creativity are the Ying and Yang of generating important new research results. One's research output will be treasured not only for its novelty (the effect of creativity) but also for its plausibility (the effect of skepticism).

Historical Examples of Extraordinary Research from Creativity and Skepticism

One simply cannot formulate the probing questions that will lead to fecund research results if one accepts, without serious challenge, and *en masse*, the "current wisdom" in the subject at issue. In fact, it is not an exaggeration to state that the primary characteristic of earth-shaking research (as judged by its paradigm-changing effects on the subject field) is the profundity of one's challenge to the underlying foundations of that field. Here are some relatively well known examples[93] of where progressive skepticism led to earth-shaking contributions to human understanding:

Example 1.– Creative Skeptics who Transformed Time, Space, and Motion.

Case 1: Copernicus. Nicolaus Copernicus (1473–1543) was the first European (Polish) astronomer to formulate a modern heliocentric theory of the solar system. In 1514, Copernicus made available to friends his *Commentariolus* (Little Commentary)—a short handwritten text describing his heliocentric conception—the audacious idea that the earth revolved around the sun, rather than the other way around.

Thereafter he continued gathering data for a more detailed work. It is difficult to appreciate now that this conception arose from a profoundly skeptical mind, seemingly at odds with everything that was "known for sure" at the time and surely heretical to the prevailing religion that had the conti-

---

93 There are surely many hundreds of such examples. The authors hope the reader will forgive as understandable that the centroid of these examples tend to be not far removed from the authors' own fields of research, yet generally well known. Readers will be able to cite similar examples more proximate to their own fields.

CHAPTER 4: THE EMINENT SCHOLAR

nent in its grip at the time. His epochal book, *On the Revolutions of the Celestial Spheres*, is often conceived as the starting point of modern astronomy, as well as a central and defining epiphany in all the history of science.

Despite urgings from many quarters, Copernicus did not publish his book for fear of criticism (and worse). This fear was delicately expressed in the subsequent "Dedication to Pope Paul III" in his great book, whose publication he delayed until his death in 1543, which put him beyond the trials of proving his case[94] to non-scientific religious credulists.

Case 2: Galileo. Galileo Galilei (1564–1642) was an Italian physicist, astronomer, and philosopher who is closely associated with the scientific revolution. His achievements include the first systematic studies of uniformly accelerated motion, improvements to the telescope, a variety of astronomical observations, and support for the discoveries of Copernicus. Galileo's experiment-based [or, as they say nowadays, evidence-based] work is a significant break from the abstract approach of Aristotle.

The motion of uniformly accelerated objects, treated now in all high school and introductory college kinematics courses, was explicated by Galileo. Galileo made signal contributions both to astronomy—for example, he discovered the moons of Jupiter—and to the fundamental laws of dynamics. He was also a profoundly practical researcher—the inventor of the telescope—who chose to focus on getting actual experimental data, even if he had to invent new devices for measurement, rather than engage in extravagant speculation. Galileo laid the philosophical/scientific foundation for someone who was born the year after his death—Isaac Newton.

Case 3: Kepler. Johannes Kepler (1571–1630) was a German astronomer and astrologer (the profound distinction between astrology and astronomy had not yet been made in

---

94 A heliocentric theory had been formulated by Greek and Muslim savants centuries before Copernicus, but this was not the prevailing view in the European Dark Ages.

this pre-scientific 16th century) who was well-intentioned, though almost chained to pre-scientific belief systems. Fortunately, Kepler and his supervisor (Tycho Brahe) realized that observational (experimental) data were crucial. He made detailed astronomical measurements which indicated that the planets (members of our own solar system) did not actually travel in circular orbits (the perfect geometrical paths of God) around the sun.

Note the brilliant question: "What sort of orbits do planets, including the earth, have around the sun?" which would not have been possible without Copernicus having earlier asked "Is the earth really stationary, with the sun moving around it?" The old politically-correct taxonomy had to be destroyed one step at a time. First step [Copernicus]: The planets move around the sun, not *vice versa*. Second step [Kepler]: The shape of these trajectories around the sun are not circles; they are not regular polygons; they are not polygons at all; they seem to be ellipses.

Perhaps to gain the most benefit from this long example we should pause and reflect on the epochal research contributions of Copernicus, Galileo and Kepler. When Copernicus began his audacious journey to truth, the prevailing "facts" were that the ancient Ptolemaic structure was beyond criticism. It was anchored to the seeming assailable truth that the sun was the immobile center of the known universe. Ptolemy was the author of several scientific treatises, of continuing importance to later Islamic and European science. However, whatever their importance, these treatises were wrong about what went around what.

Let us now continue with these historic examples of making quantum leaps in a research area, provided one is skeptical and creative:

Case 4: Newton. Sir Isaac Newton (1643–1727) was an English physicist, mathematician, astronomer and natural philosopher (and alchemist as well, since chemistry had not yet been invented). Newton is regarded by many as the greatest figure in the history of science. His most famous treatise is *Philosophiae Naturalis Principia Mathematica* [1687], in which

CHAPTER 4: THE EMINENT SCHOLAR

he developed—in highly mathematical,[95] highly rational detail—several of his most important contributions to "natural[96] philosophy," including his Universal Law of Gravitation and his "three laws of motion."

Through these and other contributions (Newton's studies in optics[97] alone would have won him a Nobel Prize in the modern era), Newton laid the groundwork for classical mechanics. He demonstrated the consistency between his own work and the observational data of Kepler (see Case 3 above). Newton was the first to show that the motion of objects on Earth and of celestial bodies in space are governed by the same set of natural laws. The unifying and predictive power of his laws was central to the scientific revolution, the advancement of heliocentrism, and the broader acceptance of the notion that rational investigation can reveal the inner workings of nature.

<u>*Case 5:*</u> *Einstein.* Albert Einstein (1879–1955) was a German-born theoretical physicist, widely considered to have been one of the greatest physicists of all time. While best known for the theory of relativity (and specifically the mass-energy equivalence, $E=mc^2$), he was awarded the 1921 Nobel Prize in Physics "for his discovery of the law of the

---

95 To support his studies of celestial mechanics, Newton developed, for the first time and as an incidental necessity, what would now be recognized as the differential calculus.

96 In Newton's time, the precise idea of science was many decades away. Even though Newton was one of the greatest "scientists" (to use the more modern term), he still thought in terms of *Philosophiae Naturalis*, which is to say, the Philosophy of Nature. One of the ironies of philosophy is that, as soon as philosophers have solved the key problem in a particular philosophical area, that problem, perforce, becomes its own scientific field, with further developments to be made by research in that field—but that field is no longer called "philosophy." Philosophy, by definition, must eternally grapple with problems that are unsolved!

97 Wordsworth wrote the following for the statue of Newton at Trinity College, Cambridge:

Where the statue stood
Of Newton with his prism and silent face,
The marble index of a mind for ever
Voyaging through strange seas of thought, alone.

photoelectric effect." Einstein's many contributions to physics include his special theory of relativity, which reconciled mechanics with electromagnetism, and his general theory of relativity, which extended the principle of relativity to non-uniform motion, creating a new theory of gravitation.

Notably, he was not an academic at the time that some of his most creative work took place, although he possessed both curiosity and skepticism aplenty. He was able to ask himself extraordinary questions. His other contributions include relativistic cosmology, capillary action, critical opalescence, classical problems of statistical mechanics and their application to quantum theory, an explanation of the Brownian movement of molecules, atomic transition probabilities, the quantum theory of a monatomic gas, thermal properties of light with low radiation density (which laid the foundation for the photon theory). The word "Einstein" has now become synonymous with genius.

Example 2.– A Creative Skeptic who Transformed Perception.

Case 6: McLuhan. Herbert Marshall McLuhan (1911--1980), known as the "oracle of the electronic age," was a Canadian educator, philosopher and scholar, and professor of English literature. As a communications theorist, McLuhan's work transformed our understanding of how people and their culture are affected by new technology in a media-dominated society. His pioneering study on *Understanding Media: The Extensions of Man (1964)* forms the theoretical foundation for modern media theory. His world-famous comment that "the medium is the message" defines his view that it is the medium and its characteristics that affect society, and not the content within the medium. McLuhan was always concerned about the individual's perception of the world as a result of the emergence of "new media." He theorized that electronic media unifies society and that the human race would become essentially a "global village," which has in fact occurred. At

CHAPTER 4: THE EMINENT SCHOLAR

the same time, he was concerned with the plethora of new technologies and how they affect people and their relationship to society. His contributions may be summed up by his lifelong quest to make people aware of the hidden consequences of the technologies they develop.

Example 3.— Creative Skeptics who Transformed Medicine.

Case 7: Harvey. William Harvey (1578–1657) was an English physician who began his life at a time when there were strange, unscientific views of the blood pump we call the heart. (Some of these views still have echoes in our own time.) The Greeks believed the heart was the seat of the "spirit"; the Egyptians believed the heart was the center of the emotions and the intellect; the Chinese believed the heart was the center of happiness. Anatomically, blood was believed to be continuously created by the liver and then pumped through the body by the lungs.

In all this philosophizing, apparently no one bothered to estimate the total volume or mass of blood pumped through the body per day. Had they done so—it would have been an extraordinary question—they might have been led to ask further questions, such as "Where does all this blood come from?" and "Where does all this blood go?" Harvey's experiments on humans and animals led him eventually to propose the closed circuit that the cardiovascular system is now known to be. Harvey's lecture notes show that he believed in the role of the heart in circulation of blood through a closed system as early as 1615. Yet he waited 13 years before publishing his work so as not to challenge the semi-sacred beliefs of his contemporaries.

Case 8: Warren & Marshall. Our stomachs exist in a highly acidic environment whose purpose is to dissolve large steaks in a few hours. Why does not the stomach digest itself? Surely we should at least suffer all our lives with intractable ulcers. When Robin Warren, an Australian pathologist, first observed in 1979 the presence of strange, small, curved bacteria on a biopsy of the gastric mucosa of some of his patients, he was well aware that the cause of stomach ulcers in general—and duodenal ulcers in particular—was not a hot subject for medical debate. Everyone "knew" that ulcers were the result of irritation by certain foods and medicines, with genetic predisposition as a risk factor.

At the time Warren made these findings, ulcers could be fatal if they progressed to the perforation stage, wherein a hole was corroded right through the stomach or duodenal wall, spilling gastric contents into the peritoneal cavity. A perforated ulcer was a medical emergency, with surgery mandatory in a few hours. In 1981, Warren joined forces with Barry Marshall, an Australian gastroenterologist, and their ensuing partnership demonstrated the clinical significance of this bacterium, a new species now called *Helicobacter pylori*. They demonstrated the association of *H-pylori* and peptic ulcers, particularly duodenal ulcers. Elimination of these bacteria resulted in curing the gastritis; the ulcers rarely recurred.

When Warren first presented his findings to the medical community, he was greeted with considerable skepticism—exactly as he should have been. Then other medical researchers successfully replicated Warren's findings. *H-pylori* infection is now known to be present in 90% of patients who have intestinal ulcers and 80% of patients with stomach ulcers. The skepticism has melted away in the light of irrefutable evidence, and hardly a year now goes by that Warren and Marshall are not awarded medals and honors of the most prestigious kind in the developed parts of the world, culminating in the Nobel Prize in medicine in 2005.

Although we have had room above for only a few major examples of how extraordinary research works, there are hundreds of other similar stories, each easily deserving a complete book in itself, not just a few hundred words. Readers will be able to cite similar transformative research examples from their own disciplines.

CHAPTER 4: THE EMINENT SCHOLAR

What Have We Learned about Extraordinary Research?

In Chapter 2 we pointed out the relatively well-known fact that, to be successful in any career, one must have the combination of distinguished ability and personal passion. In the present discussion of a research career in particular, we have demonstrated that two related habits of thought are essential to the creation of new research results—*creativity* and *skepticism*. For many other careers, these characteristics are not essential,[98] and in fact may lead to ruin.

In considering the glorious strides made by the individuals just profiled briefly above, it is difficult to empathize as we should, and at a visceral level, with their thought processes. The largest impediment to doing so is simply that we are fortunate enough to have their results now available, widely understood, and generally accepted (especially by educated persons). The contrast with the great barriers they faced can only be perceived by reflecting carefully on the environments in which their research was initiated—without results available, without understanding by colleagues or the "powers that be," and with the degree of acceptance varying from derogation (at best) to the forfeiture of one's life (at worst). The intellectual achievement in many of these cases is surely equivalent to the physical equivalent of climbing Everest.

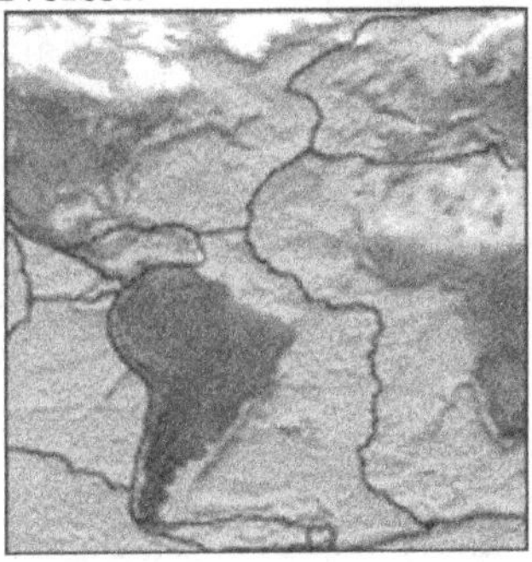

Figure 4.3: Why Do Africa and South America Fit So Well? (An Extraordinary Question.)

And speaking of matters geological, a further example has some important lessons for us. Innumerable people, looking at the modern world map, have mused that the two adjacent continents Africa and South America

---

98 It is hard, for example, to visualize a super-salesperson who demonstrates a strong seam of skepticism; however, other personal traits, not needed for research, are essential to a sales career.

look like they fit together (Fig. 4.3) and wondered, perhaps just subconsciously, why this is so. This is the seminal beginning[99] of an extraordinary question, but here, talking as we are about research, an extraordinary question does not mean merely a casual speculation on a summer's day. It means a full-court press by a dedicated, talented, creative, skeptical researcher. It means that the author of the extraordinary question must also do everything in his or her power to answer that question.

Alfred Wegener (1880–1930), a German meteorologist and geologist, did more than wonder about maps. He was the first person to propose the theory of continental drift. In his book, *Origin of Continents and Oceans*, he calculated that 200 million years ago the continents were originally joined together, forming a large super-continent. He was the father of plate tectonics, now well confirmed by data from space (and other evidence). Suddenly,[100] the human race began to understand the causes of volcanism and earthquakes, and that lunar craters are the result of meteoric impacts rather than of volcanism.

Perhaps the humanities are about to enter their golden age. One can only hope that these vast and more difficult research areas will find their Copernicus, their Galileo, their Kepler, their Newton, Einstein, Harvey, and so on. One thing is certain: Without fundamental researchers who are willing to ask original, audacious questions, and who are equally willing to risk their approval and their careers finding the answers, these subjects are unlikely ever to attain the human significance they deserve.

---

99 Sir Francis Bacon first noticed this peculiarity in the 17th century, when reasonably good maps were becoming available. Many young men and women after Bacon (but before Wegener) did much the same thing in geography class. (Did these young budding scientists ask their teachers about this idea? If so, how did the teachers respond?) Not only were world maps not the best back in Bacon's time, Bacon had none of the experimental tools necessary to support any hypotheses that were rattling around in his brain. However, Bacon is justly known as one of the fathers of the scientific method. The *Stanford Encyclopedia of Philosophy* gives a detailed account of how Bacon spent most of his life trying to convince powerful others that hard evidence and unbreakable logic were the necessary and sufficient conditions for knowing what was actually so. In other words, Bacon was one of the earliest champions of what we would now recognize as the scientific method.

100 The authors also noticed the Africa-South America fit in secondary school geography, but got only suspicious stares when they asked about it. This may shed some light on how long it takes profound scientific results to get into the school classroom. (The authors attended secondary school in the 1950s, yet Wegener's ideas were published well before his death in 1930.)

CHAPTER 4: THE EMINENT SCHOLAR

> **Diversity is Good**
> (other things being equal)
> The most important dimension
> of diversity in the academy is the
> **diversity of intellectual ideas.**

It doesn't help that the phrase "politically correct" has entered the modern vocabulary, which seems to mean, "I'm not sure this opinion or action makes sense, but I'm not in the mood for rocking the boat, so I'll just stifle my natural powers of creativity and skepticism." Sometimes it even means "I'm virtually certain that this opinion or action makes no sense, but I know my view is frowned upon so I will hold my tongue and still my pen." The university, with its special mission to develop new knowledge (including tenure as further protection) should be the last institutions in modern society to stifle free speech. The above block crystallizes the key idea.

Relationship between Research Debates and the Teaching Curriculum

The latitude[101] given to *teachers* in the classroom should be more circumscribed than the opinions and attitudes of legitimate *researchers*. This latter freedom is in accordance with the absolute need for skepticism and creativity. Of course, we are here defending and indeed promoting views and opinions that have been developed using the rigorous methods of the academia—sound reasoning, real data properly acquired and interpreted, and peer review of scholarly argument. This is one of the things that the caveat "other things being equal" refers to in the above block.

Further, the earlier the classroom situation, the narrower the latitude given. This may seem to contradict a willingness to be tolerant of offside ideas, but it is not. In the early post-secondary teaching levels—see the identification of teaching levels in the last chapter, §3.3—the primary classroom job is to present to students those ideas that have been accepted by the vast majority of the best specialists in a particular field as being almost certainly correct, while still creating a respect for skepticism and creativity

---

101 Meaning the latitude permitted with respect to the prevailing tenets of "correctness."

at the boundaries of those ideas. It would be perverse to teach academic subjects backwards (i.e. starting with ideas on the knowledge-ignorance boundary instead of with the established fundamentals), and dangerous too, since adolescent minds are untrained in the rigorous filtering processes mentioned in the last paragraph and ill equipped to distinguish between solid material and fiddle-faddle.

Still, even in the undergraduate classroom, it is dangerous to make absolute claims to infallibility, especially with respect to views that have not undergone the severe tests of rationality, empirical support, and broad agreement. Wm Brennan, a former Justice of the U.S. Supreme Court, once remarked that the U.S. Constitution "does not tolerate laws that cast a pall of orthodoxy over the classroom." A degree of diversity is still appropriate, but crackpot opinions or ill-considered ideas cannot be given the same weight as serious, seminal insights.

Closing Comments on Skepticism and Creativity

Most of all, one must cast a jaundiced eye on all claims based on "evidence where there is no evidence." In other words, on secular religions. Especially when detailed behavior patterns are educed form these claims, including pressures to take certain "correct" positions in pursuing one's academic research. Fortunately, political correctness has no central authority, no persistent or society-wide agreed creed, no holy book, and can threaten its flouters with nothing more than mild social scorn. In the long flow of human history, political correctness was destined to be replaced by more concrete bases for opinion and behavior. The likely sources for such positive relocations would seem to be academic researchers—the only sources with the high intellect, the secure funding, the decades-long timeframes, and the intellectual integrity to ask the needed extraordinary questions.

4.5 Some Nuts and Bolts of Successful Research

Though the previous section has been somewhat esoteric, its importance can scarcely be derogated because it did identify some of the most important (though sometimes neglected) mental frameworks that are mandatory to the most original, most noteworthy levels of research. We have flown with the eagles in §4.4 and, although many of us will never attain these lofty levels in our own investigations, it would be folly not to at least learn from and attempt to emulate the historic geniuses. This section returns to earth and examines some of the tactical and strategic issues that one encounters in shaping a career in academic research.

One approach to this examination is to review the many types and styles of academic research, as introduced in §4.3, and more especially to the wide array of vocational sub-choices and strategies that this variety implies. Other issues—including tactics, strategy, time management, the role of luck, and grantsmanship—are also raised and comments made that should be helpful to a recently tenured academic who is thinking about research as the centroid of his or her academic career.

Tactics vis-à-vis Strategy

One again, we pause and make sure that we have milked all the relevant meaning from key words—in this case, *tactics* and *strategy*. A brief summary of their meanings and inter-relationships is shown in the accompanying box. The actual length of time referred to by "short term" and "long term" depends on the application. In a football[102] match, the short term for the players is typically one play (one down) and the long term is the length of the game. For the team management, the short term may be as short as one game, with the long term as stretched out as a decade (for rebuilding the team or building a new stadium, for example). For much of industrial research, the short term may be a month or so, and the long term may be from one year (software company) to one decade (pharma company). For academic research, the short term might be from a few weeks to an academic term in length, while the long term may be a decade or more. By definition, the long term for an academic research *career* is the length of that career (forty years or perhaps many years longer).

Tactics, Strategy—and In Between?
- Tactics—The Plan for the **Short** Term.
- Strategy—The Plan for the **Long** Term.
- In Between—Where the game is usually won or lost.
---

[102] Meaning the North American game, not what the rest of the world calls "football."

Tactics is said to be the plan for the short term. Often, however, tactics is not so much about planning as it is about hand-to-hand combat. To continue the football analogy, there is the huddle, where tactics for the next play are briefly established, based on an understood playbook; but even in football, if time on the play clock is seriously dwindling, a team may go "without a huddle," and the tactical plan becomes the intuitive reflexive situational response (an "audible") from the quarterback. Ice hockey is another game analogy where, one the puck is dropped, everyone including the most senior management must sit back and rely on the players to do what they reflexively do; the idea of planning has no place in these tactical goings-on.

In contrast, *strategy*—the longer term plan—*always* involves a plan. Sometimes it may not be written down, but it must at least be worked out and be Priority 1 in the mind of the Leader. For small teams, who enjoy intimate communication, the strategic plan may be just a mutual understanding, with no formal written document, but for large teams a document of some kind is mandatory.[103]

Having a strategic plan for, say, five years, does not mean that one does not update the plan until the five years have elapsed! A strategic plan should be a living document, responsive to new information, new opportunities, and new threats. One does not, of course, spend a great deal of one's time doing strategic planning; that would leave no time for actually executing the plan! The usual foible is at the other extreme: not to update the plan at all (at suitable intervals), or not to plan at all. Those with enough talent always seem to do quite well without a plan, but it seems highly likely that they would have done even better *with* a plan.

Finally, the third category in the above box—vaguely named *in between*—is similar to what is sometimes called the "middle term," which is logically accurate but fails to catch the mystery involved.

> Readers who play chess will benefit from this analogy and its associated terminology. Tactics means, "Given the current board position, what is my best move, based on all the moves I can clearly see ahead?" (For a beginner, this is, at most, one

---

103 Indeed, we recommend some sort of written document in all cases. This eliminates confusion between team members—and also between what might be thought now and what was thought earlier.

move.) Strategy refers to issues like, "How can I ensure that I can castle, and on which side (King's or Queen's)?", "Is my pawn structure healthy?", "Am I trying to promote a closed position or an open position?", and so on.

There is in chess what is called the *middle game*. Books written about the *opening,* meaning the first few moves, can analyze all the remotely helpful possibilities—although despite this limited coverage such books are typically a few inches thick. Then there are chess books written about the *end game*, meaning the last few moves of the game, when only a few pieces remain on the board, and when you, the likely winner, finish off your opponent. These books explain what to do in more or less standard situations.

But, as one world champion remarked, "Between the opening and the end game, the gods have placed the middle game." This is where, for expert players, the game is won or lost. There are books also on the middle game, but they don't show a repertoire of standard situations, because, in the middle game, there are none. Instead, these books show actual games between top-level players, usually world champions, with commentary by the author. One cannot really explain, totally, what's going on. The author can only hope that, by watching the best players, aided by his commentary, readers can somehow improve their understanding of how to play better. One wag remarked that the difference between a grandmaster and a world champion is that the latter throws a pawn in the air and it lands on the right square. A true myth in the literary sense—meaning that it contains a fundamental truth, though not literally true. Who can explain how the greatest players keep on winning?

In summary, there are tactics, meaning short term actions, which deal with the future as far ahead as one can confidently predict with great accuracy. There is strategy, meaning a plan for as far ahead as one can even pretend to guess. And in between is the middle game, the part where most of one's time is spent, continually in action, immersed in complexity, beyond the range of simple policies, and engaged in continual decision-making. Over the longer term, these non-stop tactics sequentially constitute, for better or worse, the execution of one's strategic plan.

Time Management: The Importance-Urgency Dilemma

Figure 4.4 illustrates what we shall refer to as the "importance-urgency dilemma." Common sense would indicate that one should do things that are important or urgent. The problem arises when one must choose between actions that are one or the other, not both. Items on one's To Do list that lie in the northeast quadrant are not a puzzle: do them right away, and the more northeast, the sooner. Similarly, candidate actions in the southwest quadrant pose no problem: skip them altogether or, if they are done at all, pass them down to someone with more time and less experience.

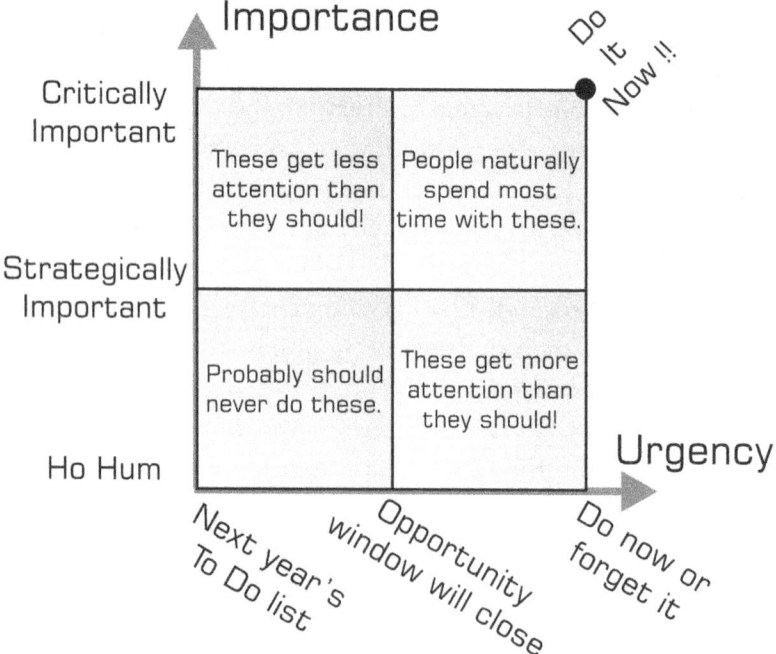

Figure 4.4: Time Management: The Tension between Importance and Urgency.

The interesting issue is how one decides, in one's time management behavior, between items in the northwest quadrant vs. items in the south-

CHAPTER 4: THE EMINENT SCHOLAR

east quadrant. The former are important but not particularly urgent; the latter are urgent but not particularly important. Or, to state the dilemma another way: The former are strategically important, while the latter are tactically relevant. Unless one is mature and well-disciplined the "urgent" issues will get all the attention. The phone keeps ringing; the e-mail keeps dinging; one wants to have an open door policy and be always available to those with whom one works. And so on.

Most of all, the items that are important (but not urgent) are susceptible to the *temptation to procrastinate*. Few enticements ever invented for going badly off the rails in one's professional activity are as alluring as simple procrastination. "After all (one says to oneself), it doesn't actually have to be done quite yet, does it?" As everyone knows, the problem with procrastination isn't that a lot of good stuff doesn't get done, it's that really important stuff *never* gets done if it's never urgent.

Career preparation of whatever sort—and especially the broadly based, highly reflective, activist kind of career planning discussed in this book—is the ideal candidate to be labeled "important but not urgent." It meekly succumbs to procrastination, sometimes fatally, for tenured academics.

Consider a common example: Most academics, just post-tenure, inevitably decide what their research program is next going to be, at least tactically if not strategically. Ideally, having just gotten tenure and with most of one's career ahead, this would be an ideal time to settle back and pause to focus on extraordinary research and the extraordinary questions one needs to ask to have one's research judged to be so. Here, one is faced with the importance-urgency dilemma (not too mention other assorted human foibles, such as the almost universal temptation to procrastinate).

One is often tempted to carry on with further elaborations of one's doctoral thesis. This may be an excellent path if such elaborations are of fundamental interest to the field. On the other hand, if they are merely more of the same, they may inhibit the process of planning a more exciting (and more demanding) research thrust. As with many other important decisions in life, pure passion may not be the most reliable guide. Perhaps a more rational methodology would produce results whose advantages would persist longer. The strategic response may well be, "I'll let someone else spend his precious time doing this simpler stuff. Instead, I will plot and execute a research plan that asks more audacious questions and that may well lead to answers that will grab the attention of many more people."

Of course, many of the driving forces that lead to a stunted view of one's true research horizons are not internal. They are external, and some are near and forceful:

External Pressure 1. One has been used, all one's life, to being regarded as among the best and the brightest and one also realizes that one is now in the most competitive situation in one's life. Any pause would surely be regarded as dropping the ball and losing one's advantage. Colleagues would say, "What's she done lately?" Relatives might lament that "He was a meteor that flashed across the sky but seems now to be burnt out."

External Pressure 2. During the brevity of one's academic career, as a graduate student and as a tenure-track professor, one has had occasion to meet some of the other academic researchers in one's field. One is now swimming in a larger pond, with bigger fish. Most of these individuals are awfully impressive and one does not relish the thought of being excommunicated from among the faithful merely by not chalking up some quick publications. After all, if one does not present a "paper," one is likely to attend the next conference at one's own expense.

The external influence likely to be most importunate is one's boss (not a word frequently used in academia but a word that accurately conveys a strategic relationship nonetheless). One can have the best habits of personal planning; one can explain to colleagues the extraordinary notion that one is taking a brief pause in one's research activities to reflect on what those activities should, in fact, be; and one can shrug off the short-term response of distant colleagues to a break from public appearances by visualizing their enthusiastic applause when one is given, two decades hence, a national award for one's research. But it is entirely another matter to ignore the cajoling one's Chair, the person who signs one's paycheck and who controls other departmental resources. While you're thinking about several decades of research, your boss is thinking about next year's external departmental evaluation and she wants more grant income—as Jack Bauer would say, "NOW."

CHAPTER 4: THE EMINENT SCHOLAR

All these (and more) temptations to procrastinate with respect to proper planning[104] should be resisted, and tenure permits one to do this. Otherwise, why have tenure? One of the authors recalls thus:

> When I started, I did not look for the long-term big problem, but rather started to be concerned about grants and contracts, to meet [the department Chair's] requirement to stay valued on staff. So I settled for extensions of my thesis work—profitable, interesting, and very publishable. However, with the same effort and more thought, I could have taken more time to plot a path down the road and look to the larger picture.
>
> Fortunately, this migration to larger, more important research issues happened later in my career when I got into a contiguous field and became acquainted with the leader in that field. Eventually, I was able to convince NASA to put my experiment on the space shuttle, as part of LDEF (Long Duration Exposure Facility).
>
> Although there is some short-term risk in going for the strategic (and big picture) research problems early in one's career, if the professor has tenure then he or she can take that moment in time to settle back and focus on the big one.

We are not talking here about years of fallow nonperformance—like years of writer's block, or the endless months while a painter changes styles from impressionism to cubism, or César Franck thinking about his second symphony until his death. On the contrary, this relatively brief pause should be seen as a highly creative and productive period, a time to assess one's research alternatives and to ask questions. If even *one* of those questions is an extraordinary one, the time has been very well spent and one's research course has been set.

Regarding Luck

This brings us to the role of luck in one's career. Luck is the great leveler. When colleagues or others have done better than we have, obviously

---

[104] The *DSM IV (Diagnostic and Statistical Manual of Mental Disorders, Fourth Edition)*, the ever lengthening list of mental disorders used by the psychiatry profession, includes "impulsivity, failure to plan ahead," as one key symptom of "antisocial personality disorder."

they were just lucky. (Or were they?) When we fail to achieve the levels of performance we have set for ourselves, clearly we were the victims of cruel fortune. (Or were we?) According to this fatalist view, everything that happens, good and bad, is controlled by some mystical providence, divine or natural. If this is the extent of one's worldview, why bother to plan at all? Or even work, for that matter?

Another attitude, closely related to the "everything is luck" virus, and one that is poison to the discipline of good planning, is the view that no one can predict the future, so why even try? Highly intelligent people are known for their ability to make fine distinctions. The distinction called for here is not even fine; it's a *gross* distinction: the truism that nobody, anywhere, ever, can predict the complete future with perfect accuracy does not mean that nobody can ever predict anything with useful accuracy. Very helpful predictions *can* be made, with helpful though not perfect precision,[105] about some things more than others, with near-term being easier than far-term—if one is willing to take the trouble. The fact that perfect prophesy is unavailable does not mean that one should not have a plan, updated perhaps annually or semiannually.

> **Deconstructing "Luck"**
> Luck occurs when **preparation** meets **opportunity**.

When it comes to career planning, which involves only one person, a *written* plan is not strictly necessary. Indeed, some very successful individuals claim they had no plan at all. It seems likely that, while they had no formal plan, they at least had a "strategic stance," that is, they usually did the sorts of things that led to career advancement over the long term. Part of this strategic stance is to comport oneself so as to be prepared for, and to quickly become aware of, career opportunities. Is this a "plan"? In the sense of a written document, perhaps one would say not.

In the sense that one is actively looking for higher rungs on the ladder, that one is laying the foundation for being a strong candidate to be considered for that higher rung, and that one spends a little time developing

---

[105] This is where the branch of mathematics that is most helpful (after arithmetic) on a daily basis, namely *probability and statistics*, comes in. It is often invaluable for making predictions with errors whose boundaries are known.

the communications channels (including informal networking) that would alert one to an attractive possibility—in that sense alone—one is indeed planning. One has some idea about future developments (though not a complete picture) and one has put in place a set of tools that make such career developments plausible.

Two final thought on "luck." First, risks have occasionally to be taken, for greater reward in the future. It is unlikely that people who are extremely risk averse will ever reach their career potential. They may value a "career" in some abstract sense but they aren't interested in doing anything personally to make it happen. What they really value is comfort and security, to the exclusion of almost everything else. If they became aware of the greatest possible opportunity in another city (or country), they would not welcome it; in fact, they would work to bury it and ignore it. Second, highly talented, highly successful academics can always say, "I didn't have a plan, and I did just fine, thank you." Still, in some cases, one can be forgiven for wondering, "Would their careers have been even more successful—using their own standards and definitions for perfection—had they done a bit more planning?"

Types of Research—Some Strategic Implications

Here we review the various types of research defined and discussed in §4.3 and offer some more detailed comments on their attributes from a strategic planning viewpoint.

Re-Search (Searching Again) vs. Original Research. We have remarked earlier that this form of research—examining what is already known—is crucial to being a great postsecondary teacher. How can one properly mentor the next generation in a field if one's own view is restricted and myopic? Re-Search is also essential to the conduct of original research: How can one build on the edifice of current knowledge if one has no idea what that edifice is?

Research students, especially at the doctoral level, are expected to have a "literature survey" chapter early in their dissertation, and it wouldn't hurt their research supervisors to spend more time on this kind of activity either. (One might, in this connection, review the discussion in §3.1 of "input overbalance disorder" and "output overbalance disorder" to gain insight as to how much time should be spent on original research vs. reading.)

In terms of financial implications, library and other similar media sources are usually supplied as part of the institutional infrastructure and do not represent a major draw on the researcher's financial means. Students are not strictly necessary to this task, although graduate students (and bright undergraduates) can frequently help with the organization, summarization and presentation of the material.

Fundamental Research vs. Applied Research. This is not a binary distinction, but a spectrum of possibilities, ranging from the most obscure developments to the frankly pedestrian. Academics tend to spend most of their research time closer to the fundamental end of the range than researchers in other organizations, and for several good reasons:

- Fundamental research carries more risk. One is never sure whether the investigation will turn out badly, or will take much longer, than originally envisioned. By contrast, in a commercial setting, where these additional costs are not being borne by the taxpayer or by a benefactor, these high risks, with their associated high costs, can rarely be tolerated.
- Fundamental research, as the name implies, requires a complete understanding of the fundamentals—the opposite of rules of thumb or a cookbook approach. When those who are not academics—or who don't think like academics—attempt to engage in fundamental research, there is often no discernable output of real value.
- Academic researchers who also teach (the current norm) must teach the fundamentals to their students. Nothing else will last through the decades.

All great fundamental research requires the *skepticism* and *curiosity* discussed in §4.4. Then, too, almost all fundamental research involves largely thinking—office work, usually with

CHAPTER 4: THE EMINENT SCHOLAR

the aid of a laptop, although some academics might still prefer pen and paper. This is not a heavy financial burden on the researcher, although one's salary and associated administrative expenses do add up and have to be accounted for.

Even at this extreme end of fundamentality, however, researchers should not be surprised at doubt on the part of an external inquirer if they cannot offer any explanation at all for how the results of their research might possibly be used by anyone else. Indeed, researchers should be pro-active in informing outside interested parties of any important utilizations or implications. It would be difficult to find a more poignant example of this latter responsibility that Albert Einstein's 02Aug1939 letter to U.S. President Roosevelt stating as follows (excerpted):

". . . recent work . . . leads me to expect that the element uranium may be turned into a new and important source of energy in the immediate future. Certain aspects . . . call for watchfulness and, if necessary, quick action on the part of the administration.

"I believe that it is my duty to bring to your attention the following facts and recommendations . . .

"This new phenomenon would . . . lead to the construction of bombs, and it is conceivable . . . that extremely powerful bombs of a new type may thus be constructed. . . . "

Theoretical vs. Analytical Research. The distinction here is, in principle, straightforward. If you are using Maxwell's Equations and your name isn't Maxwell, you are not doing *theory*; you are doing *analysis* based on Maxwell's theory. Very few humans have the theoretical talent (and the benefit of timing) to make an epochal theoretical contribution to their subject, but if these contributions are truly epochal, they will be used to great and good effect by countless researchers that follow after them.

Not all "theory" involves mathematical expression, however. Where are Darwin's equations? Exactly. Yet he founded the Theory of Evolution—"Theory" in the scientific sense, which seems almost to have the opposite meaning to the popular usage—but not a mathematical theory. A cause-and-effect theory, not a quantitative relationships theory, so mathematics is not the appropriate language. But a theory that changed (and enabled) biology and many other sectors of science. Another example of a non-mathematical theory is the scientific contribution of William Harvey mentioned in §4.4. Surely, to prove that the human heart is the primary blood pump in a circulatory system (rather than, as previously believed, relegated to erroneous and mystical functions, while all blood was continuously manufactured by the liver and pumped by the lungs) is a momentous theory of anatomy. Where are Harvey's equations? Sorry, not appropriate.

Nowadays, "analysis" depends more and more on "computation." The simple formulas have been propagated years ago, and the need is for more accurate, more complete, results for more complex cases. This makes new demands on the researcher to understand the ever more intricate world of electronic computation. There is also the question of whether the operating costs of such powerful computers (and their supporting technologists) are charged to the researcher's personal research income or whether they are provided as part of the institutional infrastructure.

Library/E-Research vs. Laboratory (Experimental) Research. Many researchers in the traditional 'humanities' and social sciences now have access to their literature and statistics from extensive data bases located at various educational and government institutions that are accessible on the internet. Although some academics might enjoy the quiet intimacy of a library, digital content is now exploding on the internet to offer these same researchers many new research applications.

Many university professors who choose experimental research (whether through planning or by drifting) as their chosen modality of contribution quickly find that they are not researchers in any sense they foresaw. They have become,

CHAPTER 4: THE EMINENT SCHOLAR

instead, research *managers*. They spend all their time writing proposals, making pitches for cash, reporting on contract deliverables, hiring personnel and sorting out problems of an essentially human resources sort, editing staff research progress reports, and of course reporting on major developments (often at conferences in idyllic settings).

We must hasten to say that we are *not* implying that there is anything wrong with becoming an "academic research manager." Indeed, there are individuals who make better research managers than researchers; their skill-set leads more naturally to leading a research laboratory. However, there is an important caveat: many professors who set out to do experimental research as their practical and needed contribution to their field never realized when they embarked on their "laboratory facility" path that they might never do any personal research for the rest of their career. The big research questions and the answers thereto become increasingly asked by research technologists and other research staff, and senior graduate students. These are uploaded to the research manager so that he/she can report results and make good grant and contract proposals.

The research manager may come to view his research staff as his personal acolytes, hirelings who owe their very professional lives to him. There is some truth to this from the standpoint of traditional management structural norms. But if the "research manager" was someone who had a passion for research, who had spent a decade training himself to do it, and who wanted to spend his life's work doing it, a transmogrification has arguably occurred whereby he is now working for his laboratory staff. (It is they who are actually doing the research.) He thinks he might have a new research idea on Monday morning? Perish the thought. It will have to wait. First, he must send quarterly cash flow reports to central administration.

Platform Research vs. Incremental Research. The words are chosen to imply what one might simply call "important" vs. "less important" research, but using more precise language.

"Platform" research can be used to build upon, with many further developments. "Incremental" research is similar in meaning to "same old, same old." Nothing really new is happening.

Workaday research for an incrementalist academic may be a good tactical notion, but is a strategically weak, if stronger performance is possible. When the big promotions[106] are later considered, people will ask, "Who used this person's work? Who even *read* this person's work? Has anyone heard of this person?" The answers mean that it's pretty much all over.

High-Risk Research vs. Low-Risk Research. At this point it's worth reviewing Fig. 4.2. The trick is to find research problems (or ask questions) about an area in one's field that are **(a)** low risk (likely to be successful) and **(b)** of high reward (likely to have significant results). This initial process takes a lot of study and thought in order to fill the diagram in Fig. 4.2. These are some of the main components of strategic planning that occur during the pause for strategic planning that is recommended after getting tenure.

Other Stratagems for More Effective Research

We conclude this section with observations on some final issues that deserve thought in planning a noteworthy research career.

The Hot Topic vs. the New Topic. Working on the same problems as many others is likely low risk, since most people, including academics (perhaps especially academics?), are risk averse. You will likely get some results and your papers will probably be published. But the glory for the success in this hot topic will also have to be spread among the many participants or assigned to the first to arrive in the area (and that's not you). Unless you speak and write so well and so often that others tend differentially to gravitate toward you, you will just be one of the herd.

Hiring Graduate Students. It stands to reason that you should get the best graduate students you can into your

---

106 Academic promotions are themselves questionable entities. See next chapter.

research group. But don't just look at a transcript, as though that little document was all one ever needs or wants to know. Have a proper job interview, meaning in person if possible. Sense the body language that is the nonverbal eighty percent of conversation. Assess the personality fit. Ask about the student's plans and goals. Ask good interview questions, like "Give me an example of something you did wrong in your career (or life) and what you think about that now," or, "Tell me about your greatest academic (or life) achievement and why you think it is," or, "Why did you decide to go on to graduate school instead of seeking full-time employment?" If you are to spend many hours closely supervising someone, a half-hour spent in an entrance interview is an excellent investment.

A Few Outstanding Grad Students or Many Grad Students. You may be tempted to accept too many graduate students. Perhaps you feel that this will raise your rewards in the eyes of the department Chair; or perhaps you are just too sympathetic to the pleadings of students who want to join your group. In any case, there are many important differences between brilliant students and so-so students. The former will bring some of their own scholarship funding, while the latter will expect you to find a way to pay them. The best students are coachable; the worst students are intransigent. The best students can work both on courses and on their research topic; the worst students must struggle just to pass their courses and whole terms can fly by without any research progress. The best students will take your intellectual contribution and build further upon it; the worst students never really understand your ideas and must have them explained repeatedly. The best students can write and speak fluently, perhaps even elegantly (check this at the job interview!); the worst students take extraordinary lengths of time to write their dissertations—and it's not that great when they've finished it. The best students could give a paper at a conference; the worst students should never be allowed on stage (especially if there is a question period). And on and on it goes.

Having read this paragraph, how many weak students do you now plan to have?

Grad Students vs Professional Assistants. Once your research program is up and running, one might consider hiring some non-student help. Among these are post-doctoral fellows, who can assist you and your students with the research. (They are awaiting tenure track positions somewhere.) Another class is professionally trained assistants who look after laboratory facilities, keep the computers humming (perhaps shared with colleagues), or have other specialized skills. They think of their positions in your group as full-time and permanent. This requires that you have more serious long-term research funding, and you must be willing to get more into "human resources" mode. One is slowly transisting from being a researcher to being a research manager (see above). However, such individuals can be of enormous assistance: They keep things running smoothly; they help to teach the graduate students via daily advice; they can help fill in while you're on sabbatical; they can even assist with generating new research ideas. As an epilog, it should also be mentioned that a university research group that consists of one professor and a collection of professionals—but no graduate students—may have forgotten that teaching, not research, is the first mission of a university.

Networking. Get to know other academics in your research area—especially the leaders and eminent scholars. Go to conferences, but don't be chained in a chair watching someone drone on in the dark, hour after hour. Before the conference starts, find out who is going to be there and with whom among the attendees you would like to speak. (Imagine that—conferring at a conference!) The idea is to spend ninety percent of your time with them finding out how they think and what they're doing. It's not about ego; it's about learning. Some of these mini-meetings may be low-grade success, but others will be dynamite. For the latter, exchange some papers, suggest mutual visits and/or seminars, etc. Go to the conference banquet and try to sit at a table that seems to be engaged in enjoyable conversation. Avoid tables where everybody is quietly masticating, waiting to judge what someone else says (if anyone else eventually says anything). If there's an opportunity to go out for a drink or a coffee with some group you'd like to learn from and get to know, take it. Leave the conference with new ideas and new professional associates. Perhaps suggest writing a joint paper with them. There are many benefits to thoughtful networking.

A Few Outstanding Papers or Many Mediocre Papers. (Compare with "A Few Outstanding Grad Students or Many Grad Students," above.) Clearly, trying to write a few landmark papers in strong journals is the high-risk high-reward strategy. As with investing, if one has only a few years (one kick at the can) perhaps the low-risk strategy is better, also yielding less reward. But if one has many years to go (as an academic does who has just received tenure) the high-risk strategy should produce better long-term rewards. There are so many academic journals around these days that just getting published is not all that difficult, but publishing a truly seminal paper takes real effort and skill. Also, many think, naively, that content is all that matters. Readers will never come to appreciate the finer points of your work if they are not drawn to the paper through erudition, superior writing, logical organization, etc. Even the title is important.[107] Take at least an hour to compose it. Take four hours to write the summary or abstract. Send reprints to your personal network of colleagues with a brief hand-written note seeking comments.

Interact with More Than Academia. Find opportunities to interact with other interested parties who are not academics. If your research has some wider societal implications,

---

107 In a long list of titles on sub-city zoology, which of the following might most catch a reader's interest: "On the Copulational Tendencies of Vermin," or "Why Rats Are Better Lovers Than the Rest of Us"?

find a non-academic publication in which to express them (and avoid narrowly understood dialects) or give a public address or a TV appearance on the subject. Be available to the press (but check what they say you said). Offer to advise and consult for agencies and politicians who have a stake in these issues. If you suspect that some of your research results may have commercial possibilities, talk to commercial and business interests, but remember, whip your ego for at least an hour before starting: the purpose of this talk is *not to show how smart you are*—and certainly *not to explain how you did everything,* which would wreck your later intellectual property position—but to suggest certain general capabilities and product functionalities that could result from your research and that may be of mutual interest. Listen a lot as well; perhaps you don't have that opportunity very often. Signing a non-disclosure agreement is ideal but may not always be necessary or possible.

Consider Writing a Book. Writing a book is certainly not essential and most highly successful academics never[108] write one. However, it should be at least considered as part of your strategic planning activity. This subject could take a chapter by itself, so here we say only that you need three new characteristics to write a successful academic book: **(i)** the ability to write fluently and rapidly (everyone thinks they have this talent but most don't), **(ii)** a strong, coherent point of view on a reasonably broad subject (something, in other words, that takes a whole book to express), and **(iii)** the passion and drive to complete such a task. Even if these three additional attributes check out, it will take at least a year of your time to complete the whole book project.

Several additional issues of interest are dealt with in the second half of Chapter 7 of Goldsmith *et al.* [2001].

---

108 Writing a paper in a book of collected papers or editing a book of conference proceedings written by others don't count here. Looking like a book is not enough. It must be a book!

CHAPTER 4: THE EMINENT SCHOLAR

Grantsmanship

We shall not dwell here on detailed questions regarding how to get specific research grants and contracts, although clearly this is of the greatest importance for those academics who need them to conduct their research. The details of all the potential sources (granting agencies) and their rules and regulations; the documented policies and unwritten conventions of the school applying; and the special understandings and expectations within each of the hundreds of research fields covered by the modern university—a compendium with all these dimensions would look like the Manhattan telephone directory.

If there's one thing that you, the aspiring researcher, and your employer agree[109] on in most academic departments, it's that you must raise funds to support your work. For that reason, your own university will likely have a research office of some kind in central administration, with additional information compiled at the faculty or departmental level. At a more general level, Chapters 8 and 9 by Darley *et al.* [2004] give helpful guidance on how the research grant process looks, from both the agency's view and from the applicant's view.

We close this section with a comment on some of the important differences between grants and contracts. First, most university granting agencies deal exclusively with providing research funds to academia. Thus they have a much better understanding of the strengths and limitations of university research. (Sample strength: bright person who really understands the material. Sample weakness: predictions of hard milestones turn out to be more than a mile apart.) The basic sections of the typical research grant proposal are these:

1. State past research contributions.
2. Give a survey of the subject to be researched. This has two purposes: (a) shows your profound understanding of the subject, and (b) raises the possibility that the earth may stop in its orbit if your proposed work does not get funded.

---

109 A reader who has bought into collegiality dogma ("We, the professors and the administrators, are all in this together, one big happy group of colleagues") may ask, "When would we ever disagree?" Here are four easy examples: **(a)** your teaching/researching ratio, **(b)** your level of compensation, **(c)** your opportunities for (real) promotion, and **(d)** whether you should stay or leave.

3. Give a list of the objectives and methodology of your proposed work.
4. Give a budget (ask for the money).

A research contract is an animal of quite a different sort. It is not Party A proposing to Party B; it is a legally binding document between Party A and Party B. Its main subjects are

1. **Deliverables.** What's going to be done?
2. **Staffing.** Who's going to do it? (And major facilities used, if any.)
3. **Budget.** What are the uses of funds? (And what is the total funding?)
4. **Schedule.** What are the milestones and by when will they be completed?

	Research Grants	Research Contracts
Signatories	Proposal signed by the academic researcher(s), endorsed by admin heads, and finally signed by at least one Officer of the university.	Contract (Legal Agreement) signed by Officer of the university plus Officer of the party providing the funds (plus perhaps some other unimportant signatures).
Are Words Important?	Statements made in a grant proposal are gilded assertions, optimistic promises, and pious expectations.	Terms and conditions in a legal agreement (contract) have the force of law.
Cash Flow	First send the money and well do the best we can. If we need more later, we'll ask for more.	Will specify milestones, and a milestone payment will be paid when the milestone is reached.
Deliverables	Usually research reports, which can later be the basis for academic papers if granting agency agrees.	Research reports, in language that can be read by nonspecialists, and possibly hardware, software or other deliverables.
Staffing	Emphasis on the professor who leads the group, but advanced training of young people may also be a focus.	Professor still main attraction but other professionals will be seen as a definite plus.
Budget	Often treated as a Grant-in-Aid, expecting university to get most of the indirect costs elsewhere. Indeed, sometimes expects collateral funds from other sources.	Focused on research. Takes a dim view of cash bleeding into other academic activities. On the other hand, may pay some indirect expenses (overhead) for the research.
Schedule	Some hint of timeframe required, but the unpredictability of fundamental research understood by grantor. Actual achievements are noted, not their precise date.	Time is money and these people know this. Well-missed milestones and deadlines may not lead to a lawsuit but will jeopardize further contracts.
Intellectual Property	Generally tends to favor the university.	Generally tends to favor the customer.

Figure 4.5: Research Support Comes in Two Quite Different Flavors.

Further distinctions between grants and contracts are shown in Fig. 4.5. Although the remarks given are typical circumstances and meant to be helpful, the totality of arrangements for funding research can, of course, have a very diverse character.

Escape from the Normative Paradigm

The fundamental premises of this book are these:

(a) There are serious career options for recently tenured academics to consider.

(b) If professors and other academics do not give the diligence their careers surely merit, the academic institution that employs them will decide their careers for them.

CHAPTER 4: THE EMINENT SCHOLAR

(c) Academics who wish to devote the modicum of time needed to settle some basic career strategy issues themselves—based either on the discussion in this book or from other sources—will enjoy a fine return on the time thus invested. They will be more efficiently reaching their own professional goals.[110]

It has already been suggested in Chapter 3 that those most drawn to teaching should consider disruptive ways to escape the "research imperative," including changing academic institutions to make circumstances more conducive to the pursuit of their craft. Teachers are not the only professional academic cohort for whom a fundamental change of venue may be needed to realize its vocational dreams.

The next two chapters—Chapter 5 on the academic management ladder, and Chapter 6 on seizing the entrepreneurial excalibur to project academic research findings into the matrix of societal needs—also provide career plots for deviating in a major way from the pre-assigned Normative Paradigm.

Academic institutions vary enormously in their organizational goals, and hence in the expectations they have for their academic staff. Staff members recently tenured, with more than three decades of working life ahead of them, would seem best behooved were they to assess whether the organizational goals of their employer were really coherent with their personal goals. Here, we ask this question most poignantly for those who wish to become extraordinary researchers.

Let's talk for a moment about *star* researchers. This concept violates, incidentally, one of the fundamental tenets of socialism—namely, that everyone should be treated equally in all situations. It is instead based on the *market principle*, namely, that people are hired and compensated based on the value they add to their organizations. This is true not only of elite basketball players, or of individuals in top management of major corporations, but also of elite researchers at internationally reputed research-intensive universities. The market principle can be temporarily sabotaged or bureaucratically diverted, but it will always eventually rule.

Star researchers bring in more external research funding, are more quoted in the media, and are more sought out by competitive universities.

---

110 Their academic institutions will also become more efficient to the extent that the duties of their staff are better tuned to their talents, aptitudes, inclinations and energies.

(They may also publish more papers, though that is not a primary virtue.) They work in the "hot" areas. The best graduate students want to work in their groups. They work very hard and everyone is very excited.

University administrators get even more excited when one of these stars shows signs of leaving for a competitor university. (A signed offer is the smoking gun here.) What have these administrators got to offer as a counterweight? And for what benefits should the star negotiate? Better lab facilities? Yes, to a point. More internal funding? (Yes, although endowments vary greatly from university to university.) More salary and other compensation components? Yes.

Another enticement the stars can be offered is a diminished (possibly zero) teaching load, especially at the early undergraduate stages where their skills are not needed anyway, and where other skills that *are* required may not be present. This arrangement may be further lubricated by having the teaching component "bought out" by explicit payments to the university from the star's grants or contracts. The university can then use these teaching buy-outs to pay other professors or lecturers to do the teaching. In any case, the star researcher has just made good his or her escape from the Normative Paradigm.

4.6   Insights on Research from Our Interviewees

We conclude this chapter with some insights into academic research from our interviewees. Once again, there is no guarantee that they always agree either with the authors or with each other. This book welcomes a full range of views from its distinguished interviewees. In rare cases of widely differing opinions, the reader will be the judge—and the beneficiary.

Tom Brzustowski is perfectly positioned to comment on the subject inasmuch as he has not only been highly successful as an academic researcher, but later led for many years the Canadian government agency that oversaw all academic research grants in engineering and the natural sciences:

> "My initial research direction was to answer some questions that had arisen in my thesis work but that hadn't been answered in the thesis. These sorts of questions [asked in the interview] about strategy and publishing and so on—they never occurred

CHAPTER 4: THE EMINENT SCHOLAR

to me. It was a question of developing the context and seizing the opportunities as they arose.

"One thing about university research activity is that it tends to have long time lags, between starting an idea and eventually getting it published—a decade with no trouble at all. By the time that decade is up, something that you started nine years ago is just nicely coming to fruition and you just never get out of that situation."

Bill Buxton knows the gratification that can come from research that satisfies an outside, nonacademic need:

"Xerox had set up a famous research center in California, Xerox Park, in Palo Alto. One of their lead people came and saw what I was doing musically and was impressed. Within two weeks he sent three people from the Park up to spend a week with me and then they invited me down for a visit. That really broadened my horizons. It was more academic than most centers, especially by today's standards.

"I'd been told by my funding agencies that they would not fund if I kept using the word "music," so I used to publish papers on "multi-point touch-sensitive real-time controllers"—which is a big euphemism for a drum. I could describe what I wanted to do in the terms necessary to procure the funding needed to do it and I was happy as long as it didn't compromise me musically. One thing that universities have that's fantastic is the ability to have graduate students working with you, where you can do curiosity-driven research.

"However, my colleagues and friends who are in academic positions are lucky if they get half a day a week to do research because after they've done their teaching, then they then spend more time on research grant writing and admin than they do on research, so their productivity is really low. I'd say to anybody who has just graduated from university, 'If you can get into a good corporate research lab—and I mean research with a capital R not a small r—they're much better off because they can devote themselves to research, full time, 24 hours a day if they want, without ever looking at a grant proposal. They can build up their publication record spectacularly; they'll got a huge reputation; they'll have a back-ground in industry, and should they want to go back to academia they'll be miles ahead of the people who stayed in the academic stream."

Michael Collins is passionate about how the proper strategic research goals are set:

"Long-term goals should exemplify university research. As soon as some committee defines what the next hot thing is, that's not long-term enough. They've read *The Economist* the week before, or maybe *Nature* or *Science*, and they say, 'This is it; if we don't do this we're going to miss the boat!' You've got to find something which is, to you, deep and meaningful, and juicy and meaty—that you're going to spend your whole academic career on, working on solving part of, or, if you're really lucky, solving a lot of. You've got to find that good problem, one that shifts the field, one that actually causes future work to change direction—the seminal piece. But you don't make such a ground-breaking piece of research without taking risks that you're going to fail. And serendipity plays a big part in coming up with good ideas.

"I think to be successful in any of the kinds of academic careers you're looking at, you've got to be an expert in something. You've got to develop your own field to where you're hopefully world class if you really want to go to the top of the academic heap. In my group, we're interested in principles, not rules. In picking graduate students the thing I most look for is enthusiasm."

Barry French's experience shows how to supercharge one's career by strategic alliances with other researchers for a good fit:

"One of the ways of bootstrapping your career and getting to the next level is working with other excellent people at other institutions. The biggest advances often come from lateral thinking, from applying something that's an advance in one field to an entirely unexpected area.

CHAPTER 4: THE EMINENT SCHOLAR

> "I had a sabbatical and I remember that I spent half that sabbatical thinking, what the heck am I going to do? I'm looking at these things that are outside my expertise (or, more negatively, nobody's interested in funding the things I'm interested in doing). Then I teamed up. That was turning adversity into advantage."

Donald Mackay has an interesting twist on how to search for the extraordinary questions:

> "I think it's very difficult to predict in advance where the big developments are going to come, but you're not going to find them unless you try. I've advocated that one should undertake a fairly central area of research but dabble in peripheral things as well. Sometimes they're the ones that take off. I think a little diversity is good but not to the extent that you dabble in far too many things and do none well. By attending scientific meetings and reading the scientific literature you can sense what some of these areas are going to be in the future.
>
> I found it fascinating to go and visit authorities in the field and hear what their priorities are and how they're setting about doing things. Contact with leaders in the field is very important and I think that's best done through scientific meetings—the more contact you have with these people the better. By forming partnerships with people in government departments, I was able to get a fairly continuous source of money, and also from associated industry groups. So if I wanted to do some work on oil spills, for example, my strategy was to go to Environment Canada and say, 'If I get money from the petroleum industry, will you match it?' then I would go to industry and say, 'I've got this etc.' So building a community of research supporters is a good way to go."

Heather Monroe-Blum conducted her research in the humanities, but her sage advice is transferable to many other fields as well:

> "It was clear at the time that the faculty of social work [at the University of Toronto] ought to be research based and should be academic to the core. Its research should inform the

profession, not only the other way around. Sometimes, it's easier to do big transformative things than small incremental things, so why go for a little grant here, a little grant there? Go and plan, and get, a huge project. And in so doing, one should be trying to maximize total government investment and commitment, and that of other partners as well."

Molly Shoichet believes that universities should concentrate on big strategic questions in fundamental research:

"Part of what I love about research is that it's always changing. I'm very comfortable with change. It's exciting and invigorating. You realize pretty early on that you might have a great idea but if you don't have any data to support it you're not going to get funded. So I think it's extremely important to work on big questions; in fact, I think that's our mandate because if you're working on the incremental questions, well, business can do those. The funding mechanisms driven by the private sector are inherently going to be shorter-term. But if it's shorter-term, I think that would be a problem. We academics have to look at the big questions because nobody else is. At the same time, if you're looking at a big question, there's a series of smaller questions. You go from the big vision down and it gets you into some really interesting basic science questions."

Chapter 5: The Academic Executive

From Bureaucratic Administrator to Inspiring Leader

Chapter Overview

Careers that emphasize teaching or research, as discussed in the preceding two chapters, are natural accentuations of what are already fundamental academic activities. Everyone receiving tenure is already familiar with, and has demonstrated strong skills for performing, these functions.

In this chapter, we turn to an area that is quite different—administration, management and leadership in academia. The primary skills required are distinct from those needed in teaching and research, and may well be lacking in many professors. This makes many academics shun such careers; they are already doing what they love and what they worked many years to attain. Why would they veer off onto a new course, one in which they won't realistically be able to continue to enjoy the kind of accomplishments they have made in the past, while entering into new responsibilities for which neither the aptitude nor the interest is present.

This response is the most common one, but it is not universal. (This is fortunate; else our institutions would be leaderless.) Some academics do not wish to end their careers doing exactly the same thing they were doing 35 years earlier when they achieved tenure. This perplexity prompts, in §5.1, a discussion about what is, and what is not, a promotion. Then in §5.2, a generic overview is given of some paths less trodden, paths to academic leadership.

A concrete approach to investigating these possibilities is given in §§5.3 & 5.4, using skill set concepts. What skills are needed and what skills do you have? Of those skills needed that you don't have, which can be successfully learned? These explorations will be fascinating to some and perhaps boring to others. The latter are not advised to follow these career paths. For the former, §5.5 makes several practical suggestions on how to approach the task of entering the management/leadership path. Finally, §5.6 is devoted to the extensive and insightful comments made by our interviewees.

5.1 Careers Measured by Promotions

Many academics—including some of our interviewees—have said that it may not be appropriate to use the word *career* with reference to one's sojourn in academia. One version of this stance harkens back to §1.3, where it was observed that many academics "do not think of a professorship as a career position; they think of it as a calling." Perhaps *sacred* is too strong a word to use, but clearly there is just a whiff here of something much more than making a fine living in an interesting job.

Another version is represented by the view that the whole business of "planning" a career in academia is essentially impossible. Surely (the argument would go), nobody can predict what will happen over three or four decades; and whatever one's views may be on the desirability of planning, the complexity of the problem must make it refractory to solution by any sort of reasonable meaning of the word.

Forethought is a Good Thing

The authors have an understanding of, and a respect for, these views. With respect to the *vocation* argument, we agree that society (if not providence) has bequeathed to professors an awesome responsibility and opportunity, namely, to transfer the best of human knowledge to the next generation and to augment still further that body of knowledge. One should not be too self-centered in the discharge of this responsibility. This touches the gravamen of the points made by Donald Kennedy [1997], in his book *Academic Duty*, referred to in §2.1.

With regard to the *complexity* issue, we are mature enough to realize that one cannot plan, in detail, and long in advance, a four-decade assault on the bastions of academic immortality—except in broadest of terms. In fact, the strategy of working hard, doing the best one can, and being alert to opportunities that present themselves, is not too far off the best one can do. It may not be "far off the best one can do," but it is *not* the best one can do! (Not to mention that many academics are not even alert to opportunities.) When it comes to the contemplation of one's dwelling in academia for almost all of one's adult life, one should do no less that one's best. One should, in a general sense at least, *plan*, with the plan being subject to constant revision, as important new facts come to light and as new opportunities present themselves.

Promotion—Another Vexed Word in This Discussion

Perhaps the brilliant amongst us do not need to plan. Perhaps they are so ineffably dazzling that mere planning would imply some sort of finiteness. For the rest of us, some planning would not go amiss. Thus we do not shrink herein from words like "career" and "plan"—and here's a new one: *promotion*.

Assuming one agrees that there is such a thing as an academic *career*, and assuming further that some sort of *planning* of said career is an authentic exercise, how does one measure one's progress along the planned career path? The generic methodology for any such measurement, whether one is referring to an academic career or a legal contract to measure the sludge in a waste disposal basin, is to identify *milestones*, an obvious metaphorical reference to progress along a literal prescribed path. That promotions are the generally agreed milestones of career progression—whatever the career—scarcely needs further defense here. Indeed, one could argue that, in academe, once tenure has been granted it is fair to say that many academics see a "promotion" to the rank of "Full Professor' as the pinnacle in their career. Unfortunately, the word "promotion," as used in academia, does not measure up to its meaning everywhere else.

So what *is* an (academic) promotion? Perhaps something, but sometimes perhaps nothing. It should immediately be clarified that the Academic Promotion Debate in the accompanying block refers to the so-called "academic" promotions (typically) from assistant professor to associate professor, from associate professor to full professor, and so on. Is anything of substance really happening here? The following two subsections contain the main elements of the debate.

Case for the Affirmative—Academic Promotions are Real Promotions

Again we emphasize that the "promotions" referred to in this debate are the fiddling-with-job-titles sorts of promotions. (A different, and more substantive, type of promotion will be discussed in the next section, §5.2.) Are these promotions real?

> The Academic Promotion Debate
> Resolved: That academic promotions are, indeed, real promotions.

Certainly they are meant to seem real to academics. Every professor knows when he or she is being considered for promotion because, in addition to many other evidences, he or she is asked to prepare[111] his or her dossier or résumé. Superficially, this seems sensible enough: Who knows better than the putative promotee the myriad details that constitute one's CV? One might, however, ask this. Why such a flood of minute details? The answer seems to be that the paper record is objectively the truth, and thus much to be preferred over, say, a face-to-face interview with a promotion committee. Perhaps some universities physically interview their candidates for promotion,[112] but most, it seems, do not. Never mind that psychologists have determined that 80% of communication is non-verbal. The committee will stand by the verbal (meaning, in this case, "written") 20%, since that information is objective and less subject to challenge.

So, one might simply argue that, if all academics think, down to their core, that these "promotions" really are promotions, then, for all practical

---

111 This document is quaintly referred to as the CV. Interestingly, CV is short for the Latin *curriculum vitae*, meaning, *life story*. Not much confusion here: One's academic job is one's life; there is none other. Echoes of *vocation*, one's *calling*. The CV is also different from a normal résumé in other respects as well. Unlike the latter, which is regarded as being excessively verbose if it runs to more than five pages (in fact, two pages is max for a résumé accompanying a non-academic application by a young person with a few degrees or an older person with serious experience), a CV can go on for miles, with every course taught, every paper published, every thesis supervised, every speech given, and much else, meticulously recorded. A résumé chronicles one's major career achievements; a CV logs all one's past academic activities.

112 It is, one hopes, unnecessary to note yet again that we are here discussing the title-fiddling promotions.

CHAPTER 5: THE ACADEMIC EXECUTIVE

purposes, they *are* promotions. The employers say they are. The employees believe that they are. What else matters?

Moreover, most of the people outside the immediate workplace, with whom professors deal, have adopted, or at least understand the academic terminology. Other professors at other institutions (with job titles signifying various altitudes within their own system) are happy with the vocabulary. Journal editors who publish academic papers by professors recognize the lingo, especially when, as often the case, these editors are themselves academics. Organizations that normally (or exclusively) award grants and contracts to academics represent another group fluent in the academic argot.

Still, do academic "promotions" connote real promotions? What is the *process* that leads to these alleged promotions? While the process undoubtedly varies considerably from institution to institution (and even from one academic unit to another within the same institution), the following process may be not far off the mark:

> A committee of academics—individuals whose academic ranks are at least that of the potential rank being considered for the candidate—gather together to mull over the matter. This group is typically chaired by the unit administrator—that is, the department Chair if this is a departmental promotion committee, or the Dean if this is a faculty promotion committee, and so on.
>
> Back in the day, the "Chair" would be called the "Head," and he or she would have the final decision. The decision of the committee was treated[113] as being *advisory*. Nowadays, it is more common for the committee's consensus or vote to be the final word at that academic level. The committee chair acts as a non-executive chair: organizing, providing materials, guiding the meetings, and ensuring that the meeting outcome is implemented to the next level.
>
> Committee members have been provided with copious written material in advance of the meeting, material with which they are therefore assumed to be familiar. The largest

---

113 Still, it would take a fierce head indeed to take a decision that ran counter to the unanimous or near-unanimous advice of his or her committee.

document is the candidate's *curriculum vitae* (CV). The advantages of this approach, it is felt, are (a) nothing important will be missed, (b) all items can be checked for their authenticity, (c) items in various categories are itemized numerically, so that a count of outputs is very straightforward,[114] (d) no committee member can be accused of being biased by intellectual side issues or personal bias. In short, the CV is very complete and seen to be objective.

For some committees, candidates will also have been asked to provide a brief overview of their work and strategic statements about their future academic directions. There may also be a statement from the departmental Chair in support of promotion.

This above process underlies the typical organizational act of approving (or denying) "academic promotion."

Guest Witness for the Affirmative—Dr. Tom Brzustowski

One of our interviewees, Dr. Tom Brzustowski, is in an unusually fine position to comment on this subject. He has experienced many academic promotions personally but has also observed, from very senior positions in academia, government, and the private sector, those of others. The following is an excerpt from Dr. Brzustowski's interview for this book:

Authors: *On the subject of academic promotions, you would be an excellent person to comment. Suppose we said to you that these so-called promotions in university are actually somewhat phony, the ones from assistant to associate, from associate to whatever . . . because if you look at how most people in society would define a promotion, none of those characteristics actually accompanies the average academic promotion. If a Prof says, "So, how do I even know it's a promotion?" the answer seems to be just, "Well, we used to call you Thing A and now we're calling you Thing B." Yet everyone seems to really go for these things in a big way.*

---

114 No evaluation of the importance of research papers is required, because that function has (supposedly) been provided by the editors and reviewers of the various journals involved.

CHAPTER 5: THE ACADEMIC EXECUTIVE

As you know, there's the other kind of promotion—of which you yourself have had many prestigious ones—in which one does receive a promotion by the normal use of the word, where you're doing new things, maybe some of the old things as well, but you're getting a change of scenery, perhaps a chance to flex some new muscles, develop some new capabilities, including people skills. Do you think that so-called academic promotions have any real function at all other than to lull people into the belief that they're getting somewhere when in fact they're not?

Brzustowski: I don't look at these promotions that way. I think the academic culture is one where one's status is tied to a number of indicators—publications, invitations, prizes and so on—and these are bundled into internal recognition through the labels associated with the promotions. And these labels are very important, both internally in defining an internal pecking order, and in representations of the university to the outside.

This issue occurs not only in universities. Let me give you an example. At NSERC, programs are run by people whose title was Director-General. Within the public service, that is a very high position in the pecking order, clearly understood, clearly identified. However, when these people were dealing with the university vice presidents for research, and also with people from industry like VP Technology or Chief Technology Officer, there was the question, What does Director-General mean? If you read John LeCarre, the Director-General of MI6 was God or slightly higher. So we changed the title of our Directors-General to VPs. The difference that made was enormous. So I agree that labeling is important.

As far as I'm concerned, the titles associate professor and professor are simply bundles of the indicators that are important in universities, and while there isn't much more money and so on, in some universities of course you are promoted from assistant to associate or you leave. But even if that isn't the case, it's still a useful indicator of the prestige or the acceptance or the recognition that the institution (meaning colleagues) has given this individual. I don't take the view that you do on that one. I think they're real.

Authors: *What is your attitude toward the other kind of promotion where one does take on new duties and starts in a leadership role involving other people of the same type one recently was? Do you think a person doesn't really need any of that, or do you view it as a successful career by the time someone reaches 65 (or whenever they retire), even if they've never been promoted in that way, they've never been anything other than a professor? Haven't they had a rather truncated experience?*

Brzustowski: Well, that depends on the individual and where the individual derives satisfaction. I know people who have gone through the academic ranks, ended that position with the title of professor, retired from that position, and have gotten most of their satisfaction from teaching good students and seeing them succeed, and from recognition by colleagues in the discipline. When I was young and more iconoclastic, I used to joke that we should have a progression: assistant professor, associate professor, full professor, distinguished professor, and finally extinguished professor! That sort of comment wasn't appreciated.

Look, I think this is a very highly personal thing. I think some are completely and utterly satisfied with the recognition of their colleagues inside the university and outside, as expressed through the academic ranks, citations, and the odd fellowship. I've known others who were totally unsatisfied by that and in fact began to put their effort at the level of associate professor translating their research into potential products, starting a business, becoming very successful, never making professor, becoming adjunct professor but becoming very wealthy and well-recognized in the business world.

But that's a very small group. The majority of academics that I knew had their ambitions focused on recognition,

CHAPTER 5: THE ACADEMIC EXECUTIVE

benchmarked by these academic ranks and supported with some external citations.

Through these comments, we begin to see that the wisest answer to the Promotion Debate is neither an absolute "yes," nor an absolute "no." We'll summarize our final viewpoint, below, at the end of the debate. This will enable us to make concrete recommendations to academics considering their post-tenure careers.

Case for the Negative—Academic Promotions are Not Real Promotions

To present the case for the negative, we begin, not surprisingly, from a different direction, namely, defining the word "promotion" carefully and then examining whether the so-called academic promotions actually satisfy this definition. This process is clearly legitimate, and in fact academics are often disparaged for insisting that rational debate cannot proceed without the key words used being defined in an agreed manner.

Promotion: Definition
1. Change to a (higher) function within an organization.
2. Advancement, as from one position to a higher position.
3. Growth in relevance or importance.
4. Movement from one location in an organizational chart to a higher location in that chart.

What makes sense in the context of a career within an organization? Even minor organizations, if they are not chaotic, have organizational charts and major organizations such as academic institutions always and must have them.[115] So when we say that a promotion means a substantive change in one's position on the org chart, this presupposes that we all know what a "position" and an "org chart" are.

An org chart conveys the key information as to who reports to whom. It makes the best single depiction of what the "positions" are, and therefore of what the (real) promotions are, since a (real) promotion must be an upward

---

115 Exercise for the reader: Find all the organizational charts for your learning institution that are of interest to you. Sometimes these are not easily acquired, but be assured that the people at the top do have them and know them well.

SO YOU WANT TO BE A PROFESSOR?

movement from one position to another. Note in passing that authority and responsibility tend to go hand in hand. A promotion carrying increased authority but no increase in responsibility is unstable and will eventually be restructured. And a promotion carrying increased responsibility but no increase in authority is a recipe for frustration.

If we compare the notion of an academic promotion with the above criteria, one quickly finds that it satisfies not one of the critical requirements of a promotion! Only the job title has been changed, to make matters more decorative. However, at the top rank of Full Professor it must be admitted that this status opens the doors to the Academic Executive suite.

Authors' Conclusions on "Academic Promotions"

Having reviewed the cases both for the affirmative and the negative, what are we to conclude? The reader, of course, is free to conclude as he or she wishes, but the authors believe that the following take-away is balanced and reasonable: An "academic promotion" is clearly not a promotion in any normal sense of the word, although it does play a somewhat similar role with many academics.

DILBERT

It does represent something concrete. A rather thorough review of the professor's performance has been made, and if the professor is deemed worthy, his or her job title is adjusted in a manner that is agreed to be upwards. It must be emphasized that attaining the rank of "Full Professor" is an essential prerequisite to move into most senior academic executive positions, as described in the remainder of this chapter.

If assistant professors reported to associate professors, and the latter similarly all reported to "full" professors, these would indeed be promotions. But they don't, so they're not. The academic quasi-promotions are a direct consequence of the Normative Paradigm. If all academic careers must traverse through a common Tube of Progress, then all that is needed is a signpost every so often along the road that says, "You're fine. You're making progress. Legions have trod this path before you and more legions will follow. Keep up the good work."

When Dr. Brzustowski was asked what he thought of [more genuine] promotions, ones that involved performing higher functions in the organization, he said, simply, "Well, that depends on the individual and where the individual derives satisfaction." Exactly. Most people are happy in The Tube, but some people are at least willing to learn about other vocational models and, having done so, to entertain the notion that they may be in the exceptional category. One such class of non-Tubers is examined for the remainder of this chapter—academic managers, executives, and leaders.

5.2 Academic Management and Leadership— Could This Be a Career?

The purpose of the preceding section was to direct a strong beam of light on how one might measure career progress. Normally, in the wider world, it is measured most directly by epochal events called *promotions*, but as we saw above, this measurement in academia may be contaminated by the persistent use of unusual meanings for the word "promotion." In this Chapter 5, we shall insist on being quite usual, when it comes to how we use this important word.

Unconventional Views May Hold the Key to Success

Performance evaluations, when successful, do serve as a sort of proxy promotion for those who are in the academic[116] Tube. Those who don't

---

116 Recall from §4.2 that the Normative Paradigm requires all professors to be active, in more-or-less the same way and to more-or-less the same degree, in teaching, research and other more minor categories (such as service to the university, professional involvement, etc.). This is precisely the sort of archaic structure that the Scottish economist Adam Smith wished to improve upon when, in *An Inquiry*

realize they're in The Tube, are blissfully happy. Those who know they're in The Tube, but are content to stay there, are informedly happy and we do not quarrel with these personal decisions. Still, using the normal meaning of "promotion" in an academic setting is what we insist on discussing.

Thus, in this and the following chapters we shall proceed with enthusiasm to examine some of the most interesting career possibilities for academics.

A Family of Escape Routes from The Tube—Academic Management

We have now arrived at the point where the reader has agreed, at least for the sake of argument, that he or she is considerably interested in an academic *career* (and is not ashamed to use the word "career"). In addition, he or she is willing to use the usual scheme for measuring his or her progress in this career, based on the *promotion*, as used generally in society. With the semantics thus cleaned, sharpened and ready for action, what can we learn about such opportunities?

We now depart from the image of all professors moving through their careers in unison, with little to distinguish them in their duties except whether they are assisting, or associating, or fully filled. We did note in §4.5 that if one is not just a competent researcher, but a *star* researcher, one can on that basis enter a career path that is no longer in The Tube. A star researcher can spend more time on research (and less time on teaching), attract a higher salary, and enter a zone of being semi-worshiped to a degree not enjoyed by one's colleagues who are merely competent or excellent researchers. The metric here may not always be research excellence *per se*. Often it is based on the vastness of one's grant and contract income, which, dollar for dollar, justifies a higher salary and also buys out teaching time to be performed by juniors and one's professional colleagues.

There may also be stratagems to break out from The Tube if one is interested primarily in teaching. However, it is unlikely that this can be accomplished at most academic institutions unless their reputation is based

---

into the *Nature and Causes of the Wealth of Nations* (1776), he explained the benefits of the *Division of Labor!*

primarily on teaching. On the other hand, if one converted all the institutional courses from just a classroom-based to an internet-based business model, one might find oneself suddenly well outside The Tube, especially if the institution was suddenly deriving serious amounts of revenue from one's efforts. Ultimately, one's compensation should be based on the value one adds to the enterprise; thus, one should always try to be aware of how the value of one's contribution is assessed, and how one's value-added is quantified.

Scarcity of Academic Management Positions

To return to the focus of this chapter, we shall discuss another generic career path that diverges, post-tenure, from the Normative Paradigm (The Tube): a career in academic management. To state a self-evident truth immediately: This career path is not for everyone. (Thank goodness! Can we picture the academic output of a 20-person department comprising 19 "administrators" and one professor?)

The institutional challenge is not to ensure that the correct fraction of professors will be promoted (*really* promoted, this time) to the available "administrative" slots. That will happen automatically: a (real) promotion will be made only if there is a slot to fill. In contrast, the institutional challenge is (or should be) to promote the right people into these positions as they become available. The challenge for the individual[117] is to know in advance whether such promotions are of interest to him or her and to be able to respond energetically to such opportunities.

Academic Leadership—The Roads Less Traveled

We shall therefore now begin to consider more explicitly the career paths in academic leadership. There are two stark differences between these paths and the careers in teaching or research examined in Chapters 3 and 4, respectively. First, the skill-sets really are quite different. Every academic is skilled in research and at least reasonably competent in teaching, and

---

[117] Several books have been written from the viewpoint of the academic institution: What is good for the university? What will make the college thrive? This book is, by contrast, written from the standpoint of the individual who is being (or who plans to be) considered for a more senior post in the academic management structure. Fortunately, these two viewpoints need not be disjoint.

in fact the Normative Paradigm, whose wisdom was questioned early in Chapter 4 (§4.2), essentially says that all professors have the same skills, or at least that they all possess, somewhat homogeneously (if not quite believably), the skill-subsets necessary for excellent teaching and research.

Yet many academics—owing to their aptitudes, inclinations and experiences—are critically deficient in at least some of the critical skills needed for academic *leadership*. This is not to their debit; not everyone can be great at everything, and we must further admit—readily, since it is so obviously true—that not all of us are as good as the best of us. Many of the skills so needed for leadership are of the so-called "soft" variety, and we shall explore these further presently.

The second stark difference between the leadership career path and the research and/or teaching path, is that the former are, indeed, roads less traveled. (This has led to the semi-serious semi-humorous observation that "It's so lonely at the top.") Some may think that the explanation for this thinness of population lies in the relative unattractiveness of these positions for most professors. Some may hold that these positions are sufficiently demanding that only a few can successfully qualify to fill them. But of one basic mathematical fact we may all be certain: There is room only for a very few (one would hope a very *well selected* few) in these positions. A Faculty[118] needs only one Dean; a university needs only one President; and so on. If everyone aspired to this sort of position, there would be a great deal of disappointment in the ranks.

Better, perhaps, to imbue in the academic culture the myth that these leadership positions are not really all that desirable; that only those with a high motivation to "serve the rest" (the teachers and researchers) eventually take on these positions, though they are naturally reluctant to do so; that it's time to "take a hit for the team"; and so on. These impressions may even be true in many cases, but it should not escape notice that they do tend

---

118 Since the word "faculty" can, in ubiquitous parlance, unfortunately refer either to "the entire teaching staff" or to a "major organizational unit or division" of the institution devoted to a large relatively well-defined are of intellectual specialization (law, medicine, engineering, architecture, physical and health education, etc.), we shall distinguish the latter by an uppercase "F," signifying a proper (organizational) name.

to dampen the demand and expectations of most professors for such (real) promotions, and are thus good for university morale.

Here, however, we are not concerned primarily about what is good for the university.[119] We are concerned, instead, about what is good for the reader's career. Skip the impressions. Ignore the cultural tales. Look at your skill-set DNA (a term explained below). Look at the academic leadership possibilities, and the skill-sets these require. Do the math. Never lose sight of your long-term inclinations and preferences (whatever those may be). Make well-informed career decisions, now and continuously. And rest with the assurance that you approached your career with a mature, enlightened, thoughtful strategy.

Administration, Management, Leadership

The most common word for university management[120] is "administration," but we shall not emphasize this word in this book. In normal usage, to *administer* something does not convey the need for considered judgment, or the use of advanced intelligence, or the exercise of leadership. It must be admitted immediately that these nuances are often quite different as between the private sector and the public sector. In government, to be the "administrator" of a billion-dollar agency is clearly a top job, but no CEO of a *Fortune 500* company would wish to be called an administrator.[121] With "administrator," one might tend to picture some bureaucrat who has a huge, multi-volume policy handbook in his otherwise-empty bookcase. The job is to find the policy section appropriate to the decision, and then to

---

119 That word "primarily" is very important. Though we are not, as we say, primarily concerned with what is best for the university, what in fact could be better for the university than all professors striving to improve their skill-sets so as to better perform their duties? What could more maximize the value of the university's intellectual capital (IC) than for key IC nodes (professorial brains) working at finding the best place for their contributions, and placing themselves in nomination for the positions best suited to their skills and enthusiasms?

120 "Oh no, surely not!" we can hear some readers asking in exasperation. "Surely we are not going to have to think about the meaning of words again." Our short answer is "We're afraid so." The slightly longer answer is that "The precision and usefulness of one's verbal statements cannot exceed the precision of the words employed therein."

121 An even more poignant example of this diverse use of job titles, as between the public and private sectors, might be the observation that the highest position ever held by Dr Henry Kissinger in the U.S. government was that of a secretary!

pinpoint exactly what the policy manual says about the issue in question. Agreed, it wouldn't be hard for teaching or research—or almost anything else—to be more interesting than doing that. Universities also tend to refer to high-level managers and senior leaders as "administrators," but we shall rarely do so for the reasons given above.

· There may well be functions that an academic finds herself in—such as Deputy Assistant Chair for Community Outreach—that can legitimately be referred to as an "administrative" position, but these are not the true career advancement positions of interest in this chapter. We are more interested in positions that can legitimately be called "management," like Head, Chair, Dean, and so on up the ladder. The higher these positions become, the more leadership is required.

A Canonical Academic Org Chart

For example, only in local situations does one speak of a *provost*; more normally nowadays, one says *Vice President, Academic*, or, most recently, *Chief Academic Officer*. As another example, the word *Principal* can mean anything from the leader of a small group to the Big Kahuna at a major university; we shall prefer *President* or *Chief Executive Officer*. Many academic institutions that were once based on some system of religious belief still retain historical job titles that seem rather antiquated by modern standards,[122] though charming to their graduates. The inclusion of all these possibilities is difficult in as general a book as this.

There are four basic types of university governance in the USA and Canada: *uni-cameral, bi-cameral, tri-cameral,* and in some instances, a 'hybrid' arrangement.[123] Uni-cameral universities are governed by a single body, often referred to as a 'Governing Council' or a 'Board of Regents or Trustees.' Bi-cameral systems, prevalent at most Canadian universities, involve two legislative bodies—a Governing Board and an Academic Senate. A third structure involves a Board of Trustees, a Senate, and a University Council, each with different administration and management roles. Finally, the 'hybrid' concept consists of a combination of elements of the above

---

122 For some reason, the title *Dean* seems very secure, although its meaning can vary widely from one institution to the next.
123 D. Shale, "The Hybridization of Higher Education in Canada," *International Review of Research in Open and Distant Learning*, Vol. 2(2), 2002.

CHAPTER 5: THE ACADEMIC EXECUTIVE

structures in the form of an Academic Council. In the U.S., where multiple campuses exist, they often share a common board. Delegation of authority to manage the affairs of the university is given to a president or chancellor, or (for private institutions) to a Chief Executive. Further delegation of authority then trickles down to subordinate university officers.

With all the accretion of senior position titles that have naturally accumulated over one, two or three centuries,[124] we shall, to condense matters somewhat, briefly lay out a kind of semi-standard organizational chart, as shown in Fig. 5.1. The position titles used are meant to be modern rather than historically curious. They are also meant to be generic, such that tuned-in readers will have no difficulty making the adjustments necessary to produce the org charts that correspond to their own academic institutions. The Canadian Association of University Business Officers (caubo.ca) or the US National Association of College and University Business Officers (nacubo.org) can also be consulted for information on different organizational structures.

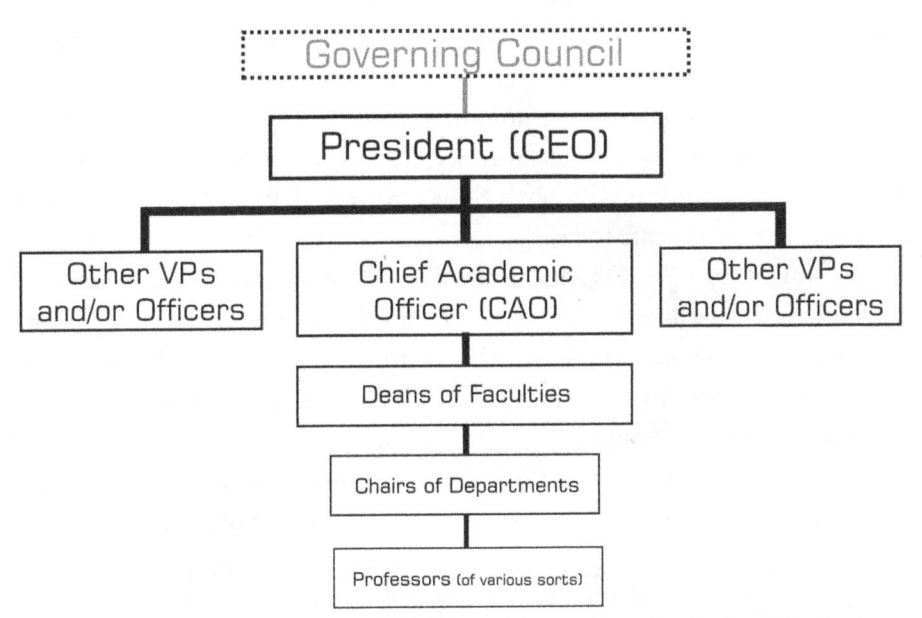

Figure 5.1: Basic Levels in a Generic Uni-Cameral Arrangement for Academic Institutions.

---

124 These titles can survey a much longer period. Teaching at the University of Oxford, claimed to be the oldest university in the English-speaking world, began about 1100 C.E.

Many important senior positions in the central administration are not shown explicitly in the above generic org chart. For example, the box labeled[125] "President" really stands for "The Office of the President," which may contain a great many positions, some of which are traditionally held be academics (professors). These are often quite interesting, and quite well paid. Similar remarks can be made regarding the Office of the Chief Academic Officer. And each of the other "Vice Presidents and/or Officers" also is a focus for authority in particular areas of importance, and can have academics as key managers in the later stages of their careers.

Many modern universities are unionized, including faculty, part-time teachers, graduate students employed as teaching assistants, and support personnel. As noted earlier, one of the major issues confronting universities and colleges is that of 'contingency faculty' (non-tenure track contract academic faculty). Aspiring university leaders must be willing and able to work effectively with unions and their leadership. This kind of experience can be obtained as one progresses through the academic ranks in various leadership positions. Avoiding debilitating strikes and their deleterious effects on students—while ensuring a reasonable workplace environment and fair remuneration for unionized staff members—is of paramount importance. Achieving this balance in the face of ideological differences and economic constraints is one of the greatest challenges facing senior academic administrators today.

By way of example, Fig. 5.2 shows a list of the chief central administration offices at the university the authors know best—their own: the University of Toronto. This example is used, not to criticize or praise, or to imply any special importance to their own university, but just to give a concrete example to emphasize the current point being made.

Also shown are the 2005–06 budgets for these central administration offices (in millions of dollars).[126] With all this money in play, and one must

---

125 The President/CEO is not an autocrat. He or she also must report to someone, that someone being the "Governing Council" in the example of Fig. 5.1. However, members of this governing body are usually from the outside community at large, not career academics; such positions are not considered here as positions that might be part of an academic career.
126 For accounting accuracy—which is exactly the opposite of the thrust here—the operating budget numbers in Fig. 5.2 are in Canadian dollars.

CHAPTER 5: THE ACADEMIC EXECUTIVE

remember that there is a whole mini-administration of people represented by each budget line in Fig. 5.2, one might speculate that there are some choice positions involved here—and one would be right. Perhaps, as part of career planning, readers would take an hour or two to familiarize themselves with the details of the central administration in their own university. They might be surprised at the attractive nuggets that are available to those who take steps to fill these positions. This process begins with knowing that they exist.

Central Administration Budget (as recommended) University of Toronto - 2005-06	$M
Office of the Governing Council	2.6
Office of the President	1.2
Office of the Vice President (Research) & Associate Provost	5.4
Office of the Vice President (Govt & Institutional Relations)	0.7
Office of the Vice President & Chief Advancement Officer	18.6
Office of the Vice President (Human Resources)	7.4
Office of the Vice President (Business Affairs)	15.6
Office of the Vice President (Provost)	3.1
Office of the Vice Provost (Planning & Budget)	2.3
Office of the Vice Provost (Students)	15.0
Office of the Vice Provost (Space & Facilities Planning)	2.8
Other Institutional	1.6
	76.3

Figure 5.2: Typical Organizational Framework at the Highest Academic Level.

What is an Executive?

The word "executive" is often misused and position title inflation can eventually create the pretense that almost everyone is an "executive." However, as used here (and in the title of this chapter), an *executive* is one who is responsible for directly *executing* the policies, strategies, budgets and plans approved by the senior governance body. For a corporation, this body is the Board of Directors. Other names for this group when charged with the governance of university management include "Board of Governors," "Governing Council," "Board of Regents," etc. This is the group to which the president reports and in fact its most important function is to choose the president. All vice presidents and officers are part of the senior management team and can legitimately be called "executives."

What is an Officer?

A university, though a "legal person," cannot write or speak for itself. A human being must do that. The humans who are legally authorized to speak on behalf of the whole university are called "officers" and they should be aware of the special legal implications of that responsibility. One can, by a parallel construction, sometimes refer to a Dean as the CEO of a Faculty.

Anyone who is an officer or executive (or both) in the central administration should understand the principal strategies and issues for the entire university.

Mobility Usually a Necessity

The simple availability arithmetic for senior leadership posts in academia means that however carefully one plans one's career to include these postings, the chances of one of them coming open timed to your peak availability are slight.

Suppose as an example that you come to regard Vice President, Research, as an ideal way to finish off your career. It fits with your career-long commitment to—and high-profile success in—research, and you are of the opinion that this position in the top management team will broaden your career in a magnificent way during, say, the last decade of your university connection. It will also involve a substantial salary increase, the benefits of which will reverberate many years (one hopes) after retirement, by virtue of a significantly enhanced pension.

However, you also realize that the current holder of this position in your university just took office about 18 months ago and seems to be doing a fine job. This means that this position will not likely come open for another seven years or more—probably too late for you.

There also are, of course, other limitations and obstacles. In addition to the usual competition from other colleagues (not just in your department, or faculty, but throughout your university), there are surely not a few individuals already in the central administration who would like to be nudged up to this plum assignment.

There may also be external candidates, not yet known, who will compete for this position (your competitors always seem to be mobile). In fact, the President and his trusted advisor, the Chief Academic Officer, at the

CHAPTER 5: THE ACADEMIC EXECUTIVE

time the VP Research position becomes open, may for various reasons decide that they definitely want an *external* candidate to fill this appointment. They will speak of "the need for new blood." Your blood is, by definition, "old," since you are an internal candidate and therefore tainted. You had one chance—and it's gone!

> **The Mobility Tug-of-War**
>
> **The Immovable Object:** Changing one's university, one's academic position, and much more, can be emotionally wrenching.
>
> **The Irresistible Force:** The attraction of a new career challenge; the desire to step up to new skill levels (and thus examine your professional breadth); the honor and distinction of a more responsible position; the higher compensation (including pension for perhaps two decades)—these may form an irresistible combination that mandates uprooting and moving.

The antidote to this syndrome of career threats is to be *mobile*. You must regard all VP Research (and similar) openings in your geographical area (or, better, the continent) as potential takeover targets, and act accordingly. If (usually for personal reasons) you decide *not* to be mobile, you must realize that this stance forecloses many, probably most, of your options. This may reverberate all the way back to a re-examination of your earlier decision to seek such a position in the first place.

There are certainly impressive examples of individuals who rose from being tenured professors, early in their career, all the way to the presidential suite in one single academic institution. But these examples are tending to become fewer. To limit oneself to this hard constraint would seem to be the kiss of death in most career paths.

Department Chair

Again with reference to Fig. 5.1, the position of academic management and leadership that is most proximate and obvious to professors is the Chair[127] of their own department. And, yes, it should be more than just

---

[127] Two quick comments. First, the Chair position was called Head until not long ago, with several important distinctions besides the name. A Head had real authority and probably no term limits either. There may still be Head positions around. Grab one while they last. Second, though basic editing calls for lower-case for a

an *administrative* position (the academic and public sector euphemism for management); the Chair can and should show *leadership*.

There is not much need, for readers of this book, to describe what a Chair does. They see one—theirs—almost every day. They can watch what is done, and how it is done, and being in a highly politicized[128] environment, they undoubtedly have strong opinions on what points should be awarded for those two sets of choices. Academics are also in an excellent position to decide, in the case of department Chairs, whether they would like to "do that sort of thing" themselves. In making this decision, however, they should bear in mind two obvious considerations: **(a)** Chair is not an end in itself, but the first main rung on a longer, more rewarding ladder, and **(b)** if you are not enthralled with the Chair's performance, might you perhaps prefer to issue the orders than to take them from someone you feel is inferior? This second question seems pretty obvious but it is astonishing how many professors complain about their departmental Chair's performance while being simultaneously bereft of ambition for doing the job (better) themselves.

As a last comment, a department Chair already must have, at least to some degree, the job skills described in more detail in §§5.3 & 5.4. This explains why a brilliant researcher or teacher in a major academic institution often finds that the door is barred from becoming Dean in even a small school of lesser prominence. The watershed question in the job interview is this: "Have you even been the Chair of a department?" If you haven't demonstrated those skills on the firing line, your other skills, however estimable, will not seal the deal for you.

---

generic position and upper-case for a specific position (a president, the President, etc.) in the case of words like head and chair, writers who are more centered on effective communication than on Miss McGillicutty's rules will perhaps be forgiven for using the upper case for both. Have you ever gotten a memo under the memohead "From the desk of the chair"?

128 Any collection of highly accomplished human beings (personal ego being highly correlated with accomplishment) is rife with political emotion, scheming and intrigue. What is unusual about the academic environment is that some profess surprise (or even shock) that this would also be so with professors. It may be better hidden, perhaps, but hardly unexpected.

CHAPTER 5: THE ACADEMIC EXECUTIVE

Faculty Dean

We are affixing the label "Dean" to the next level in the academic management hierarchy. To be so appointed, one must normally have served as a Chair somewhere comparable, or as an Associate Chair in a large department or a prestigious institution.

This may be a good time to mention an important aspect of management style—one that begins to become critical at the decanal level. At one extreme, the Dean may be rather autocratic, regarding comments from all in his or her Faculty as being advisory and reserving the right to make the final decision him- or herself. At the other extreme, the Dean may see himself in a chairmanship role, organizing meetings at which the group (department Chairs and similar) as a whole makes the decision. While any Dean (or Chair) would be foolhardy to ignore a *unanimous* vote from their Chairs (or professors) and simply overrule them, usually matters are usually less well-drawn (see the discussion of how to handle meetings in §5.4).

The non-executive Dean model simply counts the votes, or tries to achieve consensus, but makes no attempt to make any decision personally. (This may be a CYA gambit or it may be intrinsic to a Faculty culture with very strong departments.) The executive Dean model looks over all the discussion and says, in effect, and unless the discussion produced a unanimous or near-unanimous opinion), "Thanks for your help with this, and for all your valuable input. But there is a multi-dimensional range of opinion here, and you folks have not been able to agree on this. Yet we need an actual decision in order to move forward. Fortunately, I'm here, and I will reflect on what I've heard and will issue a memo on my decision Monday next."

At levels in a university's management structure higher than Dean, office holders must be decision-makers (a clear requirement of leadership). Otherwise, the whole "administration" becomes little more than a tomfoolery of ditherers. Some Deans, however, can operate by deferring to the strong Chairs in their Faculty departments, just as Chairs can, in turn, defer to the Professors in their departments who have the most forceful personalities. It's not desirable, but this dysfunction can persist for a surprising number of years before it becomes apparent that the rot has set in.

Before taking on a Deanship, make sure that your assumptions on this active-passive axis are similar to the assumptions of those to whom you will be reporting and who will be reporting to you. Are the departments supposed to conduct themselves so as to implement your vision and values? Or are you supposed merely to serve the demands of the departments in the Faculty? The former involves management and leadership; the latter is just an administrative post. Hardly anything is more important to get straight before accepting a (real) academic "promotion" than who will be pulling whose crank.

There are many further aspects of Deanship that merit careful study before applying for—much less accepting—such a position. Enough aspects to make a book on its own. Fortunately, such a book has already been written. David Bright and Mary Richards [2001] delve into many details of Deanship that will be of great interest to those readers considering this career path.

Chief Academic Officer

The Deanships just considered are still somewhat "field centered." One has the Dean of Law, the Dean of Medicine, etc., We now move to consider academic managers and leaders who are in the central university administration and who usually must, simply because of the availability of time, forsake any desires and biases consequent to their personal fields of academic excellence. It is transparently inappropriate for a central decision-maker to be accused of prejudice toward his or her original field of study. Perhaps, if one is in the Faculty of Forestry, for example, one might wish that no one from this Faculty ascends to high places in the corporate center: this "one" may actually bend over backward to avoid the suspicion of bias, leading in fact to a reverse bias.

It has already been remarked above, in connection with Figs. 5.1 and 5.2, that there are quite a number of senior central postings available, especially for large, research intensive universities. We shall focus here on the position of Chief Academic Officer (CAO) as the most important of these, other than the President position itself.[129] The CAO is in direct line

---

129 The CAO in academia is analogous to the COO (Chief Operations Officer) in private corporations.

CHAPTER 5: THE ACADEMIC EXECUTIVE

between the Faculties and the President's office, as implied by Fig. 5.1. Other positions at this general level are intended to support the CAO directly (Fig. 5.2). It is interesting to observe that matters related to teaching tend to flow through the CAO's office, while those relating to research tend to flow through the President's office. One should not jump to conclusions here, nor have the authors embarked on a research project to study a great many university budgets in this respect.

Here is a job description from an actual[130] CAO search:

> The Provost and Vice President, Academic, is responsible, in concert with the President, for providing leadership and direction to other members of the University's senior leadership team, including fellow Vice Presidents, Associate Vice Presidents, Deans, Associate and Assistant Deans, heads of major administrative units, the academic community of more than 60 Department Heads and 1,000 faculty, as well as professional and administrative staff in the colleges and reporting units. The Provost is complemented by a senior team, including the Vice Provost, the Associate Vice Presidents of Information and Communications Technology and Student and Enrolment Services, and the Assistant Provost, Integrated Planning and Analysis.

Clearly anybody who is anybody in the management structure will be no more than two or three degrees of separation from the CAO, who, in turn, must interact effectively with a large number of individuals throughout the university. (Note also the number of interesting senior management positions incidentally mentioned; these are available to professors who wish to head their careers in this direction.)

All this activity on the part of the CAO takes a great many skills, and frankly the average professor will not have many of these needed skills, although some can be learned if there is the desire and the aptitude. Here's what was said about skills in another excerpt from the above advertisement:

> The ideal candidate will possess outstanding organizational, interpersonal and communication skills to meet the needs of a dynamic and complex academic environment. The competencies

---

130 Most senior administrative posts are advertised by search firms. The above was excerpted from a newspaper advertisement by Janet Wright & Associates Inc., specializing in senior-level recruitment for the public and not-for-profit sectors.

required by the successful candidate include institutional leadership and vision, superior personal effectiveness, decisiveness, the ability to implement and support innovation and institutional change, and the effectiveness to inspire and inform a wide-ranging internal and external community.

Doesn't sound much like the advertisement a young doctoral graduate might respond to, to become a professor, does it? And yet, there is no doubt about whether this CAO, and all CAOs—like Chairs, Heads, and Presidents—must first all have been successful tenured professors. Some of these may still think of themselves as professors, because professorship, as we saw in Chapter 1 (§1.3), is, after all, a *calling* to many. Evidently, a great many additional skills must be added before professors can become senior managers and leaders. Sections 5.3 & 5.4 below are devoted to an examination of the crucial "skills issue."

James Martin, James Samels & Associates [1997] have written a very helpful book[131] on the role of the Chief Academic Officer, where a great many additional issues and ideas are presented. Readers who are taking seriously the possibility of an academic leadership career should mine this book for its information and insights. For example, a survey is quoted indicating that CAOs typically spend their weekly time as follows: meetings one-on-one and with small groups (32 hrs); mail and correspondence (7 hrs); social and ceremonial functions (6 hrs); and planning and reading (2.5 hrs). Since it is obvious that about 95% of a CAO's time is spent in one or another form of communication, it is not surprising that the skills required in the CAO advertisement (just above) begin with "The ideal candidate will possess outstanding organizational, interpersonal and communication skills . . ."

President

Finally, we have the President, the CEO of the academic institution. By the time one is considering applying for such a position, one will have a broad range of information and advice available. (This is how presidents

---

131 The book's title is *"First Among Equals: The Role of the Chief Academic Officer,"* which tends to celebrate the myth of collegiality in academic institutions rather than the clear fact that the CAO is not *"First Among Equals,"* but *"Second Only to the President."*

CHAPTER 5: THE ACADEMIC EXECUTIVE

act.) The President's Office, though perhaps not at the institution where the story began, is the natural final location[132] of a career steadfastly focused on academic leadership. This is the one position where candidates may be selected from outside the academy.

We shall, in the next two sections (§§5.3 & 5.4), examine a range of important skill-sets, involving talents and proficiencies that seem (according to innumerable counterexamples) unnecessary in the pursuit of a strong research career, and that are largely[133] unnecessary to be considered a good post-secondary teacher. However, this constellation of skills becomes more and more essential the higher the leadership position one captures—and are most numerous and mandatory in the office of President.

At least one proper study has been conducted on the subject of how college and university presidents (and other leaders) interact and communicate; how they assess their own effectiveness and that of others on the senior management team; establish goals; how they learn and transmit values; and how they make sense of the complex and dynamic organizations in which they work. This study is the ILP (Institutional Leadership Project), based on data collected over a five-year period, and reported upon by Robert Birnbaum [1992] in his book *How Academic Leadership Works: Understanding Success and Failure in the College Presidency*. This book also contains dozens of further references,[134] including many additional publications of the ILP.

Birnbaum [1992] starts at the most logical point: a consideration of *leadership* in the abstract. The best presidents don't *administer*, or even just *manage*; they *lead*. In Chapter 1, Birnbaum shows three situations where a perfectly rational, informed decision was made; yet, while it met with a cheerful response from one segment of the university community, it elicited

---

132 Some individuals have talents so prodigious, and a consequent career so meteoric, that University President is not their last job title. But these later positions are not *within* the university; they continue their career outside the ivory tower, in society at large.
133 The big exception for *teaching* is the need for some of the "soft" (i.e., human) skills. Indeed, it can be argued without fear of successful contradiction that successful teaching itself implies a sizable cluster of soft skills.
134 Yes, once again, men and women with highly gifted intellects, persons exquisitely trained and experienced in the art and science of research, may want to apply a smidgen of this talent to the subject of their own future careers. A few hours thus spent, so that they can make informed decisions on the future decades of their careers, are a wise investment.

a doleful response from another segment. A university has a great many groups and special interests within it. Getting these groups and interests on side, or at least disturbed at the sub-clinical level, is a monumental task.

Birnbaum continues with the "myths and mysteries of academic leadership." (Anyone who can rationally and factually debunk myths is worth listening to.) Just to mention one of the five "myths" for purposes of illustration—and not to mention the four "mysteries" at all—we have the Myth of Presidential Vision. The problem is not the desirability of having a vision (defining a realistic yet attractive future); the trouble arises from its *source*. If the President begins with his or her own vision, fully formed, and then spends all available energy getting everyone else to "buy into it," this is a subtle form of autocracy. Better, the results show, to have some "up" channels of communication as well, with the eventual vision becoming one that all can share. Although Birnbaum's book focuses primarily on the presidential suite, the data discussed and the lessons learned are relevant to all levels of academic management and leadership.

The role of university presidents became especially scrutinized recently when Lawrence Summers, made President of Harvard in 2001, was forced to resign in 2006 after becoming involved in controversies over several matters, including whether **(a)** a certain black professor was sufficiently committed to academic research (including the attendant academic standards), **(b)** the Army Training Corps should be banned from campus, **(c)** a petition urging Harvard to sell its securities in companies doing business in Israel might be anti-Semitic, and **(d)** there was a sufficiently factual basis for claiming that prejudice alone could explain the shortage of women in scientific leadership positions. In the contemporary argot, he touched the "third rail" (and the fourth, fifth and sixth rails as well) of left-wing dogma. In less dramatic terminology, President Summers got embroiled[135] in whether the current pillars of political correctness were, in fact, also academically correct.

The Economist opined that his (Summers's) problem was that "His affection for any agenda is less than his love of a good debate." In other words, poor old Summers viewed his position as CPO (Chief Professorial Officer).

---

135 The authors will not get similarly embroiled here, since these controversies are off topic to the present subject.

CHAPTER 5: THE ACADEMIC EXECUTIVE

At least two of the burs under his saddle should have been settled, if possible, quietly and with perhaps a slight nudge on his part to the appropriate department Chair, at a much lower level, using the academic process, which one would presume still requires, even at Harvard, a basis in fact and a reliance on rational argument.

Time sounded a familiar chord by suggesting that Harvard's undergraduate curriculum could stand improvement, although the power of being "credentialed" by Harvard is so deep that there is scant incentive to do so. This will not be the last time in this chapter when the reasonable needs of undergraduates will be in conflict with the desires of the faculty and the research (and other activities) they pursue.

Indeed, some have argued that senior leadership of an academic institution is among the most challenging of management assignments. President Peter Likins made the following observations:

"I also think that being the president of a large research university can be much more difficult than being CEO of a large corporation. First, the overall goal of the company is largely unitary (increase shareholder value) and relatively easily measured; in contrast, there are many stakeholders who have to be considered by the university leadership, including undergraduate students (teaching), graduate students (research), faculty, parents, alumni, the administrative staff, the governing board, and government (which may be contributing much of the cash, either directly or through research granting agencies). And it's not always easy to measure how well one has satisfied these various constituencies.

"Second, for a research university, there is simply more complexity involved in all the many things being done.

"And, third, a sizable fraction of university 'revenue' is controlled, not through the president's office, but by professors spending research funding. Can you imagine a CEO who would be satisfied with having no control of 40% of his company's revenue?"

These sorts of issues should touch all professors, who should develop their own informed, thoughtful responses to them. To be an academic leader, however, much more is required: He or she must develop an institutional response that is not only factually coherent (the first requirement), and rationally correct (the second requirement), but that brings along a substantial majority of the faculty into convinced support (the third, and hardest, requirement).

Why Are These Roads Less Traveled?

There is an overarching point to be made here, from the viewpoint of strategic career planning. Individuals who become academics (i.e., professors at universities and colleges) go through a process that is more-or-less logical and continuous. They study for many years, in a structured curriculum, to become an expert in their chosen field. If their gifts are sufficiently great, and if they work hard enough, they will find[136] themselves in a tenure-track position at a respected university. These positions typically require outstanding ability at research—measured, in practice, by the level of external funding for similar research conducted by one's colleagues in a similar field. They also require competent teaching, which is of course an inseparable part of the package (although, decades ago, just showing up to class with a necktie and some crumpled notes was good enough when it came to teaching).

Unlike the path to university research and teaching, which is difficult to the point of being impossible for the average person, but which is, for those with the right talents and other personal attributes, relatively smooth sailing, the path to academic management and leadership could not be more different and more difficult. University management positions are shrouded in mystery and are not widely advertised, thereby requiring an aspiring candidate to constantly search academic publications (and major newspapers) for opportunities. Often, search committees have candidates in mind, and frequently issue letters of invitation for those selected few to consider applying for the position of note, while of course the requisite advertisement is in print. Knowing this should in no way dissuade qualified candidates from expressing their interest in the position.

---

136 This is not to besmirch the large number of post-doctoral fellows (and other similarly temporary academic positions) who contribute so mightily to the academic process, en route (one hopes) to a tenure-track position.

CHAPTER 5: THE ACADEMIC EXECUTIVE

The greatest generic barrier, however, is a *skills* barrier, meaning that unless one becomes aware of these career alternatives and familiarizes oneself with the demands and requirements of these positions, one will never seriously look into them. Are any of your friends going to Department Chair School? Are any of your colleagues attending Dean College? Is that incredibly charismatic colleague spending weekends getting a CAO designation? Of course not. The academic culture not only promulgates the mythology that such positions are for aliens from some distant universe, it also encourages the value (shared by most professors) that the proper roles of professors are to remain involved in teaching and research, and that colleagues who dare to venture into academic management and leadership are rather suspect, perhaps not yet quite ready for psychological therapy, but certainly persons to keep an eye on. These strange individuals are not really *"one of us."*

So, where does one get the idea that managing might be more interesting than being managed, and that leading is more exciting than being led? Not from most of one's colleagues, who have never seriously thought about it. Not from institutional opportunities for formal training.[137] If one is going to become aware of these career opportunities, assess them and prepare for them, one must do this on one's own. Perhaps this is an entrance test for thinking outside the box after all. And the authors hope that the comments herein will prompt some creative thinking on the part of our readers.

5.3 Academic Management as a Career — A Closer Examination

This section expands at some length on the crucial subject of skills. This is the rational path that both the individual and the institution should follow in deciding on "personnel actions" like (real) promotion to a management or leadership role. By contrast, here are two quite different processes, both irrational and absurd, yet are not unknown (as they should be).

In Absurd Process #1, an outstanding researcher is promoted to Department Chair, to acknowledge and honor her contributions, and as a kind of

---

[137] Why would those who have chosen a career in academic management create competitors?

reward for her meritorious service. Problems? Twofold: One, she is now largely lost as a researcher (assuming she tries to do a good job as Chair), and Two, she will not be a good Chair—unless, of course, she has the requisite *additional skills*.

In Absurd Process #2, a professor in the department is promoted to the Chair position because "he wants it and nobody else does." Once again, this may be an impending disaster—unless he has the *needed skills*.

So, we shall spend this section on skills, the basis for reasonable promotions. In other words, and to use an old but apt phrase, real promotions (as with academic promotions) should be *based on merit*. We shall explore in the succeeding paragraphs how to evaluate merit in terms of its skill components.

The Skill Set—The DNA of Professional Functioning

In the planning of careers, few tools are as useful as the concept of the *skill set*. The underlying idea is simple enough, and important enough; the challenge is to persuade individuals who have developed a certain few skills to a high degree of proficiency—and who have begun to make a pretty good living from these few highly developed skills—to pay any attention to the many, many skills in which they are deficient, and to realize the potential career cost of neglecting these personal weaknesses.

Or, to state matters more positively, one should strive to realize the career opportunities that await those who are willing to spend 1% of their professional time identifying, and doing something about, their skill weaknesses.

Before making any further general remarks let's consider an example. The website

http://www.d.umn.edu/kmc/student/loon/car/self/career_transfer_survey.html

provides a concrete example of this sort of "professional DNA." Just as geneticists tend to group human DNA into groupings on the genome, this website has organized 62 skills into five groups, as follows:

Skill Group 1. Communication. The skillful expression, transmission and interpretation of knowledge and ideas. {13 **skills**}

CHAPTER 5: THE ACADEMIC EXECUTIVE

Skill Group 2. Research & Planning. The search for specific knowledge and the ability to conceptualize future needs and solutions for meeting those needs. [12 skills]

Skill Group 3. Human Relations. The use of interpersonal skills for resolving conflict, relating to, and helping, people. [13 skills]

Skill Group 4 Organization, Management & Leadership. The ability to supervise, direct and guide individuals and groups in the completion of tasks and the fulfillment of goals. [12 skills]

Skill Group 5. Work Survival. The day-to-day skills that promote effective production and work satisfaction. [12 skills]

All 63 skills are enumerated in Table 5.1, and the reader is invited—nay, urged—to peruse this long list of skills. The reactions to this perusal from many academics will be something like one of the following two exemplars:

Little or No Response: "What's this all about? I've had a pretty good career so far, best in my class as a student, and now considered one of the foremost experts in my field as a recently tenured academic. Surely this list is irrelevant to me, and in fact I suspect the nutniks who put this list of skills together are pushing something that is self serving and not realistic at all. In fact, I think the authors of this book are off on some wild turkey chase. The list of skills looks arbitrarily long; I know I don't have most of these "skills"; how can the authors explain how well I have done if they are trying to imply that I'm missing a lot of skills?"

Significant or High Response: Readers with a broader range of experience will instead say something more like this: "You know, I've always suspected that my own background, particularly my professional academic background, was overloaded on some skills and rather deficient in others. In professional or social situations involving a diverse group of people, I've often sensed that some of these people were very gifted in areas where, despite my academic success, I am not. And, frankly, I'd like to be. This list of skills has helped me analyze this phenomenon. I also suspect that there would be academic career opportunities open to me if I had, or could somehow develop, those missing skills I admire."

Exactly. One can always argue about the precise skills chosen[138] in the list, or about how they are defined. That's not the point. The point is that there is an impressively long list of skills and that most of these are not taught in school.

Even some of the skills mentioned in Table 5.1 have connotations different from the specialized academic meaning. As examples:
1. **Communication.** "Speaking effectively" means to an audience of peer adults.
2. **Research & Planning.** "Solving problems" does not mean "math problems."
3. **Human Relations.** "Listening" means to do so empathetically, to someone speaking with both rational and emotional content.
4. **Organization, Management & Leadership.** "Teaching" means teaching, mentoring or coaching the younger people who report to you, not the formal classroom teaching in the dark with a captive audience.
5. **Work Survival.** "Punctuality" doesn't just mean starting on time; it also means *stopping* on time!

This all suggests that academics who wish not to end their careers in exactly the same manner in which they began them, should pause and review some fundamental facts. Most academics are so obsessed with research and teaching (i.e., doing what they correctly take to be their jobs) that they give scant thought to the prospect of rising in the management structure of their employer-institution. And even those who do wonder from time to time whether there might eventually be a different life after tenure don't go about their somewhat chaotic speculations with any degree of rationality or determination.

---

138 Some skill analyzes have over 500 skills listed. This did not seem necessary to make the point here. Many of these skills—from mailing letters to filing—are too trivial to spend time on here.

CHAPTER 5: THE ACADEMIC EXECUTIVE

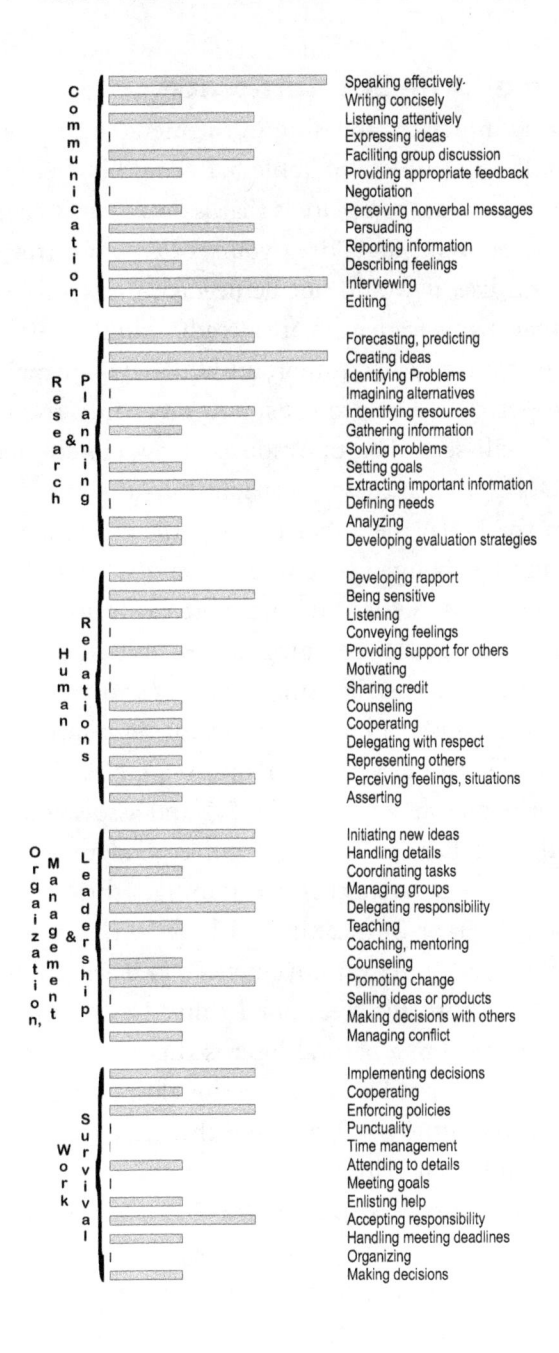

Communication
- Speaking effectively
- Writing concisely
- Listening attentively
- Expressing ideas
- Faciliting group discussion
- Providing appropriate feedback
- Negotiation
- Perceiving nonverbal messages
- Persuading
- Reporting information
- Describing feelings
- Interviewing
- Editing

Research – Planning
- Forecasting, predicting
- Creating ideas
- Identifying Problems
- Imagining alternatives
- Indentifying resources
- Gathering information
- Solving problems
- Setting goals
- Extracting important information
- Defining needs
- Analyzing
- Developing evaluation strategies

Human Relations
- Developing rapport
- Being sensitive
- Listening
- Conveying feelings
- Providing support for others
- Motivating
- Sharing credit
- Counseling
- Cooperating
- Delegating with respect
- Representing others
- Perceiving feelings, situations
- Asserting

Organization, Management & Leadership
- Initiating new ideas
- Handling details
- Coordinating tasks
- Managing groups
- Delegating responsibility
- Teaching
- Coaching, mentoring
- Counseling
- Promoting change
- Selling ideas or products
- Making decisions with others
- Managing conflict

Work Survival
- Implementing decisions
- Cooperating
- Enforcing policies
- Punctuality
- Time management
- Attending to details
- Meeting goals
- Enlisting help
- Accepting responsibility
- Handling meeting deadlines
- Organizing
- Making decisions

Table 5.1: Typical "Skill-Set DNA." This person can be a Highly Functioning Professional in some positions, but not in others.

195

How To Use a Skill-Set Template

For those truly interested in rising in the hierarchy, some further comments on the skill-set template of Table 5.1 should be helpful.[139] The elegant thing about a skill-set template is that is doesn't just have three items, such as "teach," "research," and "drag yourself to committee meetings." If this were a helpful list, it would not be needed; unfortunately, this is the skill template that many academics are already using!

There are, of course, other important skill-sets—namely, those associated with the positions you are considering heading towards. Let's call those "position" skill-sets. The question is, How closely does your "personal skill-set DNA" match these "position skill-sets"?

Fortunately, the DNA metaphor is not perfect: unlike your biological DNA, which can't be changed (not yet, anyway), your skill-set DNA can be, with effort and focus. Some skills are more easily acquired than others, depending on one's aptitude. Learning to use a computer spreadsheet is relatively easy; learning to be charismatic is almost impossible.

Here's a quick example of how to use a skill-set template:

(A). First, determine your own skill-set DNA. Go through a list like the one shown in Table. 5.1 and assess your score on each skill. The bars is Table 5.1 correspond to someone who has scored themselves either 3 (meaning, "this really is one of my strengths"); or 2 (meaning, "I have some advantage here, but could stand some improvement"); or 1 (meaning, "I'm somewhat weak in this area, but I think I can improve a lot); or 0 (meaning, "I'm a natural loser is this respect, so I'll have to be very proactive if I wish to use this skill professionally").

(B). Go through the list again, and this time assess how important you think each skill is for the kind of (real) promotion that you intend to pursue. Again use a 3-2-1-0 system, with 3 meaning "essential," 0 meaning "irrelevant," etc.

(C). Note your deficits, that is, every time your DNA in a needed skill is insufficient. It goes without saying that the whole exer-

---

[139] Table 5.1 represents only one such template of skills. There are many others. The reader who has resolved to perform an inventory of his or her skills would benefit from unearthing a skill classification system that best fits the career they wish to explore.

CHAPTER 5: THE ACADEMIC EXECUTIVE

cise is meaningless unless one is determined to be brutally honest about scoring. It might help to try our your scoring in **(A)** on a long-term friend. Similarly, why not run your estimates in **(B)** past a colleague or mentor who has "been there, done that."

(D). For those deficiencies detected through the process in **(A)**—**(C)**, decide whether there are just a few deficiencies or many, and whether the deficiencies seem correctable or not. If this process reveals many deficiencies, or several deficiencies that are critical but difficult to improve, it is likely unrealistic to pursue such a position at this point in your career. (Perhaps later, with further experience and skill development, this assessment will change for the better.) On the other hand, if you have most of the needed skills, and can readily remedy the more critical deficient ones, you are close to being a credible candidate for the position contemplated.

This skill-set approach will save you the embarrassment and trouble of pursuing the unattainable, but it may also open up some possibilities you had not previously considered.[140] One may say with accuracy that this skill-set approach is a great and useful generalization of Fig. 2.1, the 4-box of ability vs. inclination. Instead of a single attribute, "ability," we now have dozens of attributes, namely, one's personal skill-set DNA.

These ideas are equally useful on the other side of the promotion transaction, helping academic managers choose the best people for the job. The classic error is to promote a star researcher into an administrative post, thinking of this as some sort of reward, when that person is now largely lost as a researcher and may have no discernable skills as an administrator.

5.4 Academic Leadership Requires Many Special Skills

When one decides to become more specialized in one's career, one must often choose to refine and improve some of one's skills at the expense of leaving others to languish. The authors would argue that this dilemma does not really apply to the choice of academic leadership as an academic career

---

[140] There are also skill-set templates for research and for teaching, which should be helpful in the deliberations discussed in Chapters 3 and 4.

emphasis. For whatever reason, professors expect their bosses, all the way up to the top, to also be, or to have recently been, professors. In the private sector, this would like, say, all the marketing managers expecting—*and getting*—all the CEOs over all the decades to have been marketing managers.

This observation, phenomenal but true, would make sense if the position of *president* were a merely trifling variation[141] on the position of *professor*. Nothing could be farther from the truth. Sections 5.2 and 5.3 above demonstrated the enormous deficiencies that must be overcome if one possesses "merely" the skills of a great teacher or a great researcher. So long as professors have the clout they do, and as long as they insist that presidents be professors first and whatever else second, senior academic managers and leaders will have to have professorial credentials that are at least respectable, if not highly impressive.

Soft Skills, Emotional IQ

In §5.3, we examined one's personal "skill-set DNA" as a tool for a relatively rational, quantitative measurement of one's suitability for a career in academic management. Honest comparison with the skill-set required by the position under consideration was where the proverbial rubber met the road. It was mentioned that the skills exemplified by effective teachers and great researchers were not sufficient for academic leadership. Some skills are still necessary, high intelligence being an obvious example, but these are far from enough.

Lest we be too vague about all this, the types of skills most often missing from the typical academic are of the "soft" variety, the *people skills*, closely related to what may be more familiar as *Emotional IQ*. This fact is often surprising, almost to the point of disbelief, among those who have spent most of their lives in the hard sciences (and their application). "Hard" meaning "substantive and demonstrably factual," not meaning "difficult," though these areas of academic study are usually difficult as well. At least those who are schooled in the humanities and the social sciences know of what the subject consists. This doesn't always mean that they possess, to a sufficient degree, these special skills that are so important to leadership of a

---

141 It is not unusual for a university president to sign his or her letters, "President and Professor of [Whatever]" or even "Professor of [Whatever} and President."

CHAPTER 5: THE ACADEMIC EXECUTIVE

knowledge-intensive enterprise, but at least they are familiar with the concepts. They may not be virtuoso musicians, but they're not tone-deaf either.

Though it can rarely appear on a résumé, emotional intelligence[142] is a critical predictor of professional success. Indeed, some studies (admittedly not focused exclusively on academic leadership) have suggested that components of emotional intelligence may be up to twice as important for excellent performance as pure intellect and expertise, and the higher the leadership position, the more this implication holds. Most readers will have heard the saying, "Hired on experience, fired on personality."

While we shall not attempt to dwell on an detailed exposition of emotional intelligence here, it is revealing that its five components are agreed to be as follows:

1. Self-awareness
2. Self-regulation
3. Motivation
4. Empathy
5. Social skills

May we ask you, the reader, for your honest reaction to these components? Do they make you feel confident? Do you have a good idea what they mean? If so, you are probably in good shape; you either possess these skill-subsets, or at least can remedy any defects in a more-or-less straightforward manner. If you don't understand them, or don't take them seriously (which means you don't understand them), you may be quite lacking in these skills and your future prospects in academic leadership may not be bright (except perhaps leading a small group of those even more deficient).

Are Meetings a Good Idea?

This subsection title is offered only partly in jest. No multi-person organization can avoid meetings, of course, although meetings often have a "bad rep" as wastes of time. So the important question isn't whether meetings are a good idea—i.e., whether to *have* meetings—but this question: How can we make our meetings more effective as essential tools of communication and decision-making? Several books have been written on exactly this topic, usually brief and to the point, so we shall not re-plow all that

---

142 See, for example, D Goleman, *Working with Emotional Intelligence*, Bantam, 1998.

ground here. We shall, however, mention some points that seem especially appropriate for meetings in academia, most of which are not seen in general guides to meeting conduct.

> **Concrete Example (1 of 3) of an Essential Skill Cluster**
> **The Ability To Ensure that Meetings are Effective**
> The higher one rises in the leadership hierarchy, the more time will be spent in meetings of all kinds. The fact that these meetings are all with highly intelligent, knowledge-based individuals makes this especially challenging.

Professors are a breed apart; that's why they're professors. In some respects, this makes them ideal as members of committees, task forces, etc. Meeting chairs who truly wish serious input and creative ideas from their meeting groups could do a lot worse that have them populated by professors, who are knowledgeable and inventive. They can focus (if they wish to) on a single complex issue for long periods of time, and they generally respect the rules of educated, sophisticated debate (facts are better than raw opinions, and rationality is superior to vague feelings).

Meetings Are Also a Challenge

As against these advantages, professors also have some detracting characteristics. They are talkers by profession, which means that their contributions to a meeting may be, on occasion, just a bit longer than necessary. They sometimes do not make the distinction between their personal fields of specialization, in which they are indeed at the top of the game, and some of the topics that come up for discussion at meetings, about which they know no more than an average intelligent, relatively well-informed person. They also love to debate, sometimes beyond the point of necessity at meetings.

Many professors are also "alpha's" (to borrow a word from biology) or Type A personalities (to use a concept from psychology), or both. They are familiar with the idea of leadership, but with themselves, not the meeting chair, as leader. Much of their work is solitary thinking, but they have no problem with team play either, so long as their own role is quarterback, coach and general manger. The meeting chair has wonderful resources sitting around the table, but the metaphor of being a lion tamer is not inapt.

A Question for Self-Diagnosis

At this point, we pause and ask the reader a question, one that has immense diagnostic value: Are you interested in the topic now under discussion? Are you fascinated by the complexity and challenges of leading meetings comprised primarily of academics? Have you already determined that you want to learn more about this subtle subject, perhaps getting some more references and becoming skilled in the conduct of effective meetings? Do you find intriguing the prospect of exploiting the advantages of chairing academic meetings, while coping successfully with the attendant disadvantages?

If you answered affirmatively to this series of questions, you may truly be cut out for academic leadership. On the other hand, if you are just interested in the general discussion, perhaps to find out how the "other half" thinks (or if your next planned professional reading is still paper number 5,001 in your research field), then you have just made an important discovery. You probably should not aspire to academic leadership, where virtually all of your time will be spend in person-to-person communication with other academics, much of it in "meetings."

Readers who realize that leadership is about leading *people*, and who understand further that, in academia, the venues for the expression of this leadership tend to be standing committees, task forces, departmental gabfests, faculty councils, tenure and promotion committees, senior administrative confabs (and innumerable other types of *meetings*)—these readers probably have a mindset for academic leadership. They crave the opportunity to contribute to the success of their institution (or at least their academic unit). For such people, it's never too early to start. We shall see (§5.5 below) that committee work can be an important stepping stone to being given one's first academic management posting.

It's never too early to start, but it can often be too late. Compare the following two vignettes:

SO YOU WANT TO BE A PROFESSOR?

Vignette 1.   Poor Start.

Sam and Linda are walking back to their offices after a three-hours-plus marathon departmental meeting of the academic staff. Prof. Sam Block is 56 years old, a veteran of departmental faculty meetings, good and bad. He doesn't much look forward to them, but realizes they are essential and tries to make positive contributions to them, in a spirit of cooperation and consensus-building. Prof. Linda Phillips is 28 years old, a new addition to the academic staff.

Sam: "Linda, I think we can do better than that. In fact, I think we *have* to do better if we're going to put our best foot forward as a department in the announced Faculty reorganization."

Linda: "I'm relieved to hear that opinion. I thought it was just me. Surely we can have a departmental discussion that is more structured and respectful. Between you and me, I don't think Fred did a very good job guiding the discussion today. *{"Fred" is Prof. Fred Hausberger, the departmental Chair, who also acted as meeting chair}.*

Sam: "I agree that Fred is not the best meeting chair I've ever seen, but I don't primarily blame him. I think much of the negative entropy was created by Paul Haggis. After all, he started out by being a half-hour late, so he missed Fred's presentation, which laid the factual foundation for the meeting. Then Fred proceeded to ask questions to which he would have known the answers if he had been there for the presentation." *{"Paul" is Prof. Paul Haggis, 32 years old, and who is already recognized as a world authority in his field. He is one of the brightest lights in the department from a research perspective and brings Big Time research funding. Only problem: Sigmund Freud may have anticipated Paul when he developed the concept of the ego.}*

Sam [cont'd]: "I admit that Fred's a very bright, creative guy and I do think he had some good ideas. But these ideas were expressed very forcefully, including some barely hidden insults to some of his colleagues. And his comments sounded more like a lecture than a component of a dialog. Some of us were more rattled than impressed. Also, I noticed that when

CHAPTER 5: THE ACADEMIC EXECUTIVE

others ventured their opinions, Fred got into side conversations with other profs nearby. By the way, what ever happened to the ability to whisper?"

Linda: "It's a shame, really. I agree that Fred is a real brainiac, but sometimes I wonder if we might function better at departmental meetings if Fred had a dental appointment or something."

Vignette 2.   Excellent Start.

The setting and dramatis personae are identical to those of Vignette 1. "Paul," in this alternate vignette, is identical to Paul in Vignette 1, except for his consummate skills as an academic leader.

Sam: "Linda, I've been to a lot of departmental meetings in my life. Considering the complexity of the main issue today, I have a warm feeling, both about how we functioned as a department and also about how we're going to shape up in the Faculty reorganization."

Linda: "Yes, I had anticipated more chaos than we actually had. I think that Fred did a pretty good job of leading the meeting, so that's a big plus. I was also impressed with Paul Haggis's creative ideas and how he was able to quietly incorporate his colleagues' ideas into his own and build a great consensus. I think we'll be in good shape in this Faculty for some time to come. Frankly, Sam, between you and me, I wouldn't mind at all if Paul took over as departmental chair when Fred steps down next year."

So, what's the message? Readers will have correctly inferred that this vignette comparison is not about Prof. Block; he is the "old salt," a survivor in the battles at departmental meetings (both good and bad). Nor is it about Prof. Phillips, the promising young academic, newly added to the department; she is short on experience but has an unerring eye for what should happen when a group of really smart people get together to discuss and resolve something. The comparison isn't even about Hausberger, the competent if uninspiring departmental Chair. It is about Prof. Haggis, of course, whose Jekyll & Hyde personality alternatives illustrate someone who, in Vignette Version 2, could well pursue a career in academic leadership if he so chose (and someone who, in Vignette Version 1, could never do so). The message, in one sentence, is this: If you want to be noticed as academic leadership material, you must take meetings of all kinds very seriously, starting with the first one you ever have.

The Conduct of Effective Meetings

As mentioned, meetings are non-optional parts of organizational life. For academics that choose teaching or research emphases, it may be possible almost to ignore such meetings, making their primary contributions elsewhere. For academic leaders, however, their ability to lead will be highly correlated with their ability to interact with their colleagues in groups.

Many pamphlets and books have been written about the conduct of meetings. One of these, by Chan [2003], has hundreds of useful tips, and many further relevant references. Chan points out that there are several roles at a successful meeting, and nothing is left to chance. She refers to the *convener* (who decides that a meeting is necessary and sets the agenda), the *facilitator* (whom we have called the meeting chair, who runs the meeting,), the *recorder* (who records key elements of process and important decisions), and of course the other participants. Frequently, one person takes on all three roles—though this may be too difficult at large meetings. For example, that one person is usually the department Chair for departmental academic meetings, or a designated committee chair for subcommittee meetings.

Sometimes the time saved by not recording some sort of minutes is more than spent in subsequent re-hashes that would be unnecessary. (Didn't we go through all this, exactly, last year?") Not to mention the general confusion about what rules are now in place, especially as memories fade and become more divergent.

Alternative Authority Structures for Meetings

It is also important that everyone know exactly how the decision will be made, and this "how" often depends on the issue at hand. Adapted from Chan [2003], we have the following processes:
- Autocracy. Also known as "dictatorship" by those who disagree with the decisions. Here, the Head or Chair of the academic unit

simply decides[143] and then (one hopes) informs others of that decision. Examples of appropriate autocratic decisions would include dismissing a member of the support staff, and resolving an immediate crisis.
- Semi-autocracy. The Chair consults most or all of the professors in the department, one at a time, perhaps by e-mail, to get information or advice, then decides. Writing the Annual Departmental Report to the Dean would be a good example of this decision mode.
- Democracy. Only needed for some kinds of important issues, there is a motion or resolution and everyone votes. (This is a waste of time if the decision will actually be made autocratically or semi-autocratically.) Voting, after everyone has been given an opportunity to express their views, can save many hours of verbal jousting. Voting also raises many technicalities, including the definition of a quorum, whether a supermajority is needed to pass very fundamental changes, etc.
- Dysfunctional Democracy. Here, at least some participants assume the decision has been made when it really hasn't. One type of dysfunction is what the authors call "last guy talking wins." Someone who has a lot to say (and says it well) states his opinion; the meeting chair says, "Sounds good to me"; and everyone else acquiesces.
- Consensus. This is a pleasant approach and can work if the group is not too large and the general mood is collegial. If, after a period of discussion, it becomes clear that most favor the policy proposed, and that the few who aren't thrilled with it don't wish to raise a fuss about something that most colleagues are pleased with. They can live with it and move on to something else.

---

143 Often decisions that appear to be autocratic are not quite. The Chair may well have consulted her Associate Chairs, or some other particularly knowledgeable person in the department, or higher up in the management chain (e.g., the Dean's Office), before taking her decision.

If you aren't clear about how your meeting group is intended to work, it might be a good idea very early in the meeting to ask[144] politely, "Is this committee advisory or does it make the decisions?" If the committee is advisory, everyone should talk quite a bit less, giving only sage advice. If the committee is determinative, there is more talk like this: "Here's what I'd like to see, and here's why."

Financial Awareness and Accountability

The financial area is the second (of three) "essential skill clusters" that we shall briefly explore in connection with the career path to academic leadership. (There are more than three, of course, but these three catch a lot.) All professors have some skills in the financial area, but the range of these talents varies quite widely. Managing a number of grants and contracts, each with its own budget, provides some learning on the job.

> **Concrete Example (2 of 3) of an Essential Skill Cluster**
> **The Ability To Manage Financial Resources**
> The higher one rises in the leadership hierarchy, the more one must understand "accounting," meaning the rules governing the reporting and measurement of financial transactions; and "budgets," meaning the process of financial planning and the allocation of (scarce) financial resources.

Professors with mathematical training—the primary examples being, of course, professors of mathematics—are sometimes perplexed by why, with all their learning, they don't quite feel at home with budgets, accounting, auditing, and financial projections.[145] They see numbers all over the place, yet often never come to be comfortable with these subjects. How can this be? The answer is that they are focusing on the wrong skills. As *mathematics*, accounting rarely ventures beyond the four primary arithmetic operations known by Grade 5 in elementary school: addition, subtraction, multiplication and division. That's not what accounting and budgets are about.

---

144 This advice is not for the meeting chair! The meeting chair should, however, be able to answer the question.
145 Actually, financial projections, if done for a multi-year horizon, take us from *accounting* to *finance*, which can be quite sophisticated mathematically.

CHAPTER 5: THE ACADEMIC EXECUTIVE

Accounting is (or should be) about rules, conventions, objectivity, transparency, consistency, comparability, materiality, continuity, and conservative assumptions; the arithmetic is trivial. Budgets are about the allocation of scarce financial resources in a manner that optimizes the current strategic and operational priorities.

Important Question No. 1

The most immediate accounting question, for *any* organization, is this: Are we winning or losing the Battle of the Bottom Line? For a given accounting period (typically one year) we add up all the revenue, subtract all the expenses (including, in normal corporate accounting, non-cash accounting charges, like depreciation), and see whether we arrive at a plus or a minus. In the private sector, the plus-minus is called *net income* or *net loss*, respectively. In the not-for-profit sector, including universities, the plus-minus is called the *surplus* or the *deficit,* respectively.

| Projection of Operating Revenue |||
University of Toronto - 2005-06	$M	Percent
Provincial Operating Grants	511.3	44
Tuition Fees	385.3	33
Subtotal	896.6	78
All Other Revenue Sources	255.0	22
Total Operating Revenue	1,151.6	100

Figure 5.3: Typical Academic Budget –Revenue (for illustration only).

One cannot, despite the importuning pressures and pleadings from innumerable special interest groups, run a continual deficit. Anyone who has ever owned a credit card is familiar with this idea. Borrowing from the future must be done with great care, if at all, and many universities and colleges are prevented by law from doing so.

| Projection of Operating Expenditures |||
University of Toronto - 2005-06	$M	Percent
Academic	771.4	66
All Other Expenditures	396.9	34
Total Operating Budget	1,168.3	100

Figure 5.4: Typical Academic Budget –Expenditures (for illustration only).

Even with the highly simplified[146] budget information in Figs. 5.3 & 5.4, we can infer a number of important pieces of information:
1. The university's revenue is split, very roughly equally, among three main sources: the provincial[147] government, academic tuition fees, and everything else (a category that gets a great deal of attention from senior university leaders). With 44% of revenue coming from government, however, this university still more than qualifies as a *public* university.
2. The university plans on running a deficit. With revenue of $1.152B and expenditures of $1.168B, a deficit of $16M is planned for.
3. Readers familiar with corporate financial reporting will notice some divergence of terminology between the above financial data and the canonical *financial statements* of the private sector. For example, "expenditure" seems halfway between "expenditure" and "expense" as used technically by public companies; it is hard to find depreciation and amortization; and the flavor of this budget is more like that of a cash flow statement than an income statement. However, we shall not dwell on these accounting technicalities here.
4. The most interesting entry, by far, in the brief data in Figs. 5.3 & 5.4 is the entry for "academic" in Fig. 5.4. Although fully two thirds of the university's annual expense (which it calls "expenditures"), it is left deliciously vague. It is, in fact, the only one of the dozen major categories that is represented not by a noun, but by an adjective. One suspects that the missing noun is largely "salaries."

---

146 It cannot be stated strongly enough that this brief discussion, and the truncated figures and tables used, do not represent a professional discussion of the University of Toronto's budget projections. The referenced document is 72 pages long and only superficial data are used here as illustrative points in a general discussion.
147 Equivalent to state government support in the U.S.

CHAPTER 5: THE ACADEMIC EXECUTIVE

Important Question No. 2

The second important question might well be this: Given that the university is engaged in providing two categories of (somewhat related) services—namely, teaching and research—how do these two services stack up as regards the important issue of surplus/deficit? (One would simply say "profitability" in the business sector.) Alas, there is essentially no information on this clearly interesting question in the financial disclosures of a typical university.

This raises two interesting and important sub-questions:
1. Does the university *know* the answer to this question?
2. Does the university *want* to know the answer to this question?

The answer to sub-question 1 is "No." Although Fig. 5.4 shows that "academic" (salaries and benefits) consumes fully two thirds of the university's annual budget, the university has no idea[148] of how much of this is "teaching" and how much is "research." The reason is simply enough: the university has no idea how much time its professors spend on teaching vis-à-vis research. It can make some assumptions (as we shall do presently) but it doesn't *know*.

The reason it doesn't know is because professors don't fill in timecard information. Do academics, on average, spend their time {60%, 20%} on {research, teaching} or {20%, 60%}? (With 20% left to "other activities.") No one really knows. Recalling the "vocation-monastic" analogy, it would be like asking monks to list how many hours they spent in prayer and how many hours in making cheese. It would be unthinkable, a cultural insult.

"Why don't we get that information?" someone may ask. Well, one reason is that it would be easier to get the average housecat to win the Olympic breaststroke than to get professors to fill out timesheets. In their defense (professors, not housecats), some professorial activities, such as graduate student supervision, have both teaching and research components. But this could be solved with a simple assigned ratio if the will were there to measure these key outputs.

---

148 Accountants and auditors have an important concept—that of specifying the level of *materiality*—meaning that an accounting error of this magnitude could affect an important decision. Breaking down university accounting into teaching and research satisfies a *high multiple* of the materiality criterion! There is no excuse, in accounting theory, for its absence.

This brings us to the second sub-question: Does the university *want* to know the revenue-expenditure balance as between teaching and research? Perhaps. Somewhere in the senior central administration these calculations may be made (assuming elementary competence) but they are not divulged to the rest of the university community nor propagated to the public at large.

Sources & Applications of Funds	$M	Percent T	Percent R	Teaching	Research
Revenue (government)	511	70	30	358	153
Revenue (fees)	385	80	20	308	77
Revenue (other)	255	50	50	128	128
Totals	1,151			793	358
Expenditure (academic)	771	40	60	308	463
Expenditure (all other)	397	50	50	199	199
Totals	1,168			507	661
Surplus/(Deficit)				287	(303)

Figure 5.5: Teaching vis-à-vis Research (for illustration only).

Figure 5.5 shows a theoretical calculation for how research and teaching stack up in their competition for funds. The revenue lines show the funds contributed from the three primary revenue sources and how they *intend* these funds to be used as between research and teaching. The expenditure lines show the research/teaching breakdown as to how they are *actually* used. (All percentages shown are just speculative. These are not made public. That is the point.) For this illustrative example, $793M was intended for teaching, but only $507M was spent on teaching. In contrast, $358M was given for research, while $661M was spent on research. In this example, teaching is subsidizing research to a high degree.

This may or may not be happening, because we don't know the percentages. What we do know is that there are sometimes 175 students in First Year philosophy class, while very few research funding sources pay the real indirect costs of the research (and some pay none at all). These sorts of observations make one more than just suspicious.

A good reference on academic budgeting and finance is MJ Barr [2002].

CHAPTER 5: THE ACADEMIC EXECUTIVE

Legal Fluency

The legal area is the third example (of three) of an "essential skill cluster" that those who wish to enter management must take much more seriously. There are several levels of government, each with its own multitude of statutes (national or federal, provincial or state, and municipal) and each academic institution itself has countless additional rules and regulations. Granting agencies also have their own thick books of rules. No professor, unless they happen to have been a law professor, is expected to understand all this just because he or she has just become a Department Chair or a Faculty Dean, but one has to be able at least to converse, with some degree of intelligence, with those who *are* experts in these areas.

> **Concrete Example (3 of 3) of an Essential Skill Cluster**
> <u>The Ability To Understand Legal Concepts and Language</u>
> The higher one rises in the leadership hierarchy, the more one must understand terminology and concepts from law. These apply, for example, to contracts and labor law.

Once one has hire-and-fire responsibility, one has to know something about labor law. Once one has some responsibility for implementing research agreements and contracts, one has to be able to contribute to their terms and conditions (at least in lay language, while the lawyers will craft the final language) and understand what they say. If one is managing creative research, one must know something about intellectual property law. In chemistry research, perhaps, one might be ahead of the game to know some environmental law. Many other examples could be cited.

There are other significant areas of expertise as well, that suddenly loom as increasingly important as one takes on management responsibilities. All the discussion of these "new skills needed" in this and the previous section (§§5.3 & 5.4) should give one pause before making a decision to become an academic chief of some kind. Do all these new areas of knowledge frighten you or excite you? If the latter, this is a big plus and speaks well for your chances.

5.5 Some Strategies for How to Play the Game

We now give some practical advice about how to place oneself in a position to be considered for—and in fact chosen for—some of the lower levels of academic leadership. That will place one on the right initial take-off path to the higher levels later. Perhaps the title of this subsection should be called some "suggestions" for the game since there is no one foolproof approach, while contrariwise there are many slightly different strategies that will work just as well as the hints given here.

Anyone fit for this line of work will get the idea. The clues below are not a substitute for talent (i.e., the right skill-set DNA). As always in academia, being an excellent researcher (and to a somewhat lesser extent, being a good teacher) is somewhat pre-conditional to success in this quest. The reasons for this are more cultural than rational, as the skill-set discussion would indicate.

Professors at most universities should be in fine shape, as far as career opportunities and culture are concerned, if their passion is a mixture of teaching and research.[149] They will become more proficient and better rewarded as time goes on and, if they work hard and have the royal jelly for creative work, they will thrive.

However, if the reader is one who likes to put things together rather than take them apart; who welcomes the opportunity to work with others in a team environment where each member is challenged to do their best for the good of the enterprise (rather than nestling away to think their very own discipline-based thoughts); who wants to look at the forest and not just at Leaf #1 on Branch #2 on Tree #3 in Clump #4 —in short, if a reader is interested in the broad picture and playing a leadership role in painting it—these academics may be management material and should give that possibility the strategic attention it deserves.

There is, of course, a critical timing problem. In current academic culture (and for as long as one can predict into the future) one must be very strong in

---

149 However, if one wishes to emphasize teaching, as discussed in Chapter 3, one would likely settle down in an academic environment that paid teaching true deference (rather than mere lip service), and if one wishes to focus primarily on becoming a world-recognized researcher in one's field, it seems more likely that one would attain this goal if one operated from a strongly research-intensive university.

the core academic duties of one's department—usually high-level research. If one waits until one's eminence in one's research area is unassailable, one may be "too late" to capture the executive opportunities that may arise.

This situation is described, mercilessly, as "aging out." On the other hand, if one tries to speed the process up to an unseemly degree—the most important example being to short-change one's research achievements in exchange for excessive administrative duties—one can run off a cliff and end up being considered (justifiably) as having been successful at neither research nor managerial functions (much less academic leadership). Go through the stages quickly, with great competence, but don't try to skip any major stages.

Some First Steps

You must have some serious "administrative" talent; check your skill DNA. (The skill-inventory approach is meant to be helpful, but cannot perform miracles.) You must be willing to seek out a modest starter position such as Associate Chair. Try to distinguish yourself in this position, even though it is strictly a temporary staging operation to get to the positions in which you're really interested.

Do this by informing the existing Chair (or whomever is the appropriate person to recommend you for the job) that you are interested. However, don't noise your ambitions widely in the department. Prof. Collins (an Interviewee; see Appendix) says, flat out,

"If you show any sign of wanting [a leadership position], you'll disqualify yourself."

This is rather sad, but we don't shoot the messenger; it is likely also true. This means that potential leaders are forced into a hypocritical stance, pretending and acting one way, while thinking another. Other professors, who might well make excellent managers, will not even consider this career path, it being so roundly disreputed by their colleagues. It may take another decade or two to realize that the individuals who just "happened" to achieve serious promotions had often planned such a career path all along (although, to demonstrate their academic "purity,". they may still deny this).

How does one explain this cultural revulsion for professors who are willing to do more that teach and research? Partly, this may be simple envy, as would be the case in any working culture. But primarily, the authors believe, it is explicable (as is so much else in academic culture) by the Normative Paradigm.[150] Those who live in The Tube don't admire those who venture outside The Tube. The former view the latter as *just not us* anymore.

In addition, most professors do not like this sort of position; it has lots of hard work, less international exposure, and little direct credit for a job well done.[151] It also detracts from your research and teaching activity (there are only so many hours in a day). However, while this explains why some are not enthusiastic about "administration" themselves, it does not explain why some resent others seeking out such a career. (In fact, it would seem to be in everyone's interest that *somebody* take these positions.)

Second Steps

The above first steps will enable you to prove your skills and reliability. Equally important, it will also facilitate many important contacts at senior levels. As little a commitment as two years at this level will already put you in line to be considered for a Chair position.

If this plan doesn't soon bear fruit—perhaps because of the adverse timing of available Chairships—then move on to something similar, such as chairing a decanal or Faculty committee. This will keep you in the game. Interdepartmental committees get extra points (other things being equal).

Again, there will likely be few volunteers for this role, because it is an NP-less move for those enjoying (or otherwise committed to) the NP life. Assuming good performance, your new face and name recognition, supported by comments such as "she is a good [administrator]," will pave the way for a brighter path ahead.

Next Steps

Once having achieved a Chair or Director (or similar) position, the world of higher academia is now open to you. This means, at first, the possibility of higher academic management positions at your own institution—Dean, or Director of a high-profile new program, etc. (But hardly President

---

150 The Normative Paradigm, first explained in §4.2.
151 If you are an NP-confirmed person, of course, stay with the NP. We are now advising professors who wish to take un-NP-like decisions to reach un-NP-like positions in pursuit of un-NP-like careers.

CHAPTER 5: THE ACADEMIC EXECUTIVE

yet!) Your own Dean can mentor you with occasional key advice (as long as you're not aiming to usurp his or her job!).

If you can get into this sort of position by the age of forty or so, then after one term you are not only eligible to be considered for higher positions at your own university, but to be in the running for even higher positions at a smaller university elsewhere.

After a series of such important responsibility and positional increments—including at least a Deanship at a largish university or an academic executive position at a smaller university—presidential openings at other similar-sized universities are not beyond your grasp.

Develop key networks outside academia, be they in government, or in the private sector, or international. You may find that the conferences you attend are no longer exclusively in your research area, populated by your standard group of colleagues in your research field. Make your outside contacts as high in their organizations as possible.

Offer to contribute to key reports and studies whose other authors are well-placed individuals (outside you research field). There may be strategic contacts in government also; try to make these at the highest level possible.

These career sketchings are not guaranteed recipes. They merely depict a general flow of career events and some tips for how to make these events happen. Fortunately, anyone pursuing this "academic executive" career path will have no trouble improvising, as necessary, on the schemes and themes just illustrated. Those who can't quite figure out what is meant above will have just diagnosed themselves as being unsuited for the academic management and leadership competition. (This is a plus both for them and for the academic units not exposed to their weak leadership skills.)

Time is of the Essence

One does think of the interval between tenure and retirement as being quite a long time. Assuming tenure at age 30, retirement at age 65, and death at age 80, the tenure-retirement interval is 44% of one's life (or 58% of one's adult life, or 78% of one's remunerated professional life). Still, if becoming an "academic executive" is one's career choice, this is in fact a very brief time to ascend the long organizational ladder.

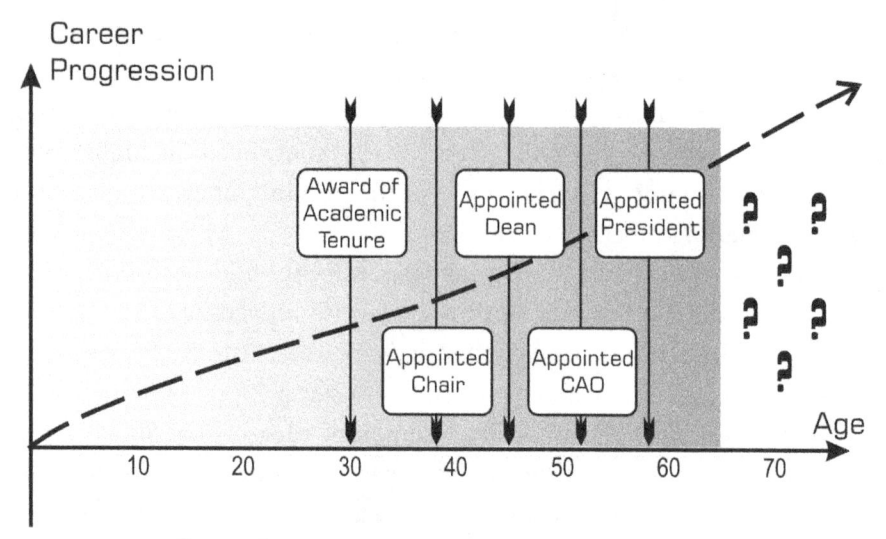

Figure 5.6: Want to Reach the Top? Time is Very Short!

We shall sketch out why this is so with some typical data, but just the fact that no one is appointed president the day before they retire should jar back to reality any reader who feels that there is "lots of time." Figure 5.6 picks up where Fig. 1.2 left off.

Only the most significant rungs in the organizational ladder[152] are shown in Fig. 5.6. No specific time is allowed for being Assistant Chair, Associate Chair, Assistant Dean, Associate Dean, Vice-Dean, Assistant Provost, Associate Provost, Assistant to the Deputy Provost, Vice-Provost, or any other intermediate position.

In addition to the obvious conclusions—that anyone who actually reaches the lofty perches of leadership in academia must be hard-working and supremely gifted in *all* the skills required (and not just be, for example, a gifted researcher)—it is also clear that such persons must be extraordinarily strategic in their outlook, and proactively aware of how well their career strategy is being executed. No time must be lost in periods of distractive unawareness. In fact, as Fig. 5.6 suggests, waiting for tenure to

---

152 The keenly observant reader will have noticed that tenure occurs at age 30 in Fig. 5.6, while it was assumed to occur at age 33 in Fig. 1.2. This is eminently reasonable. One cannot be president of a university without being on the fast track; fiddling around at the early stages makes the last stages impossible!

begin the "academic executive" campaign is probably leaving things too late.

The trick is not to over-tread the fine line between a positive, pro-active approach and the constraints of realism. Keep all communications channels open. Maintain constant touch with colleagues. Perhaps less frequently, but more importantly, gain the guidance of the decision-makers on your path to leadership. Get a sense of what is acceptable and what moves may be a trifle too early.

Some academics suggest that any intimation of one's intention to rise in the *real* hierarchy, as distinct from the "Performance Review with an Adjustment to Title" process that characterizes what are called "academic promotions" described in §5.1, should not be revealed in any way to one's colleagues. This may well be true (if sad), hence one probably should not infuse one's remarks to one's colleagues with one's personal intentions. Colleagues, even if well-liked, are not likely one's long-term friends, and certainly not one's family. The "love" of colleagues is far from unconditional. There may be many unspoken conditions, and there may be no love. Best to keep one's own counsel, which is, is fact, another key skill of top leadership.

5.6 Insights from Our Interviewees on the Academic Management Option

We conclude with the wisdom of our interviewees, details on whom are given in an appendix. Some of these comments amplify themes discussed above, while others raise new issues worthy of thought.

Michael Collins

Michael Collins advises as follows:

> "If you are interested in having some sort of academic leadership role, it's very good strategy, and helpful to the enjoyment of a rich academic life, to make as many contacts as you can outside your immediate area both within your department, outside the area of your own particular specialty, and then within the faculty, and even further afield.
>
> "I know my strengths and weaknesses. I am an effective administrator within my own little world, but I am perfectionist

and I'm a procrastinator, and those two things together are the death of someone in a very busy administrative role like a departmental chairman.

"[Our last president] was enormously successful because he had the "royal jelly," and he had enthusiasm and bounce and vigor and energy, which is needed, I think, to invigorate a huge, rather amorphous place like this. The average person would just be drained with what he had to face day by day.

"If your mind is of the sort that you can deal with three things at once then you have one of the basic talents to be a good administrator."

Molly Shoichet

Molly Shoichet also comments on the strange-but-true attitude that those who don't want leadership are offended by those who do:

"Wanting to have a position of leadership is almost reason for people not to promote you to positions of leadership. You do in a sense opt out of research when you take on these leadership roles. What's the motivation, what are their reasons? It's a difficult decision, and it's more difficult if your research is really going well. This is supposed to be your passion.

"You have leaders who tend the farm and leaders that grow the farm."

Tom Brzustowski

Tom Brzustowski, with senior management experience in academia, and in both the provincial and federal governments, first reminisces on his academic department headship:

"What I enjoyed the most was to build up the department because by that time applications from good people had started to come in. I had the opportunity to hire some first-rate people. So that drove me quite a bit. That's the thing I enjoyed the most—hiring young people.

"The thing I enjoyed the least happened very early on. I had to tell a senior colleague, somebody whom I liked very

CHAPTER 5: THE ACADEMIC EXECUTIVE

much personally and who had become a bit of a mentor to me in the department, that his work just wasn't good enough. That was very difficult to do. He was a gentleman and made it easy for me. Even better, he changed and became really active in research afterwards."

Tom raises the interesting point that, having once achieved tenure, academics are not reviewed[153] very often:

"My impression is that most faculties don't particularly do annual reviews or anything that could be considered feedback. In any well-run business, there is feedback, but in academia people can be left alone for five, ten, sometimes 15 years.

"The annual performance review—the possibility of facing somebody and saying, 'Look, your work is not good enough because . . . and then making it constructive, is something that most managers shy away from. In some places it gets to the point that, when things reach a level which is no longer acceptable, and the person has to be asked to leave, it comes as a surprise to them. There's no paper trail; they haven't been given the steering, the course corrections along the way.

"Of course, if you they have some person doing fantastically well, you compliment them in the hall!"

Tom then mentions an experience which shows that promotion/tenure committees are not completely predictable when personalities are involved (as they always are):

"When I was VP academic at Waterloo, this case came forward from one particular Faculty: It involved a man in his mid to late thirties, applying for tenure after six years. 'His thesis was so good,' the department said, 'it was edited and published as a book. He's also published six major papers—that's very good because in our field, publishing is not as frequent as in some others'. He'd developed into quite a fair teacher, accepted his share of the administrative load in the department, and all in all was, in the words of the department, 'the kind of person

---

[153] There are, of course, the performance reviews and title fiddling referred to as academic "promotions."

we like to build on for the future, so we're recommending him for tenure'.

"Two weeks later, the following case comes up from another department in the same Faculty: A man is in his late 30s, 'the only book he's got is an edited version of his PhD thesis, and he's only managed to publish six or seven papers in the last six years. And he's not an outstanding teacher . . . ' (Exactly the same data but a different interpretation.) The recommendation was to deny tenure. I said, 'Wait a minute, do you remember how we discussed that other guy last time?' Well there was some general embarrassment over this, and maybe some resentment that I raised the issue.

"It ultimately came down to the fact that one guy was liked in his department and the other guy wasn't liked in his. It was a personality thing. And yet it was being translated into an interpretation of criteria.

"If you're going to be even a department Chair, you really have to be aware of the cultural and personality aspects of what people are supposed to interpret as objective decisions under a particular policy. And you have to learn how to work your way around it. I don't think that can be taught, I think it's instinctive."

Tom on the soft skills:

"You have to use your instincts, and you have to think about the very soft (people) skills. And paradoxically, the soft skills are the hard ones. Just as examples: understanding personality clashes, recognizing that you don't want to surprise people, you can't make them lose face publicly, and that you have to account for some people being liked and other people being disliked, all of that sort of goulash of considerations. Maybe you have to develop it as you mature in an instinctive way.

"You don't just sort of tick things off on a sheet. When John Ralston Saul wrote Voltaire's Bastards, what he was saying was that in many cases decisions are made on the basis of judgment that takes a lot into account. You can't just pretend

CHAPTER 5: THE ACADEMIC EXECUTIVE

you've developed some rational system where you put numbers in, you turn the crank and the answer comes out. I think that these are aptitudes and talents and preferences that people develop not in any formal way, but they either have them or they don't."

Tom's comments on leadership in government vis-à-vis leadership in a university are also insightful (although the University of Waterloo was somewhat smaller then than it is now):

"Coming from university to government, I discovered that *process* is very often more important than *substance*. That has its positive aspects but also its negative aspects, because you often have people involved in important decisions who don't know the substance well enough. They know only the process. But quite apart from that, making sure that there are no surprises, making sure that you minimize the unintended (negative) consequences, this is terribly important. So the first thing I learned in government is it's not only the substance, process is also very important."

Heather Monroe-Blum

We have saved for last the three[154] of our interviewees who are obviously not the least, especially for the present chapter—the three who ascended to the highest position of academic leadership.

Heather Monroe-Blum describes the motivation for her present function this way:

"I never thought about this as 'administration' and I don't think I do today. I've been fortunate to have leadership opportunities and to play special roles, to make a difference, to work with great teams. So I guess if there's anything I think about, it's the opportunity for activist leadership in a time-limited but important role.

"Not so long ago, as VP, Research, there was a moment when my research grant needed to be renewed, and I knew I

---

154 Or, rather, four, not three, if Peter Likins gets his fair count of two presidencies, having been President of both Lehigh University and The University of Arizona.

could get it renewed, but I didn't believe I could fully carry out that kind of work to the standard I should continue to aim for. That was my moment of reckoning, a really tough moment of introspection. That was when I decided to keep doing intellectual work but morph it into something else completely synergistic with my previous and current roles.

"With any of these jobs—departmental Chair, Dean, VP, Provost, or President—these are jobs of influence. If they ever were, they're no longer jobs of authority. There is no workable 'command and control' leadership anywhere and especially not in a university.

"And to influence you need to inspire."

With regard to senior university positions, such as VP, CAO, and whether they can also really function as professors at the same time, Heather comments thus:

"I've seen very few of what I would call 'activist' leaders, who've also kept up as a full professor would, with a fully active research program in a traditional mode. At the same time I've also seen many former university presidents stay in the university sector and make a rich intellectual contribution—but it's of a different kind."

Heather describes some of the challenge in leading academics:

"People say there's nothing as tough as the politics in academe. You need to work hard yourself, you need to be successful yourself, and you need, most of all, to help others succeed—being able to celebrate others, to mobilize people to work together while maintaining excellence. There are a lot of very special, creative people and quite unique individuals in the university, and you cannot ignore any of them and their contributions.

"At the highest levels, it becomes the management of complexity—interpersonally, politically, and intellectually—for a greater purpose. If you're not turned on by the management and harnessing of talent and complexity, it's really tough to go this route."

Lastly, Heather comments on how all her efforts and those of colleagues in the university she leads should be of value to the outside world:
> "It's absolutely the role of leaders across the university, in their various capacities, to promote the benefits gained from the research and teaching that we do, and to be creative in thinking about what those benefits are and realizing them. Being focused on this dissemination, and how to do it productively and effectively, is extraordinarily important."

David Naylor

David Naylor paints the outline of a career that ends in academic leadership this way: Get your grounding as a departmental Chair—and, in fact, start even earlier than that.
> "No matter what discipline she or he has pursued, a junior professor should in my view focus in the first instance on developing an excellent record as a teacher and scholar. Along the way those colleagues who have an interest in administration can participate in a variety of departmental committees and task forces, and eventually take on a role such as undergraduate coordinator or graduate coordinator, where there are opportunities to "learn the ropes." Either of these latter positions may be designated as Associate Chair or Vice Chair depending on the department's traditions and structures. Having led a number of search committees that appointed Chairs during my term as Dean of Medicine, I can attest that colleagues tend to be skeptical about candidates who have not had some meaningful mileage in administration at the departmental level."

When it come to the next major step, a Deanship, matters become even more interesting:
> "There is probably more flexibility in the path to a Deanship than in the path to a Department Chair position. Particularly in any large multi-departmental faculty, the Dean's role differs quite markedly from that of a Chair, and I have seen successful Deans come from a variety of backgrounds. Some were indeed Department Chairs. Others served as Vice or Associate

Deans. Still others again led extra-departmental units, research institutes or enterprises outside the traditional lines of authority from Departments to the Dean's Office. However, it is true that the majority of Deans of multi-departmental units have served as Department Chairs or Associate/Vice Deans."

Finally, David offers his own helpful perceptions on how to consider seriously the possibility of taking a leadership role in the future in a culture that resents those academics who try to head straight for management without first paying their dues and showing their cardinal talents as academics:

"My own prejudice is that anyone who is unduly ambitious or seen to be currying favor to facilitate administrative advancement is likely to be given short shrift by colleagues on search committees. I may be naïve, but my sense is that the colleagues who make the biggest impact in administrative roles have two overriding characteristics. First, they enjoy the breadth of challenges that administrative and leadership roles bring, and are energized by the chance to work with large numbers of smart and creative people at all levels of the organization. Second, they have some burning platform, compelling vision, or overarching purpose to their pursuit of a particular position. Of course, there are some opportunists in academic administration, but I think they are a small minority."

Peter Likins

The final nuggets of wisdom from the presidential suite come from Peter Likins. To continue the views of David Naylor just above, Peter also does not counsel a straight-through "I wanna be the big guy around here" attitude or strategy. As David Naylor did, and as did Heather Monroe-Blum a bit earlier in the above discussion, Peter got his ducks in a row before heading a lot higher in the academic structure:

"My teaching, my research, and my consulting projects were all mutually supportive. Each of the three supported and was fed by the other two.

"My fixation was not with a pre-planned series of 'career moves.' Instead, I would say that my obsession was really a com-

CHAPTER 5: THE ACADEMIC EXECUTIVE

petitive one. I just wanted to do the best darned job I possibly could—whatever my job was. You know, teaching, research, consulting, and some administration —and I wanted to do it better than anybody else doing similar things.

"When I was a young person, all the way through my youth, college, early professional life, I'm sure I was perceived as a leader, although I didn't think much about leadership in those days. I just thought about doing my job better than anybody else did their job.

Peter not only suggests what should be obvious, but is rarely stated—that there may actually be some competitiveness in the academic mix—he celebrates it. But note that the competition is not about frothy distractions; it is about merit on the fundamentals. One is reminded of the arguments made by Lewis [1975] on the indispensability of merit in academia.

Unsurprisingly, networking among important contacts can often pay dividends:

"At UCLA I had by this time developed quite a network of colleagues, through my discussions at conferences, my consulting work, my invited lectures, and so on, and I had also been developing important administrative experience during my later years at UCLA. One such colleague told me that he knew the engineering Deanship at Columbia was open and he suggested I apply. Although engineering is not as important (relatively speaking) at Columbia as at some other U.S. universities, the standards of Columbia were very high so I let my name stand for the Deanship. As you know, I was successful.

"I did, however, gain the confidence of the Columbia Dean of Law, who became Columbia's provost and then president. He invited me to become co-provost with a distinguished professor of history and we served together very well until I got the call from Lehigh.

"I had to give a lot of thought to leaving Columbia, but eventually I took the 90-mile trip to Lehigh University, in Bethlehem, Pennsylvania, which I led for 15 years as its president.

"Yes, again I became aware of a search process, this time at The University of Arizona. It was a larger, more complex university, so it was definitely of interest."

Being willing to be mobile does help, and Peter goes on to compare two presidencies:

"One of the advantages of being President of Lehigh—which is a smaller and less research-intensive university than The University of Arizona—is that I was able to learn in some detail about every major sector of the university's operations. People who go straight to the presidency of a major university cannot possibly know in any detail about major segments and divisions within that university, and that does place them at quite a disadvantage.

"Compared to Lehigh, UA had other challenges in terms of complexity, but at least I had a thorough knowledge of the 'presidential control panel' from my Lehigh experience."

Peter was asked for his advice on management style at the top, and in particular to compare the best academic style with the best corporate style, government style, and even military style. In arriving at decisions, how does he balance the hands-off wisp-in-the-breeze extreme vs. the autocratic extreme?

"I think there is a slowly developing trend to a less autocratic style in all those areas. Certainly, corporate CEOs, especially those who must deal with modern, highly educated personnel, cannot just rule by decree.

"In arriving at important decisions, I work on three phases: (a) discuss; (b) decide; (c) explain. In Phase (a), everyone on the senior management team (and anyone else who is an important stakeholder) has an opportunity to give their input—to provide data, ideas, and reasoned responses. In Phase (b), I decide. I see that as being my job. The difficult task of integrating all the available information together with the many key considerations—to produce what is (I hope) the best decision—is up to me. In Phase (c), I announce my decision and explain my decision to all concerned. This last phase is very important because

CHAPTER 5: THE ACADEMIC EXECUTIVE

it has been my experience that, if people know that you value their concerns and have taken their views into account, they will tend to support your decision."

Despite the fact that virtually all university presidents were at one time professors (and many consider themselves still to so be) Peter was asked whether he could envision a military general becoming a successful university president, or—perhaps a more interesting possibility—could a successful corporate CEO move over to becoming a successful university president?

"When it comes to academic credentials, an academic 'outsider' could be accepted as a university president to the extent that he had academic credentials (and other attractive characteristics, of course). For example, I think that someone who is CEO of a highly successful public company—and who also has the qualifications and educational achievements that academic institutions value—could compete for a university presidency opening.

"With respect to the 'command and control' component in the management style of an aspirant to a university presidency, I think that a great deal depends on the current health of the university. If it's a highly successful university, much admired by other similar academic institutions, it would be difficult to impose a harsh leadership. The professoriate would say (in effect), 'Who are you to come here and tell us what to do?'

"On the other hand, if a university's most senior management board decides that its university is in trouble and that drastic measures are called for, it may well choose as president someone who has an appropriate degree of autocracy (provided, of course, that his or her other attributes are appealing)."

Asked for any further comments he might wish to make on his management or leadership style as president, Peter added the following:

"Different people manage in different ways. But I suppose I am a 'relationship-based manager.' I need to develop *relationships with people*.

"It's hard for me to imagine how anybody can rise to a position of real leadership if that person lacks a sense of, well, love, for other people. If you don't like people, if you're suspicious and distrustful of people, how can you possibly lead them? From my perspective, I may make the opposite mistake on occasion, as a manager: I may trust somebody a little too long, and have to face the harsh reality of their untrustworthiness. But I'd rather make that mistake than go through life suspicious and distrustful."

Finally, Peter was asked a question that, to some, might seem loaded: "Do you think that men and women are equally able to be university presidents?"

"Women may have an advantage in that leadership job. Men have other kinds of advantages, but what I've just been talking about, being relationship-based, is more feminine than masculine,[155] isn't it? The capacity to listen respectfully to other people's opinions is something we have come to expect from the more nurturing gender—women—and I think I'm a very nurturing person. I think I have become, as I've grown older, much less masculine in my general behavior and my management style and much more drawn to the sort of behavior that many people associate with women in management.

"Now, we're at a transition historically, of course, so that the profession now—and that of corporate CEOs and military 'CEOs'—is still dominated by males. But the student body is no longer dominated by males, the law schools are not dominated by males. I mean, you watch this next generation and I think you can look forward to—as management styles change, and as more and more emphasis is placed on understanding the needs and values and opinions of others—you may find many more women moving into positions of leadership. Now, this notion of 'servant-leadership' that I have come to embrace in

---

[155] In making these comments, Likins was well aware that the interviewer knew that he has been recognized as a college wrestling champion in the Hall of Outstanding Americans, in the (U.S.) National Wrestling Hall of Fame.

CHAPTER 5: THE ACADEMIC EXECUTIVE

my old age [Likins laughs lightly] is much more natural for women than for men."

These excerpts (taken from much longer interviews) give us all much to think about on the nuances of how best to help in the process of leading important academic institutions.

Chapter 6: The Entrepreneurial Professor

Reaching Outside the Cloister

Chapter Overview

We turn now to our fourth and final career paradigm, that of the *entrepreneurial professor*. The first two paradigms we examined (teaching in Chapter 3 and research in Chapter 4) are practiced ubiquitously in academia, and therefore have some foundation of familiarity to all readers. Our role in this book was to examine them more carefully from a career standpoint, showing how to make them more central to a successful academic career, and learning how to decide whether this would be a good choice for particular readers (i.e., particular skills, aptitudes and interests). The third paradigm, management and leadership in the academic setting, is a less common career, especially at the higher levels, and for that reason may be less familiar to readers and even more deserving of careful scrutiny.

All three paradigms above, however, have the common characteristic that they involve activities that are largely *internal* to the academic institution. Teaching is the most internal; research involves some interactions with colleagues in sister institutions and with grant and contract personnel elsewhere, but all these goings-on still take place within a culture that is either academic or academic-friendly; and academic leaders, though called upon to interact productively with others outside the cloister, are still anchored (or should be) very firmly within the academic institutions they help to lead. Entrepreneurial behavior, by contrast, relies for success on forming strong relationships with *external* individuals, organizations and cultures.

After first carefully defining the entrepreneurial phenomenon, and the many ways these impulses can apply to academics, this chapter then examines the "entrepreneurial professor" from a career standpoint, both in theoretical terms and then with a closer examination. Several levels of entrepreneurial activity are defined, with some professors migrating along this spectrum as their career progresses. Practical advice is given at each stage. Sections 6.5 and 6.6 confront the important matter of ethics—a subject more often murmured about than rationally discussed—and the challenges and resolution of ethical issues raised by entrepreneurial activity are dealt with in practical terms.

The chapter concludes with additional insights and advice from our distinguished interviewees.

6.1 What Is an Entrepreneur?

As per usual, we shall define our terms carefully, so that we may have a more precise understanding of what is being said when using those terms. In the present case, we shall define *entrepreneurial* and then say that a professor is "entrepreneurial" to the extent he or she exhibits those characteristics. To be a fully fledged entrepreneur, one must have more than a few[156] weak entrepreneurial inclinations. Nevertheless, when professors have those inclinations it is almost always a good thing—for themselves, for their university, and for society. Hence the "entrepreneurial professor," the subject of this chapter.

Earlier, we associated entrepreneurship with a desire to project research findings into the matrix of societal needs. This activity can manifest itself in many ways, from scientific discoveries to commercial products, or implementation of expertise in the form of consultancies with the private sector, government agencies or NGOs. Although the advent of new commercial products and services is generally regarded as evidence of entrepreneurship, many other academics are engaged in what we call social entrepreneurship. Their expertise is directed to improving the well being of society, not nec-

---

156 Some writers have attempted to use the English translation "enterpriser," but this has not met with general success. However, it is quite common to hear someone described as "enterprising," which usually has a broader flavor than the more business-oriented "entrepreneurial."

essarily for personal wealth creation. Examples of such contributions can be found in health care, confronting social issues of the day, addressing environmental concerns and sustainable development. The "socially conscious" professor is discussed in more detail in Chapter 7. This chapter is devoted to the commercial aspects of entrepreneurship.

Entrepreneurial—A More Precise Description

The classical definition of a "commercial" entrepreneur is shown in the accompanying box. The key words in the definition are (a) innovation, (b) market need, (c) business, and (d) risk.

Entrepreneur: Relationship of Key Ideas

1. **Innovation.** There must be a new idea that can be brought into general use so that it can benefit many. [See box below.]
2. **Market Need.** An innovation cannot succeed if no one is interested in it, or wants it, or can be moved to want it.
3. **Business.** The new idea must thus be commercialized, which requires that someone invest in it. The entrepreneur either invests himself, or convinces others to do so, or both. This creates the business.
4. **Risk.** The novelty of all aspects of this new business leads to high risks. Entrepreneurs learn to identify and quantify these risks, and by also identifying and quantifying the rewards, decide whether to go ahead.

If the reader, in perusing the above list, says something like, "This doesn't sound much like the everyday activities of a professor!", the authors are in complete agreement. The relevance of the above definition, in terms of the key ideas involved, is that they define the species *entrepreneurius* in its purist form, so that the mind is focused in the right direction in our subsequent discussion of entrepreneurial professors.

Examination of the Key Ideas

In further preparation for such discussions, let us drill one level deeper into the ideas in the above box. The purpose is to understand thoroughly these ideas and, by integrating and assimilating them, to acquire the *gestalt* of totally entrepreneurial behavior.

Key Idea 1. Innovation. This important word itself has several sub-characteristics. [See box below.] The most obvious of these is "newness." A patent attorney can quickly provide some practical advice as to what is new for patent purposes and what is not. An *innovation* should never be confused with an *invention*, because, although they have novelty in common, they are at the opposite ends of the utility spectrum. An *invention* is *micro*-creativity, quite local in nature; an *innovation* is *macro*-creativity and transforms part of society. The box below gives a useful definition of innovation.

Although most inventions don't lead to innovations, some do, and these are the ones of interest to us here. To be patented—and thus to be thought potentially an innovation—an invention must, according to patent law, be (a) *novel,* (b) *nonobvious,* and (c) *useful.* "Novel" means "new" in the simplest possible sense. "Nonobvious" means that another person specialized in the subject area will say, "I wish I'd thought of that," not "The novelty here is completely trivial and obvious to anyone who knows anything about this subject." "Useful" is again a relative term, but suggests that others might also be interested in, or benefit from, the invention. There is the whiff here of a market and perhaps much more.

Innovation (Definition):
The application of knowledge to create new or improved products, processes, and services that add value in the marketplace.
While innovation is difficult to measure, its key outcome is productivity –
– defined as getting more output per input –
and its ultimate payoff is income and quality of life.

— *Conference Board of Canada*

Key Idea 2. Market Need. Here again, we attempt to answer the widely prevalent question, "Who cares?" A "market" means a group of other people or organizations who are interested in the novelty, find it nontrivial, and find it useful (with the eminently practical meaning that they are willing to pay something for

CHAPTER 6: THE ENTREPRENEURIAL PROFESSOR

it). Sometimes a market is small (a carload); sometimes it is large (a trainload). Sometimes these folks are willing to pay almost anything for the innovation (cure for their type of cancer); sometimes they place only a small value on it (hula hoops). Sometimes the market is already mature (automobiles); sometimes it may be primitive but can grow to be gigantic (personal computers). To interest an entrepreneur, a market must be large enough and have the financial potential to make a growing business realistic and the risks worthwhile.

Key Idea 3. Business. To be successful, a business must have more than some good ideas. It must find the long path from mere invention to true innovation. It must have the means to identify (and communicate with) its market, to make and provide its products and/or services to that market, and to be able to attract all the intellectual and financial capital necessary to pull off this commercial semi-miracle. There are many ways to fail in such an *enterprise*.

Key Idea 4. Risk. Each of the many failure modes just mentioned has an associated risk. These must be known and at least semi-quantified. Some say entrepreneurs like to take risks. Nothing could be sillier. Only out-of-control gambling addicts enjoy risk. True entrepreneurs give equal emphasis to both risk and reward, and proceed to commercialize only when the former is justified by the latter. Because they like to create new enterprises, they tend to operate at the high end of the risk-reward curve.

Each of these key ideas could be discussed in much more detail—there are many books on how to be an entrepreneur (in the general, not academic, sense of the word)—but for present purposes we shall make do with the above remarks.

The Entrepreneur

An entrepreneur is one who demonstrates most, if not all, the above entrepreneurial tendencies. He first spots a new business opportunity where most would not. He does this either by noticing that there is a product or service that would be helpful but is unavailable, or by becoming aware of a new technology that could be used to satisfy unmet needs (i.e., a new market). He may well have had something to do with the development of this new technology himself, but this is not his most crucial function. It is his ability to create the vision for a brand new business that most makes him an entrepreneur.

Having had the vision, he then must ensure that the vision is realistic.[157] This is accomplished by studying several aspects of the "business model." He examines the market more thoroughly, finding out how many customers are willing to pay how much for the new product or service. He estimates all costs of production, including general and administrative costs, and makes financial projections to see whether the revenue from sales sufficiently exceed the costs of production. Only when these concerns are satisfactorily addressed does he proceed to the next step.

Assuming the vision has survived the process of due diligence sketched ever so briefly in the last paragraph, he then proceeds to assemble the necessary components of financial capital and intellectual capital. Unless he is already wealthy and can finance[158] the initial business himself, he must convince others that his business plan is sound, such that they are willing to invest in his business; this provides the financial capital. Key hires must also be made, particularly in marketing and production, and procedures must be set up so that the new staff can function as a team; this provides the human capital.

Wealth Creation

When someone (or a small group of like-minded individuals) starts a new company, they are known as *founders*, and much of their incubative work is typically unpaid (or at best paid at a subsistence rate). This labor

---

157 A majority of new businesses fail. However, this includes businesses formed by families who want to work together, persons who can't get a job unless they hire themselves, and sundry misanthropes who hate working for anyone else. Among prudent, professional entrepreneurs who are willing to follow the initial investigative processes outlined here, and who will accept the objective indications of these processes with dispassion, the success rate is much higher.

158 Some writers include 100% personal financing of the new venture as an essential part of being an "entrepreneur." This seems to be unnecessarily restrictive, although those who do finance startup companies (angel investors, venture capital investors, etc.) prefer that the entrepreneur also has a little "skin in the game" himself.

CHAPTER 6: THE ENTREPRENEURIAL PROFESSOR

for submarket compensation is frequently described as a "labor of love," and there is often some truth to this explanation. Still, apart from passion, it is often a good business decision to start such a company because, if it is successful, the founders will initially own a considerable portion—perhaps all—of the shares. Then, as the company grows in value, the shares will do likewise. When new shareholders are brought on board as investors to provide the capital to grow the business more rapidly, the fraction owned by the founders gets reduced in the process. This is called *dilution*.

Dilution raises an interesting quandary for founders. Although the value of their shares does not change with dilution,[159] eventually the founders' ownership declines below 50% as new capital is repeatedly injected into the business. The vexed question is this: Which does the founder most crave: more control but less value in a smaller business? Or greater shareholder value but less control in a larger business? Part of the solution is to choose one's investors wisely. The best investors are not speculators looking for a quick killing, but more patient sources, who also add good chemistry and much sound advice to the business, based on experience.[160]

Sweat Equity

Sometimes, new investors or recent key hires look at the founders and say, in effect, "Why do you have shares? You never paid anything for them." The answer should be obvious from the preceding narrative paragraphs. It may be stretching matters only slightly to make the analogy with the husband of a new bride saying to his mother-in-law at the wedding reception, "Frankly, madam, I don't see why you're here." It's part of the "Nothing

---

159 Assume new investment makes the (book) value of the company go up instantaneously by, say, x%. Then the *fraction* of shares owned by founder(s) must go down by precisely the same x%. Founder's value post-investment is easily calculated: Multiply ownership fraction post-investment by company value post-investment. The x% cancels out, of course, whence the just-post- and just-pre-investment founder's book values are identical. The *potential future founder's value*, however, should be enhanced by such investments. If not, don't accept the investment! The idea is not to simply make a larger pie with the founders' reduced angular share producing the same quantity of pie; it is to make a *much* larger pie, so that, even though the founders' angular fraction is reduced, the total quantity of warm juicy apple pie is larger than it would have been without the investment.

160 If one or more of the founders is independently wealthy, the value-vs-control quandary is greatly eased, at least for them. The issue remains largely similar, however, for lower-net-worth founders.

happened before I got here" syndrome from which all of us tend to suffer. We don't know the detailed history, so we assume it is irrelevant or even nonexistent. But all is right with the universe after all: The founders do have shares, and, no, they didn't pay cash for them. Instead, they either worked very hard to make it all happen in the early days or—of perhaps greater interest to academics—the credibility of the baby company rested initially on the reputation, expertise and connections of the founder with the core competence, which also were acquired through hard work. The founders have every right to an ownership stake in the company. They may not have paid cash for their shares but they paid with creativity, vision, reputation—and a major personal effort. The ownership position of founders is referred to as *sweat equity*.

One possible pitfall here: Typically, a new company does not have effective management structures in place. New hires may be left entirely to their own devices. The founder or an early manager may say, in effect, "These are really smart people [the new hires] and so I'm going to let them do whatever they want. Besides, I'm very busy with all this stuff over here." Unfortunately, the fact that these new hires are judged to be "smart"—which to an academic usually means that they have big-time university degrees—may not mean that they are straining mightily to execute the company's strategy! In fact, they may apply their alleged smartness to the problem of how to do exactly what they feel like doing without anybody noticing! They are, to use the vernacular, "not aligned." Worst of all—and the reason it is mentioned here—such a new hire may eventually say they "deserve sweat equity" in the company. They have worked long hours and they are allegedly smart, so why not? Well, if they can demonstrate that they have greatly enhanced company value far beyond that for which they have already been compensated financially, and if it really is at the very beginning, they may have a case. Otherwise, "sweat equity" is a phenomenon unique to founders.

Often the entrepreneur operates the company himself, at least at the beginning, but running the enterprise over a longer period will need professional management (especially if the business is to grow and be successful). The skill set of a manager (see, for example, §5.3 in connection with academic management) is somewhat different from that of an entrepreneur. The latter must have vision and know-how to assemble the components of a promising business, while a manager knows more about how to run an existing, larger, more complex business.

Most new ideas are exploited via small companies and most new jobs are created by small companies. While some people look to banks, government, lotteries, or goodness knows where else for economic stimulation and growth, it is to small companies—the progeny of entrepreneurs—that the gratitude is owed. However insular some institutions of higher education may be, they cannot successfully insulate themselves from this reality. And though they are rightly committed primarily to the lofty aims of advanced teaching, creative research and relevant scholarship, they find that the real world in which they operate, and from which they draw their economic sustenance, expects them to play a role, where and as appropriate, in the creation of new businesses. New graduates. New scholars. New research results. Why not also some new businesses?

6.2 Entrepreneurial Impulses Among Academics

Readers of this book are already keenly aware that being a successful professor—focused either on top-performance teaching, on world-class research, or on rapidly ascending the academic management ladder—is a full-time job. Rather more than full-time, actually, because in most cases the professors who become top-flight in any of the paradigms just cited don't work just 35 hours per week, and they don't spend a lot of time making sure they get their lunch hour and twice-daily coffee breaks.

With this awareness, readers of the last section (§6.1) must also wonder where an entrepreneur gets the time necessary to attend to all the components of his or her new enterprise. Marketing research, market strategy, establishment of marketing channels, production details, hiring key people, attracting start-up capital under reasonable terms, achieving first sales—and a thousand other details of starting and running a new business—these, in combination, require not only a full-time person but a person who is virtually obsessed with meeting the countless demands of a new business.

Readers, therefore, certainly are justified in asking: If being a professor is a full-time job (and more) and if being an entrepreneur is a full-time job (and more), how can one person simultaneously be a full-time professor and a full-time entrepreneur? The question answers itself: There is simply no way that one person can be, at one and the same time, a fully functioning professor and a fully functioning entrepreneur. Some professors do try (or pretend) to do so, but we shall postpone a discussion of this phenomenon for §6.6.

The Paradox Inspected

Having admitted the obvious—that professors cannot discharge their full duties as professors while at the same time being complete entrepreneurs—we have the explanation for the delicate hybrid terminology *entrepreneurial professor*.

When we spoke in Chapter 3 of professors who are primarily (or exclusively) teachers, we meant professors who, based on their interests and skills, have devoted their academic careers to teaching. They aren't sort-of teachers, or quasi-teachers, or almost-teachers. They are teachers in the most full-blooded and laudable use of that word.

Similarly, in Chapter 4, professors who choose research as their principal (or entire) contribution to the university are not viewed as "fooling around with research." They are accorded the stature of researchers whose eminence can only be imitated by others in other kinds of institutions; they are widely known by others in their field; they are research "stars" who blaze the investigative paths that others follow internationally.

And finally, the academic managers, executives and leaders introduced in Chapter 5 were indeed managers, executives and leaders, without qualification. Yes, it was limited to our academic context, but "managers" must manage in a bewildering breadth of organizations. While academic ones have their quirks, so do all the others.

These comments on teachers, researchers and managers (all in an academic environment) expand on the notion of *internal* vs. *external* mentioned on the first page of this chapter. Though they are drawn in quite different career directions, they all perform their duties with benefits that accrue entirely to the university, that is, *internally*. In contrast, the first loyalty of a pure entrepreneur is to his own business creation, to his customers, suppliers, employees, bankers, investors—and ultimately to himself. All very *external* to any[161] university.

---

161 In the case of entrepreneurial professors, there are clearly ethical issues that naturally arise here. We shall consider several specific issues of this kind in §§6.5 & 6.6.

CHAPTER 6: THE ENTREPRENEURIAL PROFESSOR

Entrepreneurial Professors—A Spectrum of Intensities

Though we have established that a professor cannot be a full-time entrepreneur by normal standards (§6.1), we now seek to establish, further, that a professor can have healthy entrepreneurial inclinations and that these can enrich his or her life in many ways, and not just financially. A fortune is spent every year to support the research conducted by university professors and society is justified in expecting as much return on this investment as is potentially available. One return is a flow of educated graduate students. But another would be an application, where possible, of research findings to the economy. Academic research resources are not spent, as the occasional professor seems to think, just to provide professors with an interesting, enjoyable life.

How can the benefits of this major cash outlay be returned to society? Not primarily by published papers in learnèd archive journals. These are almost entirely an internal conduit of communications within narrow technical fields. In reality, these journals are magazines published for the benefit of a small elite club of (largely) academic researchers. The papers therein rarely reach, or are read by, those who are in a position to make something of them other than fodder for ever larger libraries.

Instead, the chief channels from research discovery to societal benefit are **(a)** students who leave university and perform the transfer in person; **(b)** targeted or directed research, paid for and conducted on behalf of some external agency with a sound practical reason for valuing the results; and **(c)** the efforts of entrepreneurial academics, individuals who do not get their glows of professional satisfaction as much from seeing Paper #100 in print as they do from seeing their ideas taken beyond the journals, beyond the libraries, and into practical use by their fellow human beings.

We may distinguish several degrees of the entrepreneurial professor species:

> **Entrepreneurial Professors (Level 0):** These professors do not contemplate how their studies can be of interest to anyone beyond their colleagues in the same field at other universities. They have no vision about how their work can be more broadly useful. Perhaps they don't care; perhaps they feel

that this issue is someone else's job. These academics simply don't have an entrepreneurial bone in their body.

Entrepreneurial Professors (Level 1): These individuals do sometimes wonder what the point is of all their work, beyond their own curiosity and remuneration, and they occasionally get ideas about how their activities can be more broadly useful. From time to time they find themselves engaged in conversation with professional people outside academia who seem interested in their work. This leads to momentary entrepreneurial impulses, but these quickly subside in the days following, under the pressure of more urgent work. These academics clearly have some entrepreneurial instincts, but these have not led anywhere, at least so far.

Some academics are pleased with their outputs of teaching and/or research, but long for other avenues of contact with the broader community, avenues in which they can more personally participate. They do get original ideas concerning how their own work, or the work of colleagues, can make a positive difference to others, and they spend some time reflecting on these. They mention these ideas also to colleagues, or to their departmental Chair, and to other professionals they know outside academe. They are interested, with modest motivation, but are not pro-active. They may be waiting to see whether something might develop based on other people's efforts.

So far,[162] we have entrepreneurial flat-lining (Level 0, not much hope there), thoughts or even thoughts and talk (Level 1). But no action. Without action there will be no concrete results. With more enthusiasm we move to action categories.

---

162 Some may feel that the gradations of professorial entrepreneurship defined here are unnecessarily fine. Perhaps. Yet, entrepreneurial impulses in the academy are frightfully rare, especially if one compares actual output to potential output. As an indicator of this tendency, the authors were not able to find a single book on any aspect of academic careers that even mentioned this entrepreneurial option.

CHAPTER 6: THE ENTREPRENEURIAL PROFESSOR

Entrepreneurial Professors — at the Action Level

Some of the preceding groups of academics seem immune from any entrepreneurial impulses—particularly Level 0—but a career is a long time and one can never be certain in predicting human behavior. Those in Level 1 seem to be favorably disposed to the concept that that big campus in the center of town should have some relevance beyond its own mysterious internal goings on and beyond the fact that very malleable and relatively vulnerable young people are spending many years of their lives listening to lectures given and controlled by the occupants of its offices.

Fortunately, not all professors are described by Levels 0 & 1, above. Others are more motivated, more concerned, and more thoughtful about this issue. Let us examine some further "levels" as they exist on all campuses:

Entrepreneurial Professors (Level 2): These professors are determined that there will be, among their concrete outputs, some direct personal intellectual contribution to society. Not simply to academic journals. Not just to academic conferences. Not only to obscure monographs. But to where it can be used directly, and in a context where its benefit can be demonstrated in concrete terms. They may have become thus determined either for reasons of personal integrity, natural interest, as a secondary source of income source, or some combination of these. They identify some research results as being, at least potentially, of some commercial value to society, and contact the "technology transfer" office of their university to explore this initiative further. They are interested, motivated and pro-active and are willing to talk to VC's (venture capitalists and/or angel investors).

Some of these professors are well aware of the possibility of technology transfer[163] from their research. Indeed, they have

---

163 The authors here are using the phrase "technology transfer" in its broadest form. It thus includes much more than may at first appear. This will be discussed more fully, presently. In a similar spirit, the "technology transfer office" is a term meant here to cover whatever the university's commercial development office is called. There are many variations, but one trend is encouraging: such university bureaus, under whatever name, have been springing up ever more plentifully in recent years as academia moves to temper its isolation and expand its relevance to society.

tended increasingly to choose research goals and emphases that are likely to produce results that have some value to society at large. They contact outside organizations and businesses that might be interested and, especially if they are serious and determined, often find an interested external receptor for their work. Although they do not use the university's technology transfer machinery directly in this process, they are familiar with the university's code of ethics in these areas, and abide by these rules at all times. The organizations involved on the outside may be for-profit or not-for-profit. If commercialization is the goal, the receptor will likely be an existing private-sector[164] corporation, small or large.

These academic entrepreneurs still wish to remain university professors and realize that much of the control over the new business entity must be relinquished to others.

Entrepreneurial Professors (Level 3): These individuals take matters even more fully into their own hands. Not only are they determined to translate their university work directly into societal benefits, but they choose to do this without the help and guidance of either their university (e.g., the technology transfer office) or any existing corporation. Their preference is to create a new business dedicated to this transfer. Although it is theoretically possible that the new enterprise will be owned and managed by a group that does not include the professor him- or herself—with the professor acting solely as some sort of occasional technical advisor—this is rare and in practice the professor is one of the

---

164 The word "private" has two meanings in this context, which can lead to confusion. *Private sector* means a for-profit business, set up under a legislative act of the country, state, province, etc. The "private" modifier is to distinguish such businesses from *public sector* organizations and corporations that are set up not to create wealth but to achieve other societal aspirations (and under different legislation). The second use of "private" is the distinction between "public companies," which are still (somewhat confusingly) in the private sector and whose shares are *publicly traded*, and "private companies," also of course in the private sector but whose shares are *not publicly traded*. Most very small companies and startups are in the last category, although some opportunities for "going public" in a venture-type exchange do exist.

CHAPTER 6: THE ENTREPRENEURIAL PROFESSOR

founders. (Otherwise, why not develop the relationship with an existing small company, as in Level 2?) These professors want to establish a new company with investor money but remain within the university.

They will serve as "consultants" to NewCo (the new company). The picture here is a trifle more cloudy than the general argument for professorial consulting. There is, in fact, something of a conflict of interest going on, since it is unlikely that the professor will make him- or herself available for consultation to NewCo's competitors! (There will likely be NDAs that are legally constructed to prohibit exactly such consultation.) There are, in fact, conflicts of interest aplenty on all sides and one often chooses to anchor one's arguments to whichever of these conflicts is most congruent to one's political leanings. (Unless, of course, the critic also has a conflict of interest!) In general, compromises must be struck, with the urge to spin off high-value, high-cost university research not, one hopes, being left out of the calculus.

Entrepreneurial Professors (Level 4): These professors decide, in effect, to change careers. They form a new company to exploit—not a bad word, in this case—their commercialization ideas, based presumably on their past university research. They furthermore decide that they want to lead this new company themselves, indeed to shoulder all the responsibilities of an *entrepreneur* (discussed in §6.1). Since this is a full-time job, they have, in reality, ceased being professors. Unless this is a very-short-term arrangement (comparable to a sabbatical year), or unless the university has essentially no ethics policies for such contingencies (or for some reason fails to enforce the ethics policies it does have) such entrepreneurial professors have now crossed the River Styx: they have (or should have) resigned and are no longer professors.

The above definitions of entrepreneurial professors, by "level of intensity," will be used to organize discussion for the remainder of this chapter.

6.3 The Entrepreneurial Professor—Could This Be a Career Flavor?

For readers who are critiquing major section headings, note that being an "entrepreneurial professor" is called a "career flavor," not a "career." This introduction of a degree of ambiguity is unavoidable and intentional. We have already seen (§6.1) that a career as a true entrepreneur is itself a full-time commitment—and more. So to imply that a professor can be a full-time entrepreneur is an irresolvable paradox, not to mention a gross violation of professional ethics.

On this basis, many academics have historically regarded entrepreneurial activity—of any kind—by other academics as objectionable. They see it as a perversion, or at least a dilution, of what professors are supposed to be doing.[165] As we shall see later in this section, there are indeed a number of ethical dilemmas to be negotiated and these can entrap the unwary—or, more likely, the ethically challenged—professor. To that extent, the "no entrepreneurial activity allowed" purists do have a point. The problem is, this is just one side of a complex, important argument. The other side of the argument, whose rudiments the reader can surely surmise from the foregoing, is that the beneficial flows of technology (as defined just below) are a primary function of a university in modern society. Certainly, universities are currently much more sensitive and enthused by the prospect of technology transfer that they heretofore have been. It is not unusual for a university now to claim as one of it great achievements a successful spin-off company founded by one of its professors, when in fact the founding professor was forced to endure a degree of calumny, either direct or subtle, from colleagues at the time of the founding. While regrettable, these inconsistencies are also indicative of the profound changes that have occurred in the

---

165 No criticism is implied here of individual professors who choose to eschew entrepreneurialism in their own work. Indeed, this book is dedicated to the premise that academics can make choices and that they should not be forced to swim, stroke for stroke, within an immutable Tube, in conformity with the Normative Paradigm. The preference of the authors is that post-tenure academics, as individuals, have the right to shun all matters entrepreneurial and can choose not to participate in the direct transfer of academic-led benefits to society—other than one or more of traditional teaching and/or research and/or management (Chapters 3, 4, 5). The reference in the main text is not to those who believe that they themselves should not be involved, but that *nobody* should be involved.

past few decades. For universities, distinct transformation over (only) a few decades represents a revolution.

As intellectuals, academics are proud of their ability to tolerate ambiguity and to make fine distinctions. Here is an opportunity to do so. One the one hand we have "pure" academics, who, like monks, are determined to disdain worldly interactions, including the sale of their intellectual capital for money; on the other hand we have the "pure" entrepreneurs who are singularly focused on the creation and growth of a business enterprise, to their own financial betterment (among other motives), without caring a fig for anyone or anything else, including any universities that happen to be involved.

Surely this is a false choice. Neither of these two extremes is palatable. Neither insulated, possibly irrelevant, academism, nor rampant, ethics-free capitalism is acceptable. In the words of songwriter Johnny Mercer (and made famous by Bing Crosby) we must, and we can, find a way to "accentuate the positive, eliminate the negative." This stance opens up a new career dimension for academics. This, the authors believe, is one of the primary contributions of this book.

Technology Readiness

From the point of view of entrepreneurship, the academy can in principle convey two important kinds of value to receptors outside the university: technology and intellectual capital. As the names suggest, the former of these is primarily physical and the latter is primarily intellectual. (There are, of course, some overlaps, which do not vitiate in any respect what we shall say here.)

> Technology (Definition)
> Any man-made thing that one can use
> to assist one in doing something one wishes to do.

Let us begin with *technology*. Many definitions have been proposed for "technology," but it hard to find one that is briefer and more precise than the one shown in the accompanying box. It is a physical "thing," not an idea or a concept, and it is manufactured by one someone and sold to a second someone because the latter believes that it will help them to do something they wish to do. When a bird sharpens a long slender twig to assist it in getting the nectar from certain plants, that bird has learned[166] to use technology. When an animal who likes to find dinner, near shore, in lakes or seas, crushes a crustacean for dinner using a rock he has specially chosen for this purpose, this is also technology. When a buggy driver acquires a buggy whip to enable him to control his horsepower, this is technology; this example is also the business-school classic example of a product that is no longer commercially viable.

As would be expected, technology *transfer* is (or should be) the conveyance of some item of technology from a source to a receptor. When a person purchases a dishwasher from a retail housewares store, this is clearly a case of technology transfer, and any definition of technology transfer that fails to accommodate such examples is destined to be pretty much useless. The kinds of technology transfer of interest to us here in connection with academic careers are clearly more technically advanced but are also more commercially more primitive (see box).

Businesspeople usually underestimate the work required for real technical advances, while academics commonly underestimate the work required for successful commercialization. Having something that works in a laboratory setting and demonstrated with tender loving care by its inventor is not at all the same thing as the later version (attractive, sturdy, reliable, etc.) used by a relatively uncaring customer. That is why entrepreneurs speak of the α-version (the version that seems to work well at home) and the β-version (the version that is being field tested, so to speak, by an outside group). Even then, "β-groups" are basically friendly toward the innovation, are early adopters, are technophilic, want it to succeed, and would like to buy it when it completely commercially ready.

Commercial Readiness

Even if the academic innovation is refined to the fullest technically, the road to commercial viability (and, one hopes, eventually to commercial success) is a long one (see box).

---

166 The commercial aspects of this example are simple enough: The bird manufactures the device for itself.

CHAPTER 6: THE ENTREPRENEURIAL PROFESSOR

> **Technology from Universities
> Is Almost Always Technically Advanced,
> but Commercially Primitive**
> Intellectual Sophistication and Commercial Sophistication are
> not the same thing.

One must learn a great deal about the market—usually more complicated than the product!—and then one must decide **(a)** how to reach that market with the news (advertising and promotion), **(b)** how to produce the product reliably and efficiently, **(c)** how to get the product into the hands of willing customers (channels of distribution), and **(d)** do all this while making, not losing, money.

Several authors have made estimates of the fraction of total effort and financial resources that must go into developing a mature product vs. the remaining fraction needed to support commercial readiness. These estimates vary from 20% to 35% for the product (i.e., 65% to 80% for the commercialization). Obviously, these numbers are only very approximate and the correct answer will depend on the particular product, the specific market, etc. The important point is that if this same question were put to a group of academic researchers who were naïve about business realities, the percentages proffered would likely be the reverse of those above.

Intellectual Capital

The second of the two dynamite concepts we need in order to discuss entrepreneurship is that of *intellectual capital*. Unlike technology, which is a physical item of some sort, intellectual capital is always in one place—between the ears! It comprises ideas, concepts, perceptions, theories, thought models, vision, plans, layouts, and any and all other thought constructs that are useful, in the sense that they are useful in assist one in doing something one wishes to do.

For individuals, intellectual capital is the sum of all their (useful) ideas[167] and mental processes. This definition "for individuals" might seem to be

---

[167] Philosophers may challenge and say, "Who determines what is useful?" In a chapter on entrepreneurial behavior, this is a question easily answered. The market decides. If no one other than the owner of this "idea" can find any use or value in it, then (in this discussion) by definition it has no value.

somewhat irrelevant in a university with 100,000 students and 5,000 professors, but actually not. There may be many interconnections between the member categories of a university community, but when it comes to personal ideas that are new and possibly useful, professors are largely on their own. It is, in fact, precisely this solitary responsibility, for better or worse, of one's good ideas that sets the academy apart and makes it attractive to those whose brains are continually generating high-value intellectual capital.

For organizations, the situation is somewhat more complex. Figure 6.1 refers to private, for-profit organizations, but virtually all of it also applies[168] to academia. The total value is shown, not just based on *physical capital* and *financial capital*—the two kinds of tangible assets that accountants typically deal with—but also with intellectual capital included as well.

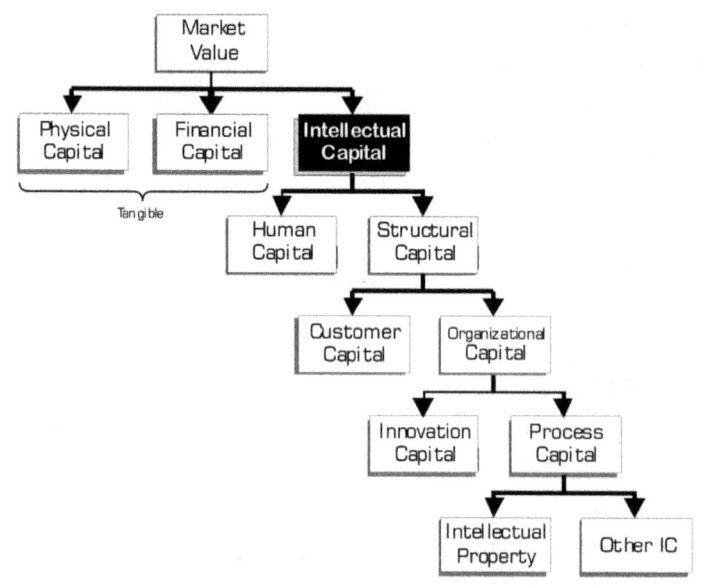

Figure 6.1: The Skandia Model for Intellectual Capital.

---

168 One does not normally speak of the "market value" of a *public* university, since without shareholders there is no one to do the selling. However, *private* universities certainly exist, and these can be sold, at which point the word "value" does have meaning. The other interesting word in Fig. 6.1 is "customer"—not easily identified for most universities. Is it the students? In some respects, yes. Is it the government? If that's where most of the funding is coming from, then, again, in some respects, yes. Is it the parents or guardians of the students? If they pay a significant portion of the tuition and also much of taxes that the government relies upon for "its" funding, then there is an argument there as well.

CHAPTER 6: THE ENTREPRENEURIAL PROFESSOR

Intellectual capital, in turn, is broken down in terms of *human capital* (what we might call the "neuronic" capital, existing aplenty in a university) plus *structural capital*. Of course, with respect to neuronic capital, the neurons must be productive towards the strategic objectives of their owners' organization. If professors are playing the violin all day—and it's not the music faculty—these otherwise admirable mental pursuits should not be counted.

Structural capital, in turn, is recognized as having external and internal components, the former called *customer capital* and the latter *organizational capital*. We have already discussed in an accompanying footnote what "customer" might mean for academic institutions. Does MIT have customer capital with respect to students studying engineering? The question answers itself. Do Harvard and Stanford gain in value on the basis of what their potential customers think of their reputation? These simple examples provide an instant notion of what customer capital means.

Into the "organizational capital" category fall *innovation capital* and *process capital*, referring respectively to (a) the capacity and processes within the institution for renewing itself and responding to change, and (b) all the other processes and intangibles (operating systems) that help the company function at a high level. One might think, as a quick opinion, that universities are overflowing with "innovation capital," but that view is to misunderstand the meaning of the term. In fact, major academic institutions have a massive inertia[169] and change anything they do only with great difficulty and after great external stimulus.

Intellectual Property (IP)

One part of "process capital" is *intellectual property*,[170] which refers to the set of legal mechanisms for recognizing, rewarding, and giving exclusive property rights, for a specific period of time, to those who innovate. This

---

169 Trying to make a major change in any fundamental process within a large academic institution has been compared to trying to make a Nimitz-class aircraft carrier "do a 180°" (which some geometrically challenged folks weirdly call "doing a 360°"). The innovation in "innovation capital" refers to how agile and creative the organization is with respect to self change.

170 Note that we must strenuously resist any tendency to confuse the terms intellectual *capital* and intellectual *property*. Such muddied thinking is clarified by Fig. 6.1, which indicates that the latter is a rather small subset of the former.

subset of intellectual capital is (or should be) of great interest to academics interested in entrepreneurial behavior.

These legal rights are the subject of legal documents and include patents, copyright, industrial designs, brands, trademarks, trade secrets[171] and similar intangibles. These rights prevent competitors from impinging; more precisely, they give the owner the right to sue competitors who impinge. To listen to some members of the legal profession who specialize in helping with the creation of patents, trade secrets, industrial designs, copyrights and trademarks, intellectual property is the only type of intellectual capital that matters—clearly a grave oversight (and an indication of vocophilia).

Patents and other similar intellectual property protections are much more important in some situations than others. They are costly to create and they divert time away from what are, in many cases, even more important activities (such as setting up marketing channels). In other cases, patents and other intellectual property protections are crucial and must be obtained.

Administrators who don't understand the commercialization process frequently emphasize patents to a manic degree. It is understandable enough. They want to point to something in their filing cabinet that indicates that something significant is happening. Still, the vast majority of patents never lead to thriving businesses, and one casually wonders whether this sad outcome would still obtain to the same degree had the money and energy spent on patents been used instead to develop the business.

Still, patents are a good idea to provide a barrier to entry from competitors when the following three conditions pertain: **(a)** the item being patented can be defined very precisely (e.g., a certain molecule), **(b)** it is relatively straightforward to copy the invention once its business potential becomes more generally known, and **(c)** many years will pass between the time of the invention and the time the economic benefits are reaped. Contrarily, if the definition of the invention is a bit blurry and arguably indistinguishable from other similar inventions that have been or that

---

171 "Trade secrets" are also referred to as "proprietary" or "organizationally confidential" information.

may be made; if great cost is needed to reproduce the invention (i.e., an alternate high barrier to entry); and if the whole business opportunity will rise and fall in less time than it takes the patent to even be processed —then it may be difficult to justify the time, expense and distraction of a patent.

Other Intellectual Capital

The last box in Fig. 6.1, labeled "other IC," is more than just a catch-all box or a miscellaneous category. It includes all the ways people in the organization interact, like a well-oiled machine, and all the technologies, standards, processes and policies used in such interactions that are not explicitly covered in the earlier categories. For example, consider the policy manual. Although this document is often the butt of derision for being followed too slavishly by unimaginative administrators and managers, it also contains the codified "rules of the game." If this manual has been well thought out, is applied with intelligence and is generally accepted as wise and fair by the affected employees, it is a dossier of great value to the corporate team, rather like a football playbook.

Some organizational intellectual capital is not codified but is contained in the behaviors of individuals. For example, the earlier discussion of how to conduct meetings (see Chapter 5, §5.4) shows that meeting skills, though unlikely to be written down, are crucial to an organization that spends a material fraction of its time involved in meetings. For a large organization, there are hundreds of other examples. All these processes, to the extent that they are smooth, efficient and effective, are part of intellectual capital.

Professors become involved in the transfer of intellectual capital to their students through teaching (Chapter 3), and to others outside their institution through their research publications and other scholarly writing (Chapter 4). They can convey intellectual capital to the outside world also through professional short courses, media appearances, magazine and newspaper articles, and consulting engagements. We shall return to these briefly in our discussion of ethics in §6.5, but this chapter is centered primarily on the transfer of technology and the creation of commercial vehicles for amplifying the significance of one's research insights.

Example: The Personal Computer

The personal computer is difficult to improve upon as an example of technology and intellectual capital. The physical electronics—growing more complicated and dazzling every day—is an important part of the technology. So too is the installed software, since without these operating systems and applications the computer is useless. However, the computer and all its hardware and software still remain useless if the user does not understand how to effectively employ them; this is where intellectual capital comes in. By contrast, the computer manufacturer's intellectual capital includes how to make the computer, and the software maker's intellectual capital includes the skills needed to create software.[172]

6.4 Entrepreneurship as an Academic Flavor— A Closer Examination

We turn now to examine some important details of the entrepreneurial "flavors" (or "levels") defined in §6.2. We shan't dwell on the first two rather tasteless flavors—some entrepreneurial thoughts, or some conversations—but no real action. Still, many professors start out quite disinterested in any form of entrepreneurship but evolve some time later into a more intense flavor. In any case, we shall confine attention here to the more action-oriented levels, namely Levels 2 through 4.

One key point that has not been mentioned explicitly yet in this chapter is the somewhat self-evident observation that some academics, by virtue of their field of expertise, are not as likely to find natural vehicles for entrepreneurial impulses as they may naturally have. Or, to state the matter positively, there are some Faculties whose residents will, with virtual certainty, have opportunities for creating value for society at large through entrepreneurial activity; whether they seize on these opportunities is, of course, less certain. Any member of a so-called "professional" Faculty will, by definition, have[173] such occasions, and many "nonprofessional" Faculties

---

172 It should now be clear that, in less precise terms, both technology transfer and intellectual capital transfer (such as occurs in lectures, among many other modalities) are loosely referred to as "technology transfer."
173 The proof is straightforward. A "professional" Faculty, by definition, deals with subject matter that is of great interest outside the academy. There are, after all, full-fledged professions that exist (outside academia) to deal with such issues. It

will not be bereft of entrepreneurial openings if they are alert for them throughout their careers.

Entrepreneurial Professors (Level 2)

The reader will recall that Level 2 professors identify a research finding that *may* be of commercial interest and they take the initiative to bring this prospect to the attention of the cognizant office in their university or college. Many such individuals do not themselves[174] have the experience or training to know how to go about reaching any sort of solid conclusion on the critical issue of commercial viability, but at least they are interested and energetic enough to catch the scent of such a possibility.

Academic institutions vary widely in their organizational responses to the entrepreneurial initiatives of their academic staff. The range runs from (at one extreme) spurning them as inappropriate anomalies in an otherwise pure and unsullied academic life, to (at the opposite extreme) permitting a completely *laissez-faire* monkey house of absentee entrepreneurs who relegate their normal academic responsibilities to their less street-smart (and more ethical) colleagues. We shall assume here that the institution of the professor in question has an organized response to potential commercialization. Even if it doesn't, there are many other ways to get counsel on the commercial value of a new technology.

Although university technology-transfer offices are generally more knowledgeable than professors about commercialization, some are quite weak. Not to be oblique about it, some occupants of such offices are quite happy just to spend the university's money on (in addition to the dubious matter of paying their salary) obtaining patents on anything and everything so that they can check off another box in their annual performance report. This is not really about commercialization; it is merely about a group of dull "administrators." Again, we shall make the positive assumption in our following discussion: not only does the academic organization

---

stands to reason that research conducted by academics in such faculties will likely be (some would say *should* be) of interest to these professions.

174 Indeed, many fall prey to the "better mousetrap" myth—that a good idea will commercialize itself. But not to worry; the professor's role is to come up with promising contenders and they may choose to leave it to others to evaluate the commercial potential of their new technology.

include a technology transfer office, but it is staffed by persons who have the training and the enthusiasm for actual commercialization.

> **Some Legal Advice**
> Before signing any legal document pertaining to intellectual property rights or to any other aspect of the commercialization of the technology based on your research, you should—absolutely—*have your own legal counsel.*

One piece of advice that may be worth from a few thousand dollars to (in the extreme) a few billion dollars is shown in the accompanying box: Make sure you have your own legal counsel and don't sign anything without it! Remember, those folks in the technology transfer office may smile a lot and seem to be nice guys and gals, but they do this for a living. You don't. That's always a loaded situation, and not loaded in your favor.

They may say, "This is just university policy." The rough translation is, "You can do boo-all about this." But that may not be strictly true. If one ascends one or two levels higher—an ascent whose success is more likely if one has an attorney present at the critical time—there is often some "flexibility" that miraculously enters the conversation.

If you don't want to pay the higher fee for counsel actually being present, at least don't sign anything without vetting it with counsel in a meeting at his or her office. If your commercialization ideas have any merit at all, they are clearly worth that expense.

Another related decision is whether to retain general legal counsel or whether to ante up the somewhat higher fee that will be asked by a specialist in intellectual property and commercialization. Our advice would be, again, get the specialist. If your ideas truly have merit, it will be an excellent investment. Entrepreneurs are known to take calculated risks. With the salary of a tenured professor to draw on, where's the big risk? There is, however, the downside risk of making a mistake for want of good advice. Some attorneys are willing to provide a fee-free initial meeting, and this alone can give you invaluable information and insight.

CHAPTER 6: THE ENTREPRENEURIAL PROFESSOR

As a last scenario to avoid, the technology transfer officials at your university may say, "You don't really need a lawyer. We have our own lawyers who deal with these issues." Exactly. They are *their* lawyers. Not yours. Lawyers always know who their client is, and if it's your employer it can't be you at the same time. If you find yourself sitting across the table from somebody else's lawyer, you should instinctively and self-defensively always ask yourself, "Where's *my* lawyer?"

One should always be mindful of the important ethical considerations. These will be sketched in §6.5.

Some Level 2 professors, it will be recalled, are quite aware of the possibility of some technology transfer from their research and they have probably arranged their past research priorities so that such opportunities would arise. The first step is to arrange a meeting with the university technology transfer office and discuss these matters frankly. This is the only way solidly to assess whether one can act independently of the university at all. Be careful to distinguish, however, which comments from the organization are actually rules and codes of ethics, and which comments are really sales pitches to let them look after it. While actual published ethical guidelines should always be respected so long as you are in the university's employ, you are not owned by the institution and your interests and its interests are not identical. On the more positive side, you may get some fine coaching in how to proceed without the formal intervention of the university.

> **Legal Advice Needed Even More**
>
> When dealing as an individual with outside corporations regarding potential technology transfers, pertaining to intellectual property rights, to your ongoing role in advising the corporation, or to any other aspect of the commercialization of the technology based on your research, you should—absolutely—*have your own legal counsel*. At the very least, have a legally advised NDA (Non-Disclosure Agreement) signed by both you and the other party before you open your mouth.

SO YOU WANT TO BE A PROFESSOR?

By definition, some Level 2 entrepreneurial professors prefer not to use the university's technology transfer machinery directly in this process,[175] either because they are interested in the whole commercialization process, or because they feel the rewards will be greater, or for some other reason. This process will take a significant amount of time, both calendar time and personal time. Further, as the attending box advises, you will need your own legal counsel if you don't want to be eaten for breakfast by the experienced business people (outside the university) with whom you must negotiate.

Always remember: You are an acknowledged expert in your academic discipline, but the folks sitting across the table from you are skilled in business awareness and parley.[176] It is not unethical for two parties in negotiation each to bargain for the best deal they can get; that means you should not enter a battle for which you are poorly armed. At the very least, make sure you require the receptors for your technology to sign a strongly worded Confidentiality Agreement,[177] which in theory prevents them from stealing your idea. It does not provide ironclad protection, but if your potential commercialization partners are themselves ethical, it will do the trick. However, if you do not even *ask* for any legal protection for your ideas, they are unprotected.

---

175 If the organization's code of behavior expressly forbids any form of commercializable technology transfer without the full involvement of the Technology Transfer Office, then what we are discussing is not permitted, period.
176 Sometimes, as the mating dance progresses between an entrepreneurial professor and his outside receptor, one suddenly feels completely out of one's depth. Or perhaps one's other university duties are already being damaged by time not spent on them. Or perhaps the whole process is no longer interesting and one yearns to quietly read a book in one's departmental library. Then this entrepreneurial avenue is not really for you. You should ask the university's Tech Transfer office to handle the details, assuming they are capable of doing so. There is no dishonor in this. Not all dances lead to consummation. As always, you should do what you love most and that you are best at, from among the actual opportunities that are open to you.
177 Also known as an NDA (Non-Disclosure Agreement).

CHAPTER 6: THE ENTREPRENEURIAL PROFESSOR

> **Further Key Points of Advice**
>
> When dealing as an individual with outside corporations, remember:
> 1. If you have already broadcast your ideas—either in papers, reports, etc., or in speeches or other oral presentations—it is probably already too late to claim that they are yours alone and cannot be mentioned to others. That boat has sailed and you were the captain. You have yourself placed them in the public domain.
> 2. When explaining your ideas to corporations, always focus on what these results can do for them—NOT on the technical details of how they are made. If you continue to get peppered with questions about the details, be suspicious but do not yield to the temptation to show how smart you are. If you tell them all you know, your are definitely not smart!
> 3. Try to become involved as an advisor (subject to university ethical guidelines) on your work as it becomes commercialized. There are many ways to do this, and good legal and independent business advice is invaluable here.
> 4. Note that one can, in many jurisdictions, and for a modest sum, file for Preliminary Patent Protection. This offers some protection. Also, from a strategic perspective, it implies higher value to the technology (or other academic material). Later, the full patent process can be undertaken if warranted.
> 5. Patents are an off-balance-sheet asset. Venture capitalists, bureaucrats and legalists are particularly enthralled with them, because they provide relatively effortless evidence of credibility by a third party. But they do consume scarce cash and valuable management time. Here are two extremes: If you are betting on a pharma drug with a 20-year payoff, get a patent. If you are betting on a software product or algorithm with a 20-week payoff, try to withstand the venture capitalists, bureaucrats and legalists.

The organizations involved on the outside may be for-profit or not-for-profit. If commercialization is the goal, the receptor will likely be an existing private-sector corporation, small or large. Small companies have some advantages. For example, they will be more agile in their decisions and responses; communication is easier and with a more senior person; they may be willing to risk more on the commercialization of your idea. On the other hand, large companies have greater financial resources; their marketing strategy and channels are established and sophisticated; and the risk of their disappearing before the commercialization is successful is much lower.

Assuming that both the professor and the receptor company have decided that the proposed arrangement is in their mutual best interests, they will then proceed through a process known as *due diligence*, meaning that they will examine the planned deal in much greater detail, asking many questions[178] to guarantee that there are no unknown deal-killers lurking in the shadows. Due diligence greatly lowers the risk that something may (or even will) go wrong. Experienced dealmakers are not just interested in the theoretical financial return; they are equally interested in eliminating the risk factors that would prevent the theoretical return from ever being realized.[179]

Entrepreneurial Professors (Level 3)

These professors throw themselves almost fully into their entrepreneurial opportunities. They should discuss their plans with the university research and technology transfer offices, to clarify what the attending rules and ethics are, but we shall presume that the university does permit this sort of full-force entrepreneurial behavior on the part of its academic staff—*at least under some circumstances, possibly tightly circumscribed ones.*

If they plan on starting a new business and acting as "leading partner" or "CEO" themselves, then one thing is quite predictable: either **(a)** they will essentially leave their university duties whole this goes on, or **(b)** the new venture will be a failure. Being a full-time professor is usually more

---

[178] Answering all these questions is somewhat tedious, but there is no real alternative for any major deal.

[179] Some readers at this point may rebel and say, "I thought we were talking about using university research to benefit mankind and now we seem to be talking about business deals. Where did this discussion go off the rails?" The answer is that nothing went off the rails; we are simply discussing a part of the puzzle that some professors never honestly contemplate. To realize the alleged potential benefits, there must be some sort of serious organization, and it must have the financial resources to produce the desired result.

CHAPTER 6: THE ENTREPRENEURIAL PROFESSOR

than a full-time job, as is being a full-time entrepreneur. To pretend, either to oneself or to others that one can combine both simultaneously is either very naïve or very deceptive.

Sometimes a potential entrepreneur starts a new company but does so, not all on his own, but as a member of a small team[180] all of whom are essentially equals. There might, for example, be four individuals, one for technical core competency (the professor) and one each for finance, marketing, and general management. All would be founding owners. This structure lightens the load on the entrepreneurial professor and makes it possible for him or her still to carry out most academic duties—though, it should be obvious, not the normal load. This version is somewhere between Level 3 (doing everything oneself with the aid of some employees) and linking up with an outside company—in this case with a small company of which the professor was a founder.

Entrepreneurial Professors (Level 4)

If an entrepreneurial professor spends all or virtually all of his time involved in a new spinoff company, and if there is no credible evidence that this is not just a very temporary anomaly but a new professional lifestyle, then it doesn't take a fine reading of a thick book of ethics rules to know what must[181] happen: the professor must resign his university post. He has ceased being an academic; he is now a "Level 4" entrepreneur. Not just an entrepreneurially-inclined academic. A full-fledged entrepreneur.

6.5 Ethical Challenges

Everything we do as human beings raises ethical issues. How we treat our family and friends—and how, more generally, we treat our fellow man and other living things. For professors, ethics also encompasses how we deal

---

180 In choosing this team, don't just choose your "buddies" because you like them; choose people who are very good at what they do.
181 Should it be a surprise that some professors in this situation, though normally ethical in most matters, try to square the circle in terms of their loyalties and relative time spent? To leave the university is an intensely jolting experience for someone who has worked their whole life to attain a well-respected, well-paying, well-pensioned, tenured university position. Yet, sometimes such entrepreneurial professors must be "pushed out" on the highly relevant grounds that, in the most practical sense, *they no longer work there*! More on this issue below, in §6.6.

with our colleagues, our students, our superiors, and the organization that pays our salary.

Some write as though *morals* and *ethics* were synonymous, or nearly so, and there clearly are strong connections between these two words. However, "morals" is tinged with religion, where rules are laid down whose truth is claimed to be absolute and whose expiry date is claimed to be eternal. The authors claim no such impressive characteristics for what they may write here. "Ethics," less impressively but more importantly, supplies a set of rules or standards governing the conduct of a person or the members of a profession. Ethics provides reliable guidelines, developed from time-honored principles, on how to behave with integrity, and these permeate every area of human activity.

In addition to one's personal ethics, we are here focused on professional ethics—most especially on how one should behave as an academic. Such ethical principles are at root a branch of philosophy. These principles and the more specific rules inferred therefrom are constantly being re-examined and updated as better alternatives are recognized and new challenges confronted. Neither the principles nor the rules are considered *absolute* in the universal sense, but it is an unwise person who flouts the ethics rules of his or her profession or institution.

Unethical Lapses vis-à-vis Illegal Lapses

Ethical constraints are less muscular but more detailed and nuanced than legal constraints. Figure 6.2 illustrates the ideas geometrically. We begin at the centre with ideal behavior, conduct that is not only completely legal but that is flawlessly ethical as well. Moving out to the next region,[182] we have personal behavior that, while it can't be easily proved unethical, does nevertheless raise some eyebrows; such people usually bear watching because they like to play close to the ethical boundaries. They are sometimes called sharp operators (in a manner not meant to be complimentary).

---

182 Each of the successfully larger volumes labeled in Fig. 6.2 excludes the inner volumes within it. Thus, for example, the "unethical" set of actions obviously excludes the inner "not unethical" set of actions.

CHAPTER 6: THE ENTREPRENEURIAL PROFESSOR

"Illegal"

"Ideal"

"Unethical"

"Not Unethical"

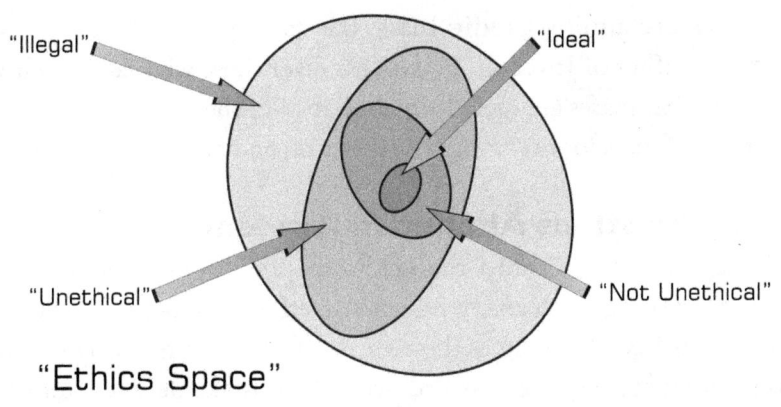

"Ethics Space"

Figure 6.2: Ethical and Legal Constraints on Behavior.

The next region in Fig. 6.2 is labeled "unethical." Such behavior, especially if it persists, will not be tolerated and will lead to some type of professional rebuke. Still, none of the behavior mentioned thus far is thought illegal. That label is reserved for the outermost region, meaning that the perpetrator can be charged with a crime. All illegal acts are assumed to be unethical.

Some people and organizations (mercifully only a few) care nothing for the niceties of ethics. If they can't be sued civilly for large monetary damages, or if they won't face steep fines or jail-time, they are quite willing to abuse ethical tenets. Professors who wish to have enviable careers in academia, however, should aim for the *ideal* behavior at the centre of Fig. 6.2, not flirt with the unethical, much less the illegal, regions.

How (Un)ethical are You?

A paper with the above title appeared in the Harvard Business Review.[183] It makes the case that most of us are less ethical than we believe ourselves to be, owing to unrecognized biases. We are not *consciously* unethical if the offending biases are unconscious.[184] The paper goes on to identify several of the leading categories:
- **Implicit Prejudice:** Biases that emerge from unconscious belief.
- **In-Group Favoritism:** Biases that favor your own group.

---

183 Banaji, Bazerman & Chugh, *Harvard Business Review*, 01Dec2003.
184 We should note especially here for academics that so-called "politically correct" biases are frequent instances of this phenomenon. Politically correct does not necessarily mean correct; it just means some group or other says so.

- **Overclaiming Credit:** Biases that favor you.
- **Conflict of Interest:** Biases that favor those who can benefit you.

These and other biases are more fully described in the cited paper, together with practical tools for becoming conscious of, and avoiding, them.

Ethical Questions Abound in Academia

Those who have climbed the ladder of professional attainment find themselves dealing with many additional ethical guidelines concerning how best to behave. Sometimes these are codified (written down explicitly); in other instances they are passed down in unmistakable ways from mentors and other more senior colleagues; and, in still further cases, usually the most subtle ones, the applicable ethics can be detected only by the most sensitive ethical antennas.

Here again, the Normative Paradigm can be useful. Most academics are fundamentally ethical, not by professional indoctrination, or by the methodical study of ethics, but as ethical human beings who possessed positive ethical impulses long before they became professors. They bring this mind-set to their academic roles, and it would be difficult to nudge them into frankly unethical behavior. To their long-held ethical stance, they add additional ethical tenets germane to academia as they become aware of them, and by so doing they preserve their reputation as ethical persons. Most professors do not become experts in all matters relating to academic ethics, nor need they do so unless they are working in an area where the context is dense in specialized ethical considerations. In this sense, they fit the Normative Paradigm.

However, if, as the accompanying box emphasizes, one chooses to specialize in one of the primary academic careers identified in this book, one should devote some time—a few hours may be all it takes—to the ethical implications of that choice.

Ethical Paradigms

When professors choose to focus intensively on one of the "career paradigms" discussed in this book—teaching, research, management/leader, or entrepreneur—they should spend the relatively brief time it takes to familiarize themselves with the special ethical considerations associated with that paradigm.

CHAPTER 6: THE ENTREPRENEURIAL PROFESSOR

Example 1 [Teaching]: Every teacher knows that it is not ethically proper to ask the most sexually attractive student in the front row out for dinner. In fact, this behavior control, for most individuals, is part of their general ethics, not derived just from their teaching ethics. Be that as it may, no one requires special study to know the ethically correct behavior in this situation. But suppose one chooses to spend all or nearly all of their professional career as a teacher (see Chapter 3). Then some further explorations into ethical territory are well worth the time spent.

First of all, are there any institutional documents (Central Admin, Faculty, or Departmental) that pronounce on ethics as related to teaching? Almost certainly there are. Read them and know them well.[185] But it is not possible to cover every situation in such documents. What does one do if a student complains that he could not perform well on an examination due to [some obviously flimsy excuse]? What does one do if a student complains that she could not perform well on an examination due to the fact that most of her family had been killed in a car crash three days prior? Does one ask for proof? What are the ethics respecting handling parental enquiries about the performance of their offspring? Is the fact that they "paid $30,000 tuition for an *A* grade" relevant? There are an unlimited number of ethical questions relating to teaching.

Shortly after entering a teaching-intensive academic career, one should have become quite expert in the ethical considerations of advanced teaching. This is not only essential to one's own career; one must become a faculty resource to younger colleagues. Just as you learned in previous years from your senior teaching colleagues, so now even younger colleagues are learning from you. You should welcome this role as a mentor, not only on ethical issues, but more broadly on all aspects of teaching. You have chosen teaching as your

---

[185] It could reasonably be argued than *anyone* teaching in the institution should be familiar with these documents.

career emphasis. You wish your colleagues and your institution to recognize and celebrate the value you are creating in this capacity. Advising colleagues about teaching (including ethical quandaries) will cement your image as a highly valued, highly skilled teacher.

Example 2 [Research]: As just one example, every researcher (see Chapter 4) knows that it is not ethically proper to blatantly plagiarize another source of intellectual value when writing up his or her research findings. This is true whether the context is an internal research report, a grant or contract report to a funding agency, a paper submitted to a learnèd archive journal, an oral presentation to the local chamber of commerce specifically on one's research, a speech receiving an award specifically for the work at issue, or any other communication modality.

Still, to "not blatantly plagiarize" is hardly a fine-tuned ethical guideline! Is it permissible to plagiarize provided the misdemeanor is not blatant? And just what does "blatant" mean anyway? Perhaps a lawyer would say, "Plagiarism, blatant or otherwise, is unethical. If blatant, this is relevant to the punishment, if detected. Plagiarism can be recognized if the alleged plagiarizee, when presented with the work of the alleged plagiarizer, and being viewed as a 'reasonable person,' objects to the reference (or lack thereof) to his or her work."

This devolves into a more basic question: "What is a reasonable person"? This is ultimately for a judge or jury to decide. Yet, even from this superficial treatment of a basic ethical dilemma, we can learn two important things: (1) as a practical matter, send the potentially offending material to the potentially offending person (the Golden Rule specifies that one should treat others how one wishes to be treated), and (2) there may be[186] unreasonable academic researchers.

---

186 Some years ago, one of the authors had a colleague at another university who was deservedly prestigious in his field, but whose ego had a growth pattern that led to suspicions of intellectual steroid use. Based on his expertise, he was frequently sent papers to review for academic journals. His review algorithm went roughly as

CHAPTER 6: THE ENTREPRENEURIAL PROFESSOR

Although we have spent several lines examining one of the fundamental academic research ethical issues (plagiarism), there are many others. Biologists who conduct research with live animals have many additional ethical protocols to observe, and professors who investigate human subjects—surely an interesting area for inquiry—have very stringent rules to follow. So stringent, in fact, that they have no opportunity to plead innocence. The issue of field trips involving students requires careful consideration of their safety and well being. Who is responsible, and do signed waivers negate legal and ethical liabilities in case of accidents? Finally, the temptation to hire family members for summer projects is of general concern and must be addressed by a faculty policy.

As a final example, academic managers/leaders/executives (Chapter 5) must be aware of all the delicate ethical details of the above career emphases (teaching, research)—otherwise they could not lead—but they must also delve into additional ethical areas as they rise in responsibility.

First Encounters with Outside Research Contracts

Now we come to consider some ethical issues that are particularly germane to the career paradigm of this chapter—the entrepreneurial professor. We begin with the first encounter with an outside collaborating organization. Most modern research-intensive universities now tend to encourage the entrepreneurial urges of their academic staff, but they also try to channel these urges within detailed ethical guidelines.

There was a time not long ago (by the pace of academic development standards) when technology transfer, spinoff companies, intellectual property development and other indications of direct contact between the university's research staff (the "suppliers") and the outside world (the

---

follows: (a) "This paper is all wrong. Don't publish it"; or, failing that, (b) "This paper is correct but I've done all this stuff already. Don't publish," or its more exasperating variant, "This paper is correct but I've done all this stuff already, and the proof is that one of my papers is referenced. Don't publish"; or, failing that, (c) "This paper is correct but I haven't worked on precisely this topic myself (although it is implied in my book), because nobody is interested in this stuff anyway. Don't publish." Not all academics are "reasonable" all the time. Several papers in Class (c), for example, went on to be praised.

"receptors") was greeted with, at best, bewilderment (by the administration) and, at worst, with palpable animosity (by one's less-entrepreneurial colleagues). There were many layers to this resistance.

Some felt that it was some sort of betrayal of one's academic purity to engage directly with "mere" users outside the cloister. Since many of these receptors had money and influence, it was feared that they would begin to have influence inward as their *quid pro quo* for the direct academic influence outward. As matters have developed, this fear was hardly an unfounded one.[187] The question often comes down to this: When, and under what conditions, should an academic conduct scholarly activity for an outside agency? If the "outside agency" is willing to pay for the activity, surely this is not unwelcome, especially if the outside agency is willing to pay for those *indirect costs* that most university-support agencies are unwilling to underwrite, and that professors (unless they have had some business experience) are almost constitutionally incapable of recognizing.[188]

Particularly sharp are the disagreements that usually arise when research work is contracted with the military. Those opposed observe, correctly, that the fruits of the research can be used to hurt or kill human beings, and those in favor observe, correctly, that those human beings that may be hurt or killed are the enemy trying to kill *us*. The public, who pay taxes to the government, have a right to expect that universities, as a high-value organizational member of society, will support the government in its objectives; the university, on the other hand, can not be ordered to do any particular government work, else it loses its intellectual freedom. We cannot argue and resolve these complex matters here, but it does comprise an excellent example of what are seen as ethical problems in the conduct of academic research for outside agencies.

---

187 We shall resist the temptation here to discuss the "corporatization of the ivory tower." It is an important, topical and controversial subject. It also touches closely the activities of entrepreneurial professors. However, this book is written for individual academics, to aid them in their career deliberations, not to give universities advice on their policies.

188 Even central administration is often fuzzy about what these costs actually are. If some customer is willing to pay only for your students' time, the consumables, the specialized equipment (at a reasonable rate)—and, hopefully, *your* time—but makes no allowance for any indirect costs (heat, light, maintenance, general and administrative, upkeep, and a thousand other costs that are indirectly affected), then that "customer" is looking for a Big Bargain.

CHAPTER 6: THE ENTREPRENEURIAL PROFESSOR

Another current dilemma cast as ethical or moral is stem-cell research. Those in favor point to its extraordinary benefits in preventing human morbidity and mortality; those opposed are concerned with the damage to the "soul" that they suppose resides in these cells. Again, the purpose here is not to argue the case but to point out current instances where the resolution of strong and contrary ethical positions may be more difficult than the research itself!

Key Contract Issues

How desperate are you for research support? In addition, the "outside agency" will almost surely ask for the Big Four of research contract specifications:
1. What is going to be done?
2. Who is going to do it?
3. When will it be completed?
4. What will it cost?

The professor's approaches to these contractual dimensions are, typically:
1. Make a long, optimistic list of things that could be done, and promise all of them.
2. Say you're going to do it personally. You're the one with the reputation and, besides, who's ever heard of your graduate students or your research associates?
3. The potential contractor wants this done a year from now. Hey, a year is a long time. Sounds fine to me.
4. Well, I'd like to be paid myself. I've worked all my life to get into this driver's seat. Nothing unethical about a day's wages for a day's work. Plus I should of course include stipends for my technical associates and graduate students involved.

Beyond that, they look to their university administration to add any other pertinent details, and to place it all in legal language, and sign it.

Rarely does the contract turn out as advertised. The *ex post facto* answers to the Big Four questions are more like this:
1. Look, this is basic research. No one can predict how it will go. We were (and still are) in principle able to do all that was promised. But in one year? That just isn't realistic.

2. One of my key graduate students suddenly left to form her own company and another one I was counting on never actually showed up. In addition, I found I couldn't spend of much of my own time on this due to a number of commitments, including ..., and ..., and ....
3. In hindsight, a one-year time frame for this challenging work was unrealistic. I teach a lot in two terms and I tend to be away a lot in the third term. And one of my graduate students was bogged down with courses. I could give you a revised schedule if you like ... .
4. I'm glad you eventually agreed to pay the final invoice, even though the contractual terms were not met.

Did anything unethical happen here? "Unethical" is too strong a word, but it would probably have been legal for the outside contractor not to pay the final invoice (or perhaps any invoices). The university clearly breached the agreement and non-payment would not have been unreasonable.

A closer look shows that there were some flaws on both sides of the contract, and professors who wish to get into entrepreneurial activities should become well aware of them. Sometimes companies try to get the most difficult[189] research work done by universities, and on the cheap at that. Fortunately, the downside will likely be much less punishing for a university professor than for a private-sector entrepreneur in the same position. In the former case, the university administration will tend to protect their professor and—likely unknown to most professors—the business world generally thinks that, *while professors are clever and leaders in their technical fields, most can't be trusted to do the work they say they are going to do, by when they say they are going to do it, for the price they quote.*

If a company finds a professor who is not only a great leader in his technical area, but who also delivers on contracts, that professor will be in high demand. In fact, that professor has the *bona fides* for being a successful entrepreneurial professor.

---

189 If the investigation weren't so difficult, the companies would probably do it themselves. Companies who ask a university to solve their most difficult research problems, while also trying to get these results at an unreasonably low price (and in an unreasonably brief timeframe), should perhaps not affect such shock and surprise when it all doesn't work out quite the way it was specified in the contract.

CHAPTER 6: THE ENTREPRENEURIAL PROFESSOR

Institutional Weaknesses

Lest the reader infer that all the flaws of research contracts between business interests and academic researchers are the fault of the latter, we hasten to add that the university itself is in many ways out of step with the process. Consider the following arrangement for a proposed academic activity, to be performed for a business corporation by a university division:

The Corporate Dilemma – A Short Play

Corp: We have the following work to be done which is on the technological leading edge. You, the university, are ideally suited to do this work, and have indicated that it falls within your strategic plans to attract such outside work, to benefit your staff, students and reputation—and to enhance the financial strength of your division. Could you please respond?

UDiv: Yes, we are interested in work like this—although not as much as we are in our "scholarly activity." However, we hope not to get embroiled in contractual issues. We'll tell you a rough guess at what your work will cost. Then you send us the money and we'll start on it.

Corp: Actually, this work is one of many subcontracts we would like to negotiate as part of a *major firm fixed-price* contact that we expect to be awarded by one of our customers. We can't treat you differently from our other subs, from whom we are also asking for fixed-price contracts, with milestone-based payments, and a 15% holdback at the end.

UDiv (quoting the VP, Research): That all sounds fine, I guess, for the business world, but the way we work is much simpler: *Send us the money, and if we need more, we'll ask for it.*

Corp (quoting the CFO): There is no survivable cash flow basis for us to pay all our subcontractors the whole shebang upfront. We are not a bank. I assume you have your own financing sources?

VP, Research: Actually, no, we do not "finance" (as you put it) our research with borrowed funds. Even if we wanted to, it would be too risky. In our framework, we just ask professors to conduct research to the best of their ability. They often don't meet deadlines or achieve objectives. So that would be much too risky for us! I'm sure you understand.

271

> **CFO:** In other words, you want **us** to shoulder all this huge risk. Unfortunately, for both cashflow and risk management reasons, I'm afraid our company cannot issue you a subcontract. We're done here. I'm sure you understand.

This playlet indicates some institutional weaknesses that the typical university and the typical company see in each other when it comes to getting business done together.

Other weaknesses of academic institutions are in the area of professorial compensation policies. Even universities that set up well-resourced technology-transfer offices and that provide clear and far-sighted ethical guidelines are still missing a central component of their entrepreneurship policy if their reward system is just the old "journal papers x research dollars" paradigm. *They must show in their compensation policies that they wish to encourage ethical technology transfer activities by their academic staff.*

Of course, the "wish to encourage" is an assumption. If an academic institution wishes to remain aloof from its societal environment, and if it determines that, in the interests of "purity," or any other idealism, it will have no interaction with the surrounding polity, that is its business. This book has no interest in this seemingly overly-antiseptic stance; what this book *is* interested in is the academic staff who populate such institutions.

If the university says it is interested in technology transfer, and wishes to support and promote it, what are the actions and policies that demonstrate that commitment? Several of these have been identified already: a well-staffed technology transfer office in the central administration, a comprehensive and fair ethics policy that is pro-actively made available to the entire university community. But here is a third policy area, equally important: compensation policy.

Compensation policy has, as its two most important outcomes, **(i)** academic promotions, and **(ii)** financial compensation. It has already been shown (§5.1) that the whole "professor" taxonomy is somewhat dubious, so **(i)** is arguable. In the end, though it may pain many career academics to read it, it is **(ii)**, namely, salary and all the other benefits components that are proportional to salary, that count.[190] In any case, when academic salary increases are decided, we must ask these questions: To what extent are they determined by "teaching" parameters? To what extent by "research" parameters? To what extent by "management/leadership" parameters? And, finally, to what extent by "entrepreneurial" parameters?

The last category is the most recent historically, so it is not surprising that the treatment of entrepreneurial professors by personnel committees is usually the most primitive component. Although indeed a complex issue, it is safe to presume that mistreatment in this area is not really due as much to new modern complexities as to old cultural clashes. Many professors, and many academic leaders, are very suspicious of their entrepreneurially-driven colleagues, and, down deep, don't wish to support them, and this prevents more enlightened compensation policies. Finally, most universities are bureaucracies with enormous inertia; changing a core policy would be akin to changing the orbit of the planet Jupiter.

6.6 Frequent Ethical Dilemmas and Concrete Solutions

In the previous discussion, ethical behavior was viewed in largely general terms, to cover the canvas with as broad a brush as possible. In this section, by contrast, we examine several specific examples of the most common (and sometimes egregious) instances of ethical dilemmas faced by entrepreneurially minded professors. These issues are "common" because they are almost always a temptation. And they can be egregious, if either **(a)** the institution has weak or nonexistent policies on these matters; or **(b)** the institution has wide ethical policy coverage but the Departmental Chair[191] is uninformed, or feeble, or perhaps even unethical; or **(c)** the individual

---

190 Especially when many academics will live into their 80's, pension levels become a matter of the highest practical importance, since they are, for defined-benefit plans, based on end-of-career salaries. Even if pensions do seem of little concern to some younger professors, such professors merely illustrate how one can be very smart and very stupid at the same time.
191 We shall use the position "Departmental Chair" generically, to refer to the supervisor of the professor involved. In specific cases it may be, instead, the "Head" of a "School," the "Dean," or some other similar and obvious generalization.

professor is pro-actively unethical, and uses subterfuge or deception to hide the nature of his activities.

The authors are also aware that they are applying their own sense of ethics to this discussion, saying from time to time that certain behaviors are "unethical." This is dangerous for us to do, because not everyone agrees on all ethical issues (an understatement). If we say or imply that something is unethical, but the reader's employer says it is indeed ethical (or at least does not rule it out as unethical), then the reader will just have to decide on his or her own how to behave. A similar remark applies to the reader's Department Chair.

However, the authors also wish to state that none of the concrete dilemmas in this section have been chosen as on the edge or difficult to interpret. On the contrary, they are mentioned because they almost always occur in academically entrepreneurial situations, and because, in our experience, there is almost complete unanimity (among the uninvolved) as to what constitutes ethical behavior.

Dilemma 1: How Do I Split My Time? — Part I

Professors are to spend their time, generally, on "scholarly activity," an expression that has the virtue of generality but (of course) the vice of non-specificity. Very few (if any) professors have an employment contract that specifies the exact percentages, or hours, of teaching, research, administration, or other activity. There is the *norm*, of course—what we have herein called the Normative Paradigm (or more succinctly, The Tube)— which specifies the acceptable levels of teaching and research, and perhaps some other permissible activities, provided they are kept to within quite restricted limits, like committee service, and some consulting. The Tube is a cultural thing, rarely a narrow legal prescription.

Of course, The Tube is precisely what this book warns against, caring nothing for minimalist cultures, and suggesting instead that individual professors find more of what they love, and are good at, and make their contribution in those areas. The outstanding teachers of Chapter 3; the star researchers of Chapter 4; the manager/leaders of Chapter 5; these are not mythical creatures created by the authors. They exist at every important academic institution. Yet younger academics are often unaware of these

CHAPTER 6: THE ENTREPRENEURIAL PROFESSOR

career potentialities until it is too late. To these, this chapter adds a fourth possibility: the entrepreneurial professor.

However, unlike the previous three paradigms, in which all the work of whatever kind was done for the professor's academic institution, entrepreneurial work is, by definition, for *somebody else*. This raises special problems, many of which are of an ethical nature—which explains why ethics is given special attention in this chapter. There is virtually nothing in the hardcover literature about the "entrepreneurial" career option for professors, and still less (if that is possible) about the attending ethical issues.

It is generally appreciated by modern university divisions that some involvement by academics in the society in which they are immersed is a good thing. If they want governments to contribute to their operating budgets, they must show serious practical significance. If they want parents of potential students to see their course offerings worthy of consideration, they must satisfy the demands of relevance. And if government research-granting agencies are asked to support their research, this research must satisfy criteria beyond the personal curiosity of the academic researchers.

Besides, courses given by professors who have contact with the "real world" do tend to have a better selection of material, and dissertation topics assigned by academics in touch with the human applications of their discipline do tend, nowadays, to be respected for their perspicacity.[192] Some departments now track how often their faculty members are interviewed on TV, or write opinion pieces in the press, or are selected for external committees, etc., and this is proof of the growing awareness that academia is not viewed as a consulate from another planet but a functioning component of society.

Though these examples do indicate the increasing importance being placed on the involvement of academics beyond the campus boundary, they are not normally of the magnitude and duration to generate major ethical problems. In fact, in many cases the professors are not even paid for these activities. Cash, as always, brings the intensity of the debate to new levels.

The next echelon of activity—one that *does* begin to include cash—is "consulting." An outside party needs some information or advice, and an

---

[192] They certainly are respected more by students who plan on finding employment after graduation!

academic has that information or can provide that advice. The outside party is willing to pay for the consultation,[193] and the academic is willing to be paid. Many professors who become entrepreneurially focused begin the entrepreneurial career road via the route of consultation.

> **Ethical Comment 1 — What Time Do I Owe my Employer?**
> If a professor provides, through consultation, advice to an Outside Party, and is paid for doing so, this is—with some conditions—an *ethical* activity. Indeed, it is a *desirable* activity in many ways, provided it satisfies the ethical guidelines of the academic institution, as consistently interpreted by the academic administrator to whom the professor reports. Normally the guidelines are specified in terms of *time spent, not cash paid.*

Is this activity ethical? Normally, yes. But there are some obvious conditions, such as this one: that the time commitment is not large compared to normal university duties, or, if it is large, it is quite temporary.[194]

If the institution has any codified ethics at all in this area, it will usually specify how much time the professor can spend as a consultant (and on related activities). Note that such rules are normally couched in terms of time, not money. It is the former that is a reasonable claim by the employer, not the latter. Everyone may be interested in how much the academic consultant is being compensated, but there is no direct justification for this curiosity becoming the basis for ethical guidelines.

Dilemma I: How Do I Split My Time? — Part II

Some academic ethical guidelines are quite jealous about the time spent by their academic employees on "consultation." It is often made scrupu-

---

193 In proper English syntax, one does not say that a professor "consults." Surely, it is the Outside Party who does the consulting! The OP consults the professor, and the professor is consulted. (One is reminded of the similar syntactical laxity in saying that Fred "graduated university." No, it is the other way around: the university graduated—i.e., measured—Fred, which led to his being graduated by and from the university.)
194 If research-focused professors are permitted to take a summer off to visit an important colleague or laboratory, it would not seem untoward for entrepreneurially-focused professors to spend a summer professionally engaged at the offices of the consulting party.

CHAPTER 6: THE ENTREPRENEURIAL PROFESSOR

lously precise that, if, say, two days a month are allowed for consulting, this allowance is made within the "total" time available to the academic employee, explicitly including evenings, weekends, holidays, and presumably that most fertile cabinet of creative thought: the shower. (This is entirely consistent, of course, with the historical professorial culture, wherein, as discussed in §1.3, to be a professor is not a job, or even a career; it is a *vocation*.) Even if this seems like a rather extreme position, there should be some sympathy for the employer's position here, since there is a sizable percentage of employees who otherwise would always claim that their breakthrough did occur in the shower.[195] Unlike the highly measurable environment of, say, manufacturing, how can anyone prove where[196] an idea did or did not occur?

Certainly the authors have heard colleagues say, in effect, "I don't give a darn about what any policy says. If I get a good idea up at the cottage that, though somewhat related to my research program, does not directly follow from it, and is hardly something I'm required to think about at the cottage, then as far as I'm concerned, I'm on my own." If this viewpoint[197] sounds at odds with the "vocation doctrine," that's because it is. One can press ahead, knowing that one may be in violation of the institutional ethical guidelines, or one can take a more subtle tack.

A major research-intensive university is a large place. In the matters under discussion, it is almost impossible to find school-wide guidelines on *anything*—including ethical guidelines—that are finely-tuned for all departments, faculties, and divisions within the school. Even if there is a set of "ethical guidelines" developed for the whole university, chances are good that more local interpretations have developed. Finding out what these home construals are, through a frank discussion with one's Chair or Dean, is clearly a more promising strategy than just saying, "I was in the shower at the cottage." (See accompanying box.)

---

195 See the subsection "How (Un)ethical are You?" in §6.5.
196 Employee contracts in the corporate sector and modern academic praxis are quite similar: If, while you are employed by us, you come up with a $1B idea, don't just say it all happened in your "magic shower."
197 In the interest of Full Disclosure: Both the authors have owned cottages. Occasionally, they have had excellent ideas at these locations, not all of them of a commercial nature.

> **Ethical Comment 1 — What Time Do I Owe my Employer?**
> **– Postscript**
>
> Find out (from the person to whom you academically report) exactly how your ethical guidelines are normally interpreted. You may be surprised at how many "variances" there are for your department or Faculty. A lot will also depend on how much you are otherwise contributing to your department. Are you normally an energy source or a boat anchor? If the former, expect some welcome latitude in how you use your talents to contribute to the department.

There are many subcultures within the university-wide culture. Some of these will be more receptive to outside involvements than others. Those most naturally involved with outside opportunities—such as the "professional" faculties—will usually have more detailed ethics policies. They may also have policies, established by practice and precedent, that appear to be inconsistent with policies promulgated for larger groups in the academic family, but that are just as real and equally pertinent, despite their wont of being less than codified.

As a final but very important remark on ethical interpretation, your departmental Chair (or Faculty Dean) may have to rule on the ethical questions you raise with respect to how you deal with your external opportunities. He or she will have to exercise intelligence and judgment in adjudicating each case. The most important two considerations for the Chair—after the "black letter" legal interpretation of the institutional ethical guidelines—should be these:

(1) What is the value generally created by this individual in this department, through his/her teaching, research and other activities? (If this value is high, that may move the decision in a more supportive direction.)

(2) What is the chance of success of this "outside" involvement? (If this chance is felt to be high, this will also improve the likelihood of a supportive decision.)

CHAPTER 6: THE ENTREPRENEURIAL PROFESSOR

Of these two criteria, the first is by far the most important. Unless the Chair has specialized knowledge of the field involved, it is unlikely that she will be able to judge the technical issues personally. In contrast, if she is competent in the position, she will be aware of the departmental value of the individual who is seeking permission that a major portion of time for the next few months (or even the next few years) be spent on an extensive entrepreneurial venture of some kind, which could lead (or has already led) to the formation of a new company dedicated to the innovation.

Anyone who wants to spend full time or nearly full time on outside activity, for an extended period (more than a year), should move to fractional time at the university, possibly the zero fraction.

Dilemma 2: Do I Owe My Colleagues Anything?

Dilemma 1 above (How do I split my time?) dealt essentially with one's ethical duties to the university. In Dilemma 2, we raise a related issue: Do I have ethical duties to my colleagues? The answer, of course, is yes.

In many ways, academics act largely as individuals. Certainly each bears primary responsibility for (as examples) the quality of one's research, the effectiveness of one's teaching, the extent of one's research funding, and the positive influence one brings to meetings and other deliberations. Yet, in other ways, the department functions as a team. The general reputation of the department is influenced by the contribution (to the department) of each professor. Departmental morale depends on the fluid functioning of all individuals in the department. And, as a final example, one should note that there are always departmental jobs and functions that are not especially popular with anyone, but when all pitch in and do their share, the work gets done with reasonable amity.

The departmental peace is dealt a damaging blow if there are one or more professors who are clearly not pulling their load because they are often (or even usually) off doing something else—however laudable that something else might be. (See accompanying box.)

> **Ethical Comment 2 — Do I Owe My Colleagues Anything?**
> Colleagues usually support the notion that there will be some variability in the contributions made by professors to the department (and if this book were very successful they would tolerate an even wider variability). But it is important to note that all these contributions, with whatever their variability, are **to the department.** Once the contribution is to some outside entity, once it has a noticeable magnitude, and once it persists for an extensive duration—this will become quite obvious to one's colleagues, who will, naturally enough, resent it.

Similarly, academics know that there will be a substantial salary spread between the junior and the senior professors, based on experience and reputation, but even a child knows that if someone is paid by A but spends their time working for B, when B has no relationship to A, that someone is committing simple larceny. Professors know it too, and they will be most distracted by this behavior if it is committed by senior professors, who get paid the big bucks on the grounds that they are the putative intellectual leaders of the department. Strong ethics should be part of this leadership.

Dilemma 3: How Should I Treat My Students? — Part I

Undergraduate students, especially in the early years, should be completely unaffected by the entrepreneurial activities of the lecturer.[198] The main ethical temptation here for the professor, of course, is to skip classes frequently, or otherwise reduce teaching load. This has to be judged by the departmental Chair in the context of the overall departmental contribution. If the individual's contribution is primarily[199] through research (as in Chapter 4), he or she may not be teaching much in the first place, so there is no problem.

When it comes to graduate students, however, there are further opportunities to slip into unethical behavior (see accompanying box). The two

---

198 Except in a positive way, as when the course content and examples chosen and are more relevant and interesting.
199 A strong research contribution can be objectively demonstrated and is not just someone's opinion. Here are some symptoms: quantity and quality of research publications; number of graduate students; relative size of research funding; etc.

proscriptions in the box are more subtle that they look, so some further comment is in order.

It is readily admitted that there are many good reasons to get graduate students involved in consulting work or similar activity. Many students want the additional experience, especially of the outside variety, thinking that this will be of a more practical nature. It helps to add to their rather sparse résumés and to improve their chances of securing employment on graduation. Last, but seldom least, most graduate students welcome an additional stream of income. The key ethical point is that a graduate student *can choose to decline such involvement, at his or her sole option, without any adverse academic consequences for so choosing.*

Ethical Comment 3 — How Should I Treat My Graduate Students?

Here are the Top Two Things **NOT** to do:
1. **Never** permit your graduate students to think that whether they contribute to your entrepreneurial activities will affect how they will be treated and judged academically by you as a professor.
2. **Never** make a graduate student's dissertation an integral part of your entrepreneurial activities.

It should go without saying (but may not) that this ethical position must be carefully explained to the student as part and parcel of the offer of extra activity. Otherwise, the student may assume, or deduce from your body language, that compliance with the offer is expected. Thus, while it is ethical to offer a student an additional work opportunity, and even to explain the benefits, there should be no doubt about whether the student must either accept or be harmed academically.

In fact, if the student asks what the *disadvantages* of accepting this opportunity are, one should be frank and helpful in reply. As a professor, you have a dual and somewhat conflicted role. You are offering the opportunity, but you are also the student's most trusted academic advisor. The latter must take precedence.

You might, for example, observe that the work will likely delay the date of graduation. Students often fight this wisdom, promising to work feverishly, but however honestly they aver this new level of dedication in the office, a good rule of thumb is that six months' of additional work will take six additional months to complete.[200] You might also mention that this graduation delay may have an associated opportunity cost. More specifically, if graduation is delayed by (say) six months, that leads to six months of salary foregone.

This leads to another key point which has some ethical considerations: What should the student be paid? Ideally, he or she should be paid at the rate of a fresh graduate[201] in the field. This rate, which will be considerably higher than the student stipend level, reduces the student's opportunity cost to zero. However, there are times when an outside opportunity presents itself, and the student (owing to the benefits mentioned a moment or two ago) wishes to undertake the work—even though being paid less than the "graduated professional" rate. Should this student be prevented from participating on ethical grounds? This seems too severe. One might rather argue that his decision was fully informed and that he is a consenting adult. Nevertheless, it would be ethically questionable if the professor did not make a good-faith effort to find a way to pay the student appropriately, even if it means a slightly diminished consulting fee.

Dilemma 3: How Should I Treat My Students? — Part II

The second prohibition in the above box was "Never make a graduate student's dissertation an integral part of your entrepreneurial activities." This is a very common dilemma. If a student and her professor are discussing a new outside opportunity, including how to find the time, how to find the money, etc., it isn't long before the student says something like this: "Look, why don't we just make this project my dissertation? That will remove the opportunity cost to me, and the dissertation would immediately be useful to someone—your client."

Whether the student suggests this stratagem or not, the idea will already be quite familiar to the professor. Though it is tempting, it is somewhat unethical—and probably against departmental rules. There are sev-

---

200 A better rule of thumb is that the time taken to complete will be π times the initial estimate.
201 The *next* graduation, not the last one!

CHAPTER 6: THE ENTREPRENEURIAL PROFESSOR

eral problems, one of which is this: "Who owns the work?" Very few clients are willing to pay for intellectual property (IP) but not own it. Indeed, further thought demonstrates that the client and academia treat the work product in an almost *diametrically opposed manner*. The university wants to publish the dissertation, and normally a journal paper of some kind as well, so that the whole world can become aware of, and potentially use, the new information. The commercial client, in contrast, has paid for what it hopes will be a competitive edge based on the new proprietary information. This issue alone seems to require a separation of the dissertation from the client activity.

A second problem is this: Who calls the shots on what gets done, and how it gets done, and by whom, and by when? The client will wish to control (or at least strongly influence) such matters, whereas academic research has a different master. Suppose, for example, that nicely into a research dissertation it is found that a much more promising line of inquiry is available. (Promising *academically*.) The client, however, may say, "We're not interested in all that general theoretical stuff. We just want you to do what you agreed to do, and we don't want any delay either." If the client is paying market rates (and if not, why not?), it has the right to make such claims.

The ethical solution is to make the dissertation and the outside work *distinct though related*. For example, the dissertation may be to examine a new method of calculating (or doing, or making) something, while the existing method will be used in the private work. The client can be told that a new method is also under study but that this IP belongs to the university and will be published. The client, along with everyone else, will be free to use the new method at that time.

But what if the new method fails to materialize? Ah, here's another disadvantage of making a dissertation a consulting deliverable! Academics are familiar with the fact that research—especially the best research—is speculative and unpredictable, and that dissertations sometimes need to be re-jigged somewhat to be fair to the student. Clients don't think that way. They think more like, "No results? No pay." A professor may be willing to take such risks with his own consulting work, but it is unfair and probably unethical to place this risk on a student whose whole career may be adversely affected.

6.7 Insights from Our Interviewees on the Entrepreneurial Option

We conclude this chapter with important insights from our interviewees, details on whom are given in the Appendix. These provide helpful real-life examples and further wisdom on the issues discussed in this chapter.

Tom Brzustowski

Tom has been around the block enough to quickly recognize the naturally entrepreneurial professor:

> "One of the very best researchers I know—fine publications with real impact, citations and awards—started a business with his graduate students, building on his and their research into a type of scientific software. They turned it into a thriving company. (With another graduate student, the same individual had previously produced a technology that he *gave away* to people who needed to use it because they couldn't afford to pay for it, and that helped a lot of people.)
>
> "However, this man never wanted to take any administrative responsibilities. Some criticized him for being 'selfish.' He simply said, 'Look, I know I wouldn't be good at it. I do have this wish to see my research turned into practical things. I saw a need for a company and we made a lot of money for a lot of people through this. This is how I am and these are my preferences.'
>
> "Would he have behaved differently if the department had sat in some sort of focus group to talk about the options? No, not at all.
>
> "He was also a very fine teacher, and a winner of teaching awards. An all-round academic—except that he chose to put the additional element of his time not into administrative service but into entrepreneurship, involving his students and others as partners."

Not quite in The Tube on admin, apparently, but a successful entrepreneurial professor. Moreover, his exemplary research record and award-winning teaching indicate that his ethics were also onside.

CHAPTER 6: THE ENTREPRENEURIAL PROFESSOR

Michael Collins

Michael has become known in his field world-wide. Not just by his academic colleagues but also through his strong involvement in challenging civil engineering projects. His thoughts:

> "Consulting has a real role to play in that it offers the possibility for the young faculty member, over a period of years, to interact with companies and become involved with lots of interesting projects. That sort of behavior made me a better engineer and gave me much more understanding of what the whole profession is all about."

In addition to the beneficial effects for one's research, Collins also believes that "for your self-respect as a professional teacher you should have professional experience wider than simply your narrow research area."

Dan Farine

Dr Dan Farine is an internationally recognized obstetrician and a professor of Ob/Gyn in the University of Toronto with cross appointments to the Departments of Medicine and Public Health. (More biographical information in the Appendix.) As a perinatologist and head of Maternal Fetal Medicine, he deals with the most difficult pregnancies, which often places him at the cutting edge of the subject.

One of Dan's first points is that physicians who are also professors have additional options beyond teaching, research, etc., to which most professors are limited. This leads to still further career variety:

> "I think you are right to distinguish between different kinds of academic careers and different kinds of people with different options. In medicine, we are lucky because we have at least one more option that most others in academia do not have—clinical work. For me, the clinical work is very rewarding on the personal side; it's also rewarding financially. My clinical earnings are much higher than my academic salary. So financially there's a difference between being a physician—or an engineer, or somebody in a hot field in economics, for example—and a professor of Sumerian languages."

SO YOU WANT TO BE A PROFESSOR?

One should perhaps pause and ask rhetorically whether *all* professional faculties should not encourage their professors to become involved regularly in the profession they profess to teach (i.e., the counterpart of clinical work). In any case, Dan was not for staying in the Normative Paradigm for very long:

"In academia you can get onto the treadmill and start running and you are so busy dealing with the next step, the next month, the next year, that you don't really plan ten years down the line. I was fortunate in the sense that things happened to me very fast. I was running, but I was running ahead of the crowd, not in the middle or in the back.

"If you are a professor and a world expert on Sumeric languages it's very unlikely that you'll find a commercial niche or a consultative opportunity or anything of that sort, where your unique skills could actually be used for something different. If you are in other fields, like business, communications, medicine, you have the option of using those skills in a different way.

"Lots of people have an academic career where they become super experts in a very small niche (more and more about less and less). I find that boring. I became the world expert in a very small niche during my fellowship and I was invited to give talks and lecture tours and everything. I could just have done that for the next 25 years and become very well known, be very prolific academically—but I just found it boring. So I got off that horse, not when it was old and beaten, but while it was still a very successful horse. It could still have won a few more races but I went to look into other things.

"Now I also use some of my time for consultative work, which provides a lateral view on my clinical and academic experience, and is not only fascinating but also financially rewarding. I ended up being a very good consultant, so I could have left medicine altogether and gone out on my own, but I decided not to. It was an eye-opener because I knew nothing about finances and nothing about how companies operated or

CHAPTER 6: THE ENTREPRENEURIAL PROFESSOR

> how money gets invested. In fact, I knew little about anything outside medicine. I had to learn."

Once one becomes a successful consultant, it usually doesn't take long before larger entrepreneurial opportunities present themselves. One then must respond at one of the levels described earlier in §6.2.

Dan's first such opportunity was when he created a disposable cervical sensor system that took much of the guesswork out of the labor/delivery process. This led to the founding of Barnev, Inc., with two friends with complimentary skills:

> "One of the things that I wanted to do was to study the way that we manage labor (delivering babies), which had been rather inefficient. So when I started I was not interested in any of the financial or administrative matters; I simply wanted to improve the way labor is managed.
>
> "Then I was invited to dinner by an old friend from high school who happens to be a professor of medical engineering at Tel Aviv University. During the dinner he confessed to me that his area of research was boring, and he was tired of doing assistant pumps for failing hearts and he was looking for something new. I said I have an idea. We discussed it and he was very interested. He said the way to do it is as a company, because then you're not depending on time constraints in which the right student has to show up; you can move forward and really get it done quickly. I said okay, sounds interesting.
>
> "He called me the next morning and said, 'You know, I've thought about it and if you and I were to go into business we would fail in about five minutes. But we have another person, a guy I've known since I was 18 and a very good friend, who is a very successful entrepreneur. He has had five start-ups of which four were successful and he's very good at business.'
>
> "The three of us met the next morning for breakfast. You have to realize that these two friends of mine were Israelis, and Israel at the time had a very different climate. This was 1998, and the government was really supportive of start-ups. We

could get very easily $300,000 to start off. It's really a one-product company, with several patents."

Barnev won a prestigious research award and its computerized labor monitoring systems were given FDA approval.

Note that the co-founders of Barnev were, in addition to Dan (the medical driver), Prof. Ofer Barnea, former Chairman of Tel Aviv University's Biomedical Engineering Department (the sensor engineering driver), and Mr. Shlomo Nevo, an experienced industrialist (the business driver). Good team structure really matters and entrepreneurial professors who try to spin off a company all by themselves quickly learn the magic of forming a small team[202] of individuals with complementary skills and good personal chemistry.

In addition to the knowledge that many young lives are being saved by his creativity, one can sense the fun (and some financial benefits) Dan has had from this area of activity. He has also learned a lot. Some last snippets:

- By doing this, many other things also opened. Now about once a year I get an offer to become involved in another medical invention that is being commercialized.
- Be careful of cultural differences when pitching your ideas: an encounter with a potential investor involves many subtle clues and much body language in addition to the right words and phrases.
- For Canadian companies, what attracts them is the fact that I'm a legit physician working in a good center within a strong university. They know I know my field, so I can actually find among the suggested applications the really useful ones.
- Networking is so important. Even if you can open the door, the door will not stay open too long. If you have nothing important to offer, it will close in no time.

Note again the benefits of networking. A professor who remains cloistered always in academe—except for the odd conference huddled with other professors in his narrow discipline—will be unlikely to possess the networking resources needed to found a successful company.

---

202 One of the authors is fond of saying that going into business with someone is pretty much the same as marriage, except for the money (more) and the sex (none).

CHAPTER 6: THE ENTREPRENEURIAL PROFESSOR

Barry French

Barry French's first degree was in chemistry, but his doctorate was in aerophysics and he soon found himself developing very sensitive instrumentation for measuring the composition of the atmosphere of Mars as part of the Viking mission. Barry's vision and creativity enabled him to connect the dots between "sniffing" for trace gases on Mars and adapting this technology to important applications here on our home planet (such as, for example, air pollutants, illicit drugs and explosives). This led him to found Sciex Ltd., and to develop the science and market for such instruments. Sciex was then acquired by, and has remained a division of, MDS Inc.,[203] and has recently become AB Sciex.

Most spinoffs have a clear moment when the professor decides to take entrepreneurial action:

> "I decided to have a PhD student work turning this [Mars instrument] into a useful device. We focused on airborne trace gas analysis. I was thinking in terms of the environment and similar applications but as it turned out that was not the major market."

Barry's further comments touch further on many of the themes discussed in this chapter:

> "You have to be a good judge of people because you've got to build a team with the right individuals. That's the way I built Sciex, with the right scientific and technical team—and most of those folks are still there 20 years later.
>
> "To create a successful start-up, you also have to have financial connections, and you have to have creative marketing ability—or work with someone who does. You have to have enough business knowledge to be able to analyze markets and market trends. And then you have to be able to collectively inspire a group of people that, hey, if we do something here, this is going to change the way things are done. I was only

---

203 MDS Sciex is a global life sciences company providing products and services used for the diagnosis and treatment of disease.

interested in something that was really going to be a platform[204] technology for major change."

As with many startups, Barry had an outside associate (Bill Breukelman, a former classmate in chemical engineering) who helped plan and execute the business aspects:

> "Bill and I together really looked at all the 'sniffing' ideas. I dug up all I could find on different forms of activity that were going on—there was bomb-sniffing, the atmospheric environment, analysis of human breath (several applications), various things like that. We found there were lots of applications, broad enough to figure that we could write a very attractive business plan. There was enough, we thought, to be able to get angel funding for example. It was also enough to convince the university that it was worth getting patents. The university paid completely for the first patents."

As things worked out, the university also made a magnificent royalty over the next 17 years. They got millions. It was divided 50/50 between the university and the inventors.

Barry also has sensible comments about patents, which are often overrated by those with primarily legal rather than business interests:

> "There's no sense in getting patents unless you have a (realistic) view that this thing is commercially useful. This means that you have to know markets. A little luck doesn't hurt either. There are business cycles and timing is everything."

One must also, as discussed in §6.2, find one's level of entrepreneurial involvement:

> "Route one is do it yourself—be everything, be the businessman and so on. That wasn't my choice, but it is a viable choice if you'd like to be a businessman. Route two is team up with people with complementary skills and that team building is just so important. And by now, being in a research-inten-

---

204 A *platform* technology is one that has many and diverse applications. It is difficult to find a better example than the modern computer.

CHAPTER 6: THE ENTREPRENEURIAL PROFESSOR

sive university, you should know whether or not you're good at building a team. You give people the vision and get them enthused—just the stuff a good academic should be able to do.

"The third route is somewhat similar to that, where you have a little core group of people, but you build up an IP company and you can just directly license it as a raw piece of IP. But that to me can be underselling the potential in general. If it is game-changing technology, something that's really important, it will have a market and that market will be exploitable and the business scalable.

"Bill and I chose to go on Route two – I was fortunate that he had skills complementary to mine. We can trust each other and we know how to work together. I trust his business judgment and he trusts my technical judgment."

Barry believes that, if done correctly, this whole process benefits all concerned:

"There's nothing mutually exclusive about the 'company's good,' the 'students' good,' and the 'university's good.' I've never heard anyone say that Sciex was not a good thing for the university and the students involved."

Entrepreneurial professors, in short, need not play a zero-sum game.

Donald Mackay

Don has been quite entrepreneurial in the application of his university research, for which he set up a company—D. Mackay Environmental Research Ltd.—as a framework for the interactions he was attracted to. His approach is via is an active, web-based consulting practice:

"I first thought of *selling* my [computer] models, but I decided not to do that—partly because when once sell it to somebody you're always on the hook for providing advice. So I gave away the models free.[205] You take a model; you use it;

---

[205] This approach would seem to work especially well for computer models since the Cost of Goods Sold (assuming the research is completed in the university) is almost zero.

it's your responsibility. I'll help you if I can, but I'm not on the hook.

"But if you want me to apply that model and modify it slightly for your purposes I will do that on a contractual basis. One can download the models from the website. This has been quite warmly supported by industry folks who use these models. We often don't know what they're doing, but we get glimpses. But the models are downloaded, ten per day, from all over the world. DMER Ltd. has been on the go for almost 20 years now and that's provided me with a steady source of consulting income."

Several issues already discussed, including ethics, lie beneath his further comments:

"I think consulting, *in moderation* [his emphasis], is very good from a financial point of view, for gaining experience, and for dealing with other people in industry and in government.

Heather Monroe-Blum

Having served at the top levels in two major universities, Heather is very familiar with the benefits and concerns of channeling the entrepreneurial urges of academics:

"I think there's enormous room for entrepreneurs to begin commercial spin-off companies and other commercialization activities.

"I'm a big believer in multi-sectoral (government, universities, private sector, NGO's) partnerships as being critically important for achieving and advancing the full mission of the university. But you do have to know what your core academic mission is, and then to define the overlapping arena of activity which defines a common cause. I feel sometimes that we start again and again, from scratch, to create these "new" platforms of productive collaboration, instead of refining the existing model(s) to be mutually productive and rewarding. This is true of everything from basic research collaboration, through interdisciplinary teaching and research with a university, to managing intellectual property effectively.

"The overlap between business and university interests may not be huge but it is critically important and it is this overlap-where you want highly productive relationships."

Chapter 7: Academic Path Planning

Different Strokes . . .

Chapter Overview

In this last chapter we wish to unite the preceding themes into a coherent view of the academic career; to express some thoughts that form the connective tissue between the four "paradigms" considered in detail in Chapters 3–6; and generally to wrap up our discussion of how to influence one of the most important voyages of one's life—one's career path.

Using the four earlier paradigms intelligently is explained further. They are not intended to be pure careers, but ingredients from which to guide one's career over time. Nor do the four paradigms exhaust the possibilities: two further flavors are described below—the "celebrity professor" and the "socially conscious professor."

It is stressed that continual career evaluation is desirable throughout one's long academic life, not just at tenure time. Some comments are also made about special end-of-career issues.

7.1 Other Academic Career Flavors

As expressed in this chapter's subtitle, the "path" metaphor does have one weakness: It suggests that one is following a path blazed by others. This is a variation on the Tube (a.k.a. the Normative Paradigm, §4.2)—which implies that all academics must behave identically, regardless of their aptitudes, their interests, their constraints, or their opportunities. In our discussion here, path does not mean "well-beaten track"; it is, instead, an analogy with the continual thought process, over decades, about what one is doing in one's work life. One's career path is—or, at any rate, *should* be—a very personal pilgrimage, where general principles have been well thought out, yet where key adjustments are made periodically. The plan always points the way, yet is subject to constant revision in the light of new external information or personal insights. The "path" forms first in the mind, then becomes objectively obvious.

Professorship as a Career Choice

Perhaps another helpful metaphor might be that of a tourist who arrives in a large city for the first time, determined to make the experience enjoyable and/or meaningful. Here are three possible options:
1. Spend most of the time sitting in the hotel room, watching sitcoms and reading novels.
2. Find the nearest tour bus, and hop on.
3. Acquire a small library of information about the city, its history, its culture, and its distinct areas, and form a plan to visit those sites and vistas that seem to meet the twin criteria of "enjoyable" and "meaningful."

Obviously, Option 1 wastes the opportunity. How does one reply when friends ask, "How did you enjoy Chicago?" Option 2 might be acceptable, especially if one has only a day or two for the visit, and it could be part of the information gathering in Option 3 for a longer visit.

But to make the visit truly memorable and significant, clearly Option 3 is the preferred choice, especially if the stopover is more than fleeting, and "fleeting" is hardly a word that describes one's lifelong relationship with academia. In academia, the visit is long—five or six decades, or even longer! Just tossing oneself into the Tube (or grabbing a tour bus driven by others to destinations prescribed by pedestrian expectations) is not the best plan that should emanate from the minds of professors.

Mix and Match Paradigms

Exercised to stimulate reader thought towards non-Tube career choices, the authors have chosen to highlight four[206] identifiable career paradigms,

---

206 These four paradigms being: Teaching (Chapter 3), Research (Chapter 4), Management/ Leadership (Chapter 5), and Entrepreneurship (Chapter 6).

CHAPTER 7: ACADEMIC PATH PLANNING

none of which is consistent with fundamental Tubism, a belief system that could be summarized as mixing the first two paradigms in a fixed proportion and ignoring the second two paradigms altogether.

Chapters 3–6 explicate these four paradigms, but there are dangers in this approach: some readers may think that these paradigms are "pure careers." After tenure, just pick one and eschew the rest. Unfortunately, it doesn't work quite that way, and readers would misapprehend our intent—and, more important, would ignore reality—were they to take that message.

Thus the first mistake would be to believe that, having achieved tenure, one should pursue, ruthlessly and single-mindedly, one of the four careers. Single-mindedness is sometimes rewarded long-term, but ruthlessness never is. Nobody is recommending a one-flavor career. The idea is, instead, that one construct a recipe from among the paradigm flavors, and that this recipe should evolve over time.

Let us pursue the recipe metaphor a bit further; it may help clarify the present intent. Typical successful recipes can be broken down into basic ingredients. Think of the paradigms as sugar, flour, eggs, etc. In this metaphor, the Normative Paradigm is itself a recipe: teaching (1 tbsp); research (2 tsp); management (~0); entrepreneurship (filter out any vestiges with a fine-screen colander). We simply say, fine, that's one recipe, but what are the chances that's it's the right one for you? What's your signature dish as executive chef of your own career?

Successful academics usually have, at any given time, more than one ingredient, at least for most of their career. In practice, the most successful academics juggle at least two of the paradigms at once—but they adjust the ingredient balance as they move toward their longer-term objectives.

Combining the "four paradigms" into various career recipes, and modifying the recipe throughout one's academic sojourn can create an exceedingly large assortment of options—but hardly ends the range of possibilities. In the remaining sections we shall look at some further creative choices with the caveat that the purpose is not to complete a finite list, but to demonstrate the ever widening range of vocational innovations.

7.2 The Celebrity Professor

One of the many joys of being a professor is the opportunity to garner external recognition for one's knowledge, not just among one's academic colleagues and in archive journals, but by becoming a recognized media expert. In addition to all the known academic skills, these individuals also have *charisma*, which by definition cannot be taught. Professors who achieve celebrity status early in their career find extra funds for research more available, salary increases above the regulated norm. While other colleagues might have trouble having a meeting with the VP-Research, usually encountering delays, followed by secretarial suggestions that it might be best if one discussed the particular issue with their Dean, celebrities are usually welcomed warmly at the highest echelons.

The reason for this behavior is self-evident: Most universities, particularly in the professional faculties, are realizing that they are not immune from the detrimental effects of bad (or no) public relations. Celebrity professors, who often begin (and remain) as star researchers or star teachers (or both), are those who provoke a very favorable response in the media—and who proactively seek such opportunities.

Internal Celebrity Status

The "celebrity" moniker usually begins internally. Some academics seek throughout their careers to be well known within their own institution, acknowledged by their peers as experts in their field. This is the first step toward recognition by the external community, nationally and then internationally, for their knowledge, wisdom, and expert commentary. To achieve this status, one must gain recognition for one's work—not just erudite specialized articles in journals of specialized circulation, but interpretations of one's work in the popular[207] press.

---

207 It helps, of course, if one has the good fortune to be an expert in a subject of intrinsic public interest. The authors might argue, however, that if professors cannot make their subject interesting to anyone save other academics like themselves, they either don't understand their subject or they are poor communicators. In the former case, they shouldn't be doing research and in the latter case they shouldn't be teaching; in combination, these attributes define someone who shouldn't be a professor in the first place. Other professors understand their research subject well and are excellent communicators, but they feel the public media is not where they should be spending their time. Now that many university administrations track

CHAPTER 7: ACADEMIC PATH PLANNING

The first opportunity to have a serious encounter with the media often begins with some high-profile news event, on which further light is sought. The professor is contacted by the media and asked to go "on," sometimes with very little notice, and usually unpaid, for a news interview. This is at once a challenge, a great opportunity, and a potentially dangerous situation. Here is some advice on how to handle the situation:

- ☐ Find out the exact news item that prompted this request, and learn as much about it as you can before the interview.
- ☐ Similarly, ascertain what related knowledge area you are being asked to support. Interviewers will ask anything—*anything*—that comes into their minds. Nothing is more embarrassing that being asked a peripheral question that has no bearing on your subject of expertise, so try to set some guidelines. Remember, this may be live TV; with a fumbling performance you could become an instant non-celebrity.
- ☐ To be proactive, contact your local (respectable) media outlets, and acquaint them of your subject of proficiency and of your willingness to support their activity if a really good fit comes along.

To reach a wider audience, write an excellent book that brings the most interesting (to the non-expert) aspects of your views to the public attention. Don't think of this as a professorial activity that is dubious and anomalous; think of it as part of your *publication* activity. Think of it as a substitute for Archive Papers #107, #108, #109, but with an audience of 10,000 or 100,000 rather than 100. The public broadcasters, seeing someone who dares to present a non-vacuous book topic to the general public, will often oblige by arranging an at-length interview, furthering your exposure, amplifying your sales, and making the "celebrity" title well deserved.

Even internally, research discoveries are great, often followed by university sponsored promotion of such noteworthy events. However, although there are benefits to this type of activity, if one wishes to extend their nominal 15 minutes of fame (which decays very quickly unless some major effort is expended to keep the interest alive), there are guidelines that can be fol-

---

references to their faculty in the media and regard such effusions as an important organizational output, old insular attitudes will likely be forced to evolve rapidly.

lowed to ensure continued interest in one's work and opinions, thus ensuring the status of a "celebrity professor."

External Celebrity Status

The following advice is offered to professors who wish to enhance their status within their universities, and who further seek to exploit such opportunities as a leaping-off point to local or national recognition. However altruistic these impulses may be, the extra internal recognition can lead to earlier promotions, leadership opportunities, and salary increases.

Consider the following more detailed scenario for achieving internal "celebrity" standing:

- Select one of your most noteworthy research results—assuming you are not yet Nobel prize material and still struggling for recognition—or choose an academic paper that has garnered some external recognition, such as an award or some major research grant.
- Make sure your departmental Chair knows about it—don't wait for annual performance reviews—and get it noted in university publications.
- If it is really special—meaning one of the few expected breakthroughs in your career—let the Dean know about it also. Don't go to the well too often with this one or it might have an effect opposite to the one desired.
- Evaluate positive responses from the Chair and Dean. Is it just faint praise or do you sense a shared excitement? If really first-rate, copy these responses to the VP-Research and the President. Don't rely on the Chair or Dean to make these upper echelon executives aware of your singular achievement. Start building your recognition factor.

The decay time for this single achievement—about six months—is time enough for a salary increase, is exhilarating for your résumé, and will help with promotions and possible leadership applications.

To lever this success further, to achieve external (but still local) celebrity status, send news releases to local media outlets such as newspapers, radio and TV stations, as mentioned above. Use the media relations people

CHAPTER 7: ACADEMIC PATH PLANNING

in your faculty or the President's office to assist and advise with this effort, although you must be seen as the focus and you must drive the process yourself. You cannot rely on them to consider your event as sufficiently newsworthy for them to publicize. If you start getting responses, make sure these same media people know about it. Then they get excited and start promoting you. Tell them you are available for interviews (see above). Don't be shy about giving interviews; this is the starting point to achieve external celebrity status.

The benefits of this type of external recognition, besides being personally satisfying, include the following:

- ☐ It gives impetus to your stature within the department and university, as well as granting agencies.
- ☐ When submitting papers for conferences, or asking the Chair, Dean or VP-Research for some special recognition in funding for a follow-on research project, you can go from being a "supplicant[208] professor" to being a "celebrity professor," who gets asked to give keynote addresses, gets a quick appointment with the VP or President for the funding pitch, and gets offered a seat on high-level university advisory committees.
- ☐ Consulting offers will also trickle in whether it is for technical advice, radio appearances or TV commentary for special events.
- ☐ Requests to give keynote lectures from local and international societies and groups will be proffered. Although one should make sure that travel and living costs are covered, expecting to get a stipend at an early stage of external recognition is premature. Don't be greedy—the money comes after you have proven to be an exciting and interesting speaker. Market forces (supply and demand) tend to become stronger than academic credentials at this stage. This is true for radio and TV commentary; early days buy recognition, then comes the demand if you are good on your feet and have mastered public speaking.
- ☐ Requests to sit on high-level presidential advisory committees, as well as government committees start to arrive, although some

---

208 For example, a "supplicant" professor is one who asks whether he can be permitted to attend; a "celebrity" professor is one who is asked whether he will be kind enough to attend.

will require considerable time commitments. Being associated with policy advice and future funding directions, for example, will enhance your "recognition factor" and add to the demand for your appearance at conferences, public enquiries, and in government and private-sector consulting.

International Celebrity Status

Other than winning a Nobel Prize, achieving international celebrity status is rather difficult[209] to achieve for a university professor. One requirement is international exposure, other than speaking at international conferences. This opportunity—created in the first instance by doing some ingenious work—can be enhanced by seeking to participate in international organizations that formulate policy, address issues of current concern, and have a high public recognition factor. One must be willing to seek a leadership position in such organizations. The celebrity status then occurs when you act as a spokesperson for that organization on matters of international interest.

Being an acknowledged expert on a specific subject will also lead to celebrity status if one is willing to write articles (technical, economic, philosophical) and get them published in magazines or journals that are of the highest standard and that enjoy an international readership. The articles, of course, cannot be of the pedantic variety; they must be seminal and provoke interest, commentary, and discussion, and generally pave the way for others to follow.

Often such articles get Radio and TV play because they are of general interest and perhaps provocative in nature. However, publication of such articles will require that you have built up high recognition. The publisher must believe that there will be a strong interest in what you have to say.

7.3 The Socially Conscious Professor

While writing this book the authors had occasion to interview Arnold M Noyek, MD, who provided an impressive—indeed inspiring—model for a creative academic career in many dimensions. Let's begin with a brief bio:

---

[209] In fact, it is impossible unless your field happens to be physics, chemistry, medicine, literature, economics or peace.

CHAPTER 7: ACADEMIC PATH PLANNING

Dr. Arnold Noyek was born in Dublin, Ireland and immigrated to Canada. He graduated from Medical School at the University of Toronto, and trained in Otolaryngology at Manhattan Eye, Ear and Throat Hospital in New York City. He was Otolaryngologist-in-Chief at Mount Sinai Hospital, Toronto, from 1989–2002, where he has been on staff since 1966. He is a consultant with the Baycrest Centre for Geriatric Care in Toronto. Dr. Noyek is a Professor of Otolaryngology-Head and Neck Surgery, a Professor of Public Health, and a Professor of Medical Imaging (Radiology) at the University of Toronto. He is also Director of International Continuing Education for the Faculty of Medicine at the University of Toronto, Director, the Peter A Silverman Centre for International Health, Mount Sinai Hospital and Senior Ashoka Fellow.

Despite appearances, that is a brief bio! A full bio would have taken many pages.

Note the many ingredients: medical doctor; ear, nose and throat specialist; otolaryngologist-in-chief; geriatrics; professor of otolaryngology; professor of public health sciences; professor of radiology; director of international continuing education; and director of an international center and Senior Ashoka Fellow. Certainly there are threads of most of the main paradigms—teaching, research, management—and that doesn't even cover the diverse involvement of an intense clinical practice.

Entrepreneur in Social Capital

"Aha," some reader may say, "I don't see any evidence of entrepreneurial behavior in this bio. Creativity, certainly. But not an entrepreneur." Strictly speaking—meaning as defined in Chapter 6—Dr Noyek is not an entrepreneur in the usual sense.[210] He does not expend effort to create a commercial success; he does not build financial capital. Noyek's riposte to this observation is shown in the accompanying box.

---

210 As an interesting side note, Dr Noyek is not tenured: "In the health sector of this university, you don't get tenured. Just the Chairs get tenure. We're in a professional stream and they think your patients support you, so you don't get tenure. I became a full professor, but having also a clinical practice I never got a penny from the university."

> **An Entrepreneur Building *Social* Capital**
> My idea of being an academic includes taking my work from the ivory tower down to the grassroots. When it comes to entrepreneurship, we're not about financial capital. The capital we build is social capital.
> I'm a powerful believer that education carries the day. It overcomes ignorance.
> — Professor Arnold Noyek, MD (excerpt from authors' interview)

That's quite a claim, but entirely justified, as it turns out. To find out what's going on, we consider a little history[211]:

> "Working in the Middle East is a little different," says Dr Noyek, a master of understatement. He's remembering March 3, 1996, the day he'd finally—after more than five months of planning at the invitation of the late King Hussein—gathered a group of Canadian, Israeli, Jordanian and Palestinian physicians and scientists under the banner of the Canada International Scientific Exchange Program (CISEPO), of which he is founder. That same day, a bomb exploded on a Jerusalem bus, killing 20 people. This tragic event is one of the many episodes of violence and the obstacle of constant conflict that Noyek and his team have overcome in order to help bring healing to a troubled region."

The organization Noyek created in 1984 is a University of Toronto-based academic and scientific network that today transcends political and religious boundaries. This Canadian umbrella program now operates in Israel, Jordan, the West Bank—and, through other linkages, with Qatar, and many other countries around the world.

But what, precisely, is it that Dr Noyek and his colleagues do? And how does it tie in to his academic and professional activity? Here's the short version:

> "Because of genetics and the commonality of consanguineous marriages, children throughout the Middle East are suffering from hereditary hearing loss six to 10 times more than in

---

211 In addition to the authors' own interview, this passage also benefits from the insight of colleague John Drake.

the Western world. The index goal of CISEPO was to educate local doctors and hearing health professionals to properly diagnose and manage hearing-loss problems in newborns, infants and children. Universal screening for hearing loss in newborns is, Noyek hopes, the first step to providing care to needy Mideast populations while building people to people relations. So far, CISEPO has impacted national hearing health policy in Jordan and Israel as well as in Qatar through a bilateral program with the Peter A Silverman Center for International Health and the University of Toronto, Faculty of Medicine (ICHEC)."

Note the many symptoms of entreprenuria:
1. The urge to bring one's expertise to those outside the university who need it.
2. The wisdom to use the resources of others, if available and not directly available.
3. The willingness to create new organizational structures, as and when needed.
4. The readiness—even enthusiasm—to work with others in an effective team, where each contribution is valued and where, if some deserve credit more than others, that will happen naturally; egos are anesthetized in the best interests of the patient.
5. The planet-wide view, wherein one can export and expand the product/service throughout the word.

The only difference—and one suspects that Dr Noyek believes this to be a difference he is proud of—is that the currency of this entrepreneurial thrust is not monetary, it is the smiles on the faces of children.

Whatever the label, a multitude of others besides the authors have appreciated this unique creativity, bringing the benefits of academic study to the most vulnerable amongst us. David Naylor, formerly Dean[212] of UofT's Faculty of Medicine, called the CISEPO program "a spectacular example of academic outreach as an activity that not only develops clinical and research capacity abroad but builds bridges among colleagues living in a conflict-ridden region of the planet. This program is internationalization at its very best." And the late King Hussein of Jordan personally urged

---

212 And now, as UofT President, one of the interviewees for this book.

Noyek "to get involved in the peace process." Through his career choices, Dr Noyek arguably already was:

> "Our team and I have carried out over 100 academic missions to the Middle East. Because of my initial bridge between ENT and radiology I'm fortunate enough to be the founder of what is now a multidisciplinary organization (CISEPO) using health as a bridge to peace across the Arab and Israeli frontier. In order to lead in this kind of enterprise, first of all you have to have the courage of your own personal convictions. You have to have a strong and large network around you who believe in and who support collectively a vision of peaceful professional cooperation where all are treated with equitable respect. It's an academic model. So we're about education and research and service.
>
> "My idea is that you build distributive academic networks to build social capital. We start with medicine but we incorporate nursing, science, students, public health—all in a continuing health educational system, and the idea is to advance society by touching the lives of ordinary people. We see the health sector—it's never been used for peace-building—as ideal. So what we're all about at the end of the day is building peaceful professional co-operation network, health based and then moving out into and impacting on the lives of kids, women, the disabled and society at large—and influencing change because you touched the lives of ordinary and needy people. When we work in the Middle East, we're doing research projects and educational projects and cross-border training, and people-to-people activities in spite of the constant conflict and violence. We just keep moving forward—it's health as a bridge to peace!"

Arnold Noyek has shown much by his actions. Although his impact will generally continue to exemplify commitments much greater than the narrower aims of this book, he does provide a stirring example of how a professor can fashion a career path that, though unique to him or her, can be held up as a model that many other colleagues may seek to emulate.

7.4 Some Closing Thoughts

We have traveled far since we embarked on an examination of academic careers at the outset of Chapter 1. By far the most important points, made time and again in the intervening pages, are these:

> **Your Academic Career Journey**
> After Tenure
>
> *Travelers, please note:–*
> 1. This is your journey, no one else's.
> 2. The navigation along this journey is your responsibility, no one else's.

The authors have endeavored to provide travel guides, first in the form of two of the most common (and often non-optional) career emphases, namely, teaching (Chapter 3) and research (Chapter 4), and then, to add to these two paradigms, the authors have urged the reader to consider other possibilities. Two of the most rewarding are academic leadership (Chapter 5) and becoming an entrepreneurial professor (Chapter 6); for those with the right skill-set and aptitude (and the proper motivation) many outstanding academic careers have included a major or minor component in these directions.

The present chapter has again emphasized that the above four academic career essences, even if combined in unusual variations, hardly exhaust the range of possibilities. Two further innovations—the celebrity professor and the socially conscious professor—were introduced to illustrate the boundless creativity that professors can apply, not just to their work but also to their choice of work. We end the presentation with some last thoughts on the diversity of academic career profiles.

Staying in The Tube

First, despite the many scoldings given earlier to those who prefer just to accept the academic cultural norm (the Normative Paradigm) in the academic institution that employs them, there is nothing criminally or ethically wrong about just "going along to get along." However, we do believe (as mentioned repeatedly) that to merely accept the norm in this as in any other matter without the same level of mature, intelligent, challenging enquiry that successful academics always apply to their own fields is to risk missing many fascinating possibilities.

However, if after an appropriate examination, The Tube is optimal (or close to it) for you, by all means swim along. You will never have to regret your decisions later. You will never have to say, "I should have known, but I didn't." You will never lament that, as millions of high-school students have done, you were mesmerized by peer pressure.

The "Doomed"

Though referred to here by a jocular designation, most of the professors in any institution cannot, by definition, be exceptional (by the standards of that institution). For those with a brushing knowledge of probability and statistics, the inescapable fact is that academic staff members fall into a talent distribution that covers, at the lower end, "those that barely made it," to, at the higher end, the "stars."

However, being "doomed" in academia is hardly a cause for sympathy. Being a grunt in the academic trench is still vastly preferable, for most, than a posting in the marines. Professors are well known to have a long life expectancy and one's remuneration is hardly at poverty level. One's colleagues may be a trifle egotistical sometimes, but what profession has perfect peers?

The Normative Professor

Speaking of probability and statistics, what does the average (or median) professorial career look like? This typical professor has a broad range of talents and advanced knowledge. These professors are good at (and enjoy) teaching, as measured by student assessments. They may also be known as good "administrators," perhaps having acted as an Associate Chair or Director for a time, respected and liked by colleagues both within and outside the department. They are frequently called upon for advice and lectures on their specialties. They work well with colleagues in several other institutions, and serve the university in non-academic roles external to the university (government committees, centers of excellence, industry consultants, etc.).

These professors choose to remain (or have the talent to realistically remain) within the norm of the distribution of attributes of a standard group of professors, neither among the "doomed" nor among the "stars." They have good research programs with a reasonable level of grant funding, permitting some graduate students and some travel to conferences; their research is of sufficient caliber to have papers accepted for presentation and subsequent publication (although star status is not a descriptor). They are willing to accept whatever committee assignments are doled out by Chairs. No real aspirations for a high management position are evident, but they would probably accept one if offered. They have a social conscience, behave in an ethical manner towards students, colleagues and department. They are liked by colleagues within the department, but are not well known outside the department. They are not publicity seeking, but are honored if it comes their way. These professors are the heart and soul of the university—they love working with students (both graduates and undergraduates), are reliable, have integrity, and love their research and the academic life style. Most often they can be found in their office or laboratory off hours, sometimes on weekends, and long holidays are not essential.

Out to Pasture? Or an Exciting End-of-Life Mini-Career?

Although most of the career planning discussed in this book is said to start immediately post-tenure, in fact it is a continuous process throughout one's career. This fact is highlighted in the accompanying box.

> It's Never Too Late to Plan (the rest of) Your Career

This raises some interesting possibilities for end-of-career choices (meaning end of *working* life). The realistic possibilities depend to some extent on which flavor of career has taken place in the past.

Professors who have been active, competent teachers throughout their career can certainly continue to teach, so long as they remain current in their teaching fields (and with modern instruction technology). In fact, some older professors enjoy a high degree of success at teaching, because they are thoroughly knowledgeable; they are more relaxed and affable than when they were young turks (they may even show some perspective and a sense of humor); and they are not as focused on covering a narrowly-defined topic, giving interesting life examples instead.

Similarly, professors who have been continuously active in research can continue successfully so long as their powers of imagination and creativity remain undiminished. They may even begin a new line of investigation that they have been interested in for decades.

Perhaps the most interesting cases are professors who have ascended to a certain level on the academic management ladder, but who are eventually prevented from continuing to hold their current position by virtue of term limits, and who have no easy choice but to return to their position of many years ago, in their home departments. These individuals, who have served their academic institutions with distinction, and who have seen themselves as highly successful in their academic careers—they are definitely and unashamedly thinking "career" at this point!—are asked to re-start and re-build their teaching and research careers, including the following tall orders:

1. Teach a course not already being given by somebody else, but one that is nevertheless in their field of expertise (or, at least was, a few decades ago).
2. Subject themselves to the class challenges and assaults from the latest generation of undergraduate students, who aren't overly impressed by their "distinguished" academic career.
3. Bring themselves up to date with the recent developments in their research area(s).
4. Come up with exciting new research topics to work on.
5. Write and win major proposals for grants and contracts.
6. Attract new graduate students, in competition with their younger colleagues.
7. Publish dynamite research papers, even though this process can take a year or two after the research process has been completed. (Which, in turn, may take many, many years after The Great Reversion to being a "mere professor" has taken place.)

How successful are professors who have taken the academic management career path but who are, not long before retirement, asked to accomplish the above tasks?

CHAPTER 7: ACADEMIC PATH PLANNING

The short answer is "not very," which is really a euphemism in most cases for "not at all." Most "former professors"—who, for cultural and job-security reasons, persist in thinking of themselves as "present professors"—cannot adapt to *any* of the boggling tasks listed above. A few further words of explanation might be required for the general reader, but for the target audience of this book, the understanding is complete, and the general response might be a shudder. The seven tasks listed above vary from difficult to impossible. Given their decades of absence from their competition in the teaching and research domains, the career academic manager simply is out of his or her element.

One always must make the exception for the extraordinarily brilliant person, even by academic standards, who can "do it all," however daunting the post-management demands may be.

Another case where teaching and research may still come easily is the person who, though hired to do an academic management job, has been fooling around all along with *earlier job descriptions,* like teaching and research. (Perhaps, this lack of complete commitment is why their academic management ascent was limited.) In any case, it seems likely that this is why even very senior university leaders continue to refer to themselves as "professors"! It is a reminder, to themselves as much as to anyone else, that they are *tenured,* and that they have a right to come back to their home departments. A hard term limit for service in any management posting is a now-entrenched feature of academic life.

In the private sector, by comparison, corporate leaders don't last forever either. They are continually judged by their performance—and by the alternatives available to their employers—a survival-of-the-fittest approach. When they are asked to leave, they are usually given a "golden parachute," a financial settlement that they will not find unpleasant.

In academia, the details are rather different, but the overall effect is much the same: the individual, by virtue of tenure, is assured a happy landing place, in which he or she becomes a senior citizen in his or her original academic department. Even if he or she accomplishes *not a single one* of the seven (at least) job requirements listed above, there is no penalty. These individuals are, after all, tenured professors. They have become the senior citizens of the department (even though they are still paid much in excess of their still-active colleagues who did not ramp up their compensation through the management channel).

In some cases, these former academic managers can contribute value to their departments through their mentoring of young staff; through their advice on academic and other matters to busy, at-their-peak professorial colleagues; and through their sage counsel to the current departmental leadership. Otherwise, not teaching anything much, and not conducting any research (other than what was called "curiosity-based" research in §4.3, by now a euphemism for reading), these professorial re-treads, with their relatively high salaries as leftovers from their previous management positions, have a financial impact that may be considerably more expensive than the golden parachute in the private sector, or the very early full-pension arrangements in many places in the public sector.

Of course, one can always retire, by which we mean *retire*, as in leaving and not coming back. Though culturally frowned upon in academia, this is hardly an unpleasant life, with a reasonably comfortable pension and a life spiced by wider reading, perhaps writing, and some travel. Perhaps one can finally take up one or more of those hobbies that were always on the list but never developed . . .

Bibliography

Barr, Margaret J: *Academic Administrator's Guide to Budgets and Financial Management*, Jossey-Bass (Wiley), 2002.

Bender, Thomas; Schorske, Carl [eds.]: *American Academic Culture in Transformation: Fifty Years, Four Disciplines*, Princeton University Press, 1998.

Birnbaum, Robert: *How Academic Leadership Works: Understanding Success and Failure in the College Presidency*, Jossey-Bass (Wiley), 1992.

Blaxter, Loraine; Hughes, Christina; Tight, Malcolm: *The Academic Career Handbook,* Open University Press, 1998.

Bright, David F; Richards, Mary P: *The Academic Deanship - Individual Careers and Institutional Roles,* Jossey-Bass (Wiley), 2001.

Chan, Janis Fisher: *Academic Administrator's Guide to Meetings*, Jossey-Bass (Wiley), 2003.

Darley, John M [ed.], et al.: *The Compleat Academic: A Career Guide* [Second Edition], American Psychological Association, 2004.

Diamond, Robert M [ed.]: *Field Guide to Academic Leadership*, Jossey-Bass (Wiley), 2002.

Eulau, Heinz: *The Politics of Academic Culture: Foibles, Fables, and Facts*, CQ Press, 1998.

Goldsmith, John A; Komlos, John: Gold, Penny Schine: *The Chicago Guide to Your Academic Career,* University of Chicago Press, 2001.

Kennedy, Donald: *Academic Duty*, Harvard University Press, 1997.

Lewis, Lionel S: *Scaling the Ivory Tower: Merit and Its Limits in Academic Careers*, Johns Hopkins University Press, 1975.

Martin, James; Samuels, James E [& Assoc.]: *First Among Equals: The Role of The Chief Academic Officer*, Johns Hopkins University Press, 1997.

Appendix

Distinguished Scholars Interviewed

(Their remarks are sprinkled throughout this book.)

Tom Brzustowski, O.C, PhD, PEng

Professor, University of Ottawa, Telfer School of Management, holds the RBC Financial Group Professorship in Commercialization; Officer of the Order of Canada; former President of the Natural Sciences and Engineering Research Council of Canada; served as Deputy Minister of Colleges and Universities of Ontario; Former Professor of Mechanical Engineering at the University of Waterloo.

MOTIVE FOR CHOOSING ACADEMIC CAREER

My father was an engineer, I wanted to be a good engineer, I was always interested in aircraft, and I got a job with Orenda engines after I graduated, working on designing afterburners in the combustion section. I discovered that nobody there really knew much about it, and myself the least of all, but the papers we were reading seemed to come from certain places, so I went to one of those places (Princeton) to get a Masters degree and while I was down there, the Canadian government chopped the Arrow (an advanced fighter aircraft being built in Canada), so I stayed on for a PhD and became a university professor. Never had a thought of that. I joined the faculty (in 1962) of a very new university (U Waterloo, Ontario, Canada). I became chairman of mechanical engineering five years after I arrived as a wet-behind-the-ear junior faculty member.

ACADEMIC LEADERSHIP

What I enjoyed the most was to build up the department . . . and I particularly enjoyed hiring young people.

The thing I enjoyed the least happened very early on. I had to tell a senior colleague, somebody whom I liked very much personally and who had become a bit of a mentor to me in the department, that his work just wasn't good enough. That was very difficult to do.

At that point I became aware of how important the human resource aspects of management were. If you aspire to be even a department chair, you really have to be aware of the cultural and personality aspects of what people eventually may be forced to interpret as objective decisions under a particular policy. And you have to learn how to work your way around it. I don't think that can be taught, I think it's instinctive. You have to think about the very soft people skills. And paradoxically, the soft skills are the hard ones

In many cases decisions are made on the basis of judgment which takes a lot into account, you can't just pretend you've developed some rational system where you put numbers in, you turn the crank and the answer come out.

I discovered a couple of things. One was that process is very often more important than substance. That has its positive aspects but also negative aspects, because you often have people involved in important decisions who don't know the substance well enough. They know only the process. That's a serious fault.

ADVICE TO YOUNG ACADEMICS

Smart people do better than people who are less smart, and smart people working together do better than smart people working separately.
Luck favors the prepared mind. I think without the hard work, luck would do nothing for you. Hard work without having the ability wouldn't achieve nearly as much as hard work with ability. I think it's a spontaneous process. Out of every situation, seek to find an opportunity and then seize it.

OTHER INSIGHTS

I think it's very important that people at the highest levels see the world from a perspective of the university at one time, government at another time, industry at another time.

Bill Buxton, MASc

Associate Professor, Department of Computer Science, University of Toronto; Senior Researcher for Microsoft Research; Chief Scientist, Bruce Mau Design; recipient of the Canadian Human-Computer Communications Society award and the New Media Visionary of the Year award; elected to the CHI Academy; consultant to Xerox PARC and SGI Inc.; past board member of the Canadian Film Centre.

WHY CHOOSE ACADEMIA

To me the only reason to be at a university is if you really love teaching. I loved supervising students, I loved one on ones, I loved small seminars. I think by the time I started my masters program I already had a research grant that I was running, to build a music system: Design Issues in Computer Based Tool for Music Composition. When I finished my masters, they offered me a teaching position right away and I started working as a lecturer. Again since I was a musician and I wanted to focus on music, it seemed no point to do a PhD and I never did do one.

CAREER IN RESEARCH

The early days at U of T were probably the best training I could have had, much better than say a normal technology degree, partially because it made me different from other people in my department. I got a multi-million dollar grant to do some work on a project called TelePresence but it was collaboration at a distance. So I was based at the University and I was paid out of that, but I actually was paying the university for the privilege of being there and supervising students. That was very successful, so that was fine, I was happy to do that.

I'd been told by my funding agencies that I would not have funding continued if I kept using the word 'music' in it so I used to do things like publish papers on multi-point touch-sensitive real-time controllers which is a really big euphemism for a drum. And I was perfectly happy to play that game. But the good news was we had by that time in Toronto one of the—if not the—most famous and best facilities for computer music

The universities have one thing that's fantastic and that's students and the ability to have a research group of students and graduate students working with you where you can do curiosity-driven research

SO YOU WANT TO BE A PROFESSOR?

Almost all of my colleagues and friends who are in academic positions are lucky if they get half a day a week or a day a week doing research because after they've done their teaching, after they've done their academic administrative departmental duties, they then spend far more time on research grant writing and administration than they do on research and so their productivity is really low. So for me, I'd say anybody who has just graduated from university if you can get into a good corporate research lab and I mean research with a capital R not a small r, they're way better off because then they can devote themselves to research full time 24 hours a day if they want, without ever looking for a grant proposal. They can build up their publication record spectacularly, then they've got a huge reputation, and have a background in industry and should they want to go back to academia they will be miles ahead of the people who stayed in the academic stream.

The problem with the university environment right now is that it's become so driven by funded research, commercially-funded research and short-term (what I would call) development rather than research objectives. We seem to be so focused on what companies are interested in, how much are they willing to pay, can you get matching funds and all this sort of stuff that the pure long term research has almost disappeared. The irony is it's in the corporate sector, the private sector, that we're looking at ideas that are 20 years out, but it's not in the university. That's what's so bizarre, that the universities are doing the short-term stuff you used to think the companies would do.

Michael Collins, PhD, PEng

University Professor and Bahen/Tanenbaum Chair, Department of Civil Engineering, University of Toronto; Canadian Council of Professional Engineers Medal for Distinction in Engineering Education; T.Y. Lin Award from the American Society of Civil Engineers.

WHY CHOOSE AN ACADEMIC CAREER

The essence of being a good academic is doing something you really love, that you would do for no money. You find a passion—I think that's the essence of both good research and good teaching . . . you find something that you obsess about and you're an enthusiast about. The ideal for which we should strive is that every professor should teach and every professor should do research . . . and if they can do one of those things superbly but not the other, they're in the wrong place. For most of us, we'd like to make a difference in life. You get a sense of accomplishment by knowing I've done this, I'm leaving this as my legacy.

ON TEACHING AND RESEARCH

University is about teaching. The epitome of teaching is to sit in a class and hear someone who understands the subject so deeply because that person is involved in actually developing the subject. You're listening to the person who writes the textbooks and you're listening to the person who develops the research in that area. If you really understand what you're doing, it doesn't matter how complex the subject is, you can put it at every level and explain it. For your self respect as a professional teacher, you should have professional experience wider than simply your narrow research area.

What should exemplify university research is long term goals not short term goals. As soon as you get to where some committee defines the next hot thing, that's not long-term. You've got to find something which is to you, deep and meaningful and juicy and meaty, that you're going to be able to spend your whole academic career working on it, hopefully solving part of it. If you're really lucky, you might solve a lot of it. But you've got to find that good problem. Serendipity plays a big part in coming up with good ideas.

I think to be successful in any of the environments you've got to be an expert in something. You've got to develop your own field where you hopefully are world class if you really want to go to the top of the academic heap. We are interested in principles, not rules so we're looking for the principles governing behavior, not empirical rules of how you design things, not handbooks . . . and behind that is quality not quantity.

ON BEING A GOOD ADMINISTRATOR

If your mind is of the sort that you can deal with three things at once, then you probably have the basic talent to be a good administrator.

Dan Farine, MD

Professor, University of Toronto, Head of Maternal Fetal Medicine Department of Obstetrics and Gynecology, Head of high risk pregnancies at Mount Sinai Hospital, Co-Founder Barnev Ltd, a company that develops ultrasound based labor monitoring devices.

MOTIVE FOR CHOOSING AN ACADEMIC CAREER

I never really had long term planning for myself, but I was still aware of a variety of different things. My father was in academic medicine, he was the chairman of orthopedics in Tel Aviv and he told me many, many years ago when I was in medical school, that if I did not make it academically, I would not be happy, but if I did make it academically there's no guarantee that I'd be happy then either. He said you have to think about other activities, other scopes in life.

First of all, I started late. I became an MD when I was 24 but then I went for five years into the Israeli Army and I actually started at 30. And the way it was in medicine there, it was four years of residency. Then I did two years of fellowship. So in a way I started my independent academic career at the age of 36. And then things moved fast.

Within two years I became head of this unit, two years later I became head of obstetrics. Then on a personal level what happened with me was, at some point, I had to stop and think, because we merged two units, and only one of us could be the head, it wasn't me. I took time off . . . this was the time that I made decisions that I didn't make before. Everything that was not interesting I cut, and I had more time.

ENTREPRENEURS IN A UNIVERSITY ENVIRONMENT

I think you have to distinguish between different kinds of academic careers and different kinds of people that have different options. In medicine in a way, we are lucky because we have at least one more option that lots of other people in academia do not have—clinical work. If you are in other fields, like business, communications, engineering, you have the option of using those skills in a different way.

Lots of people have an academic career where you become a super expert in a very small niche. One of the things that I wanted to do was to study the way that we manage labor (delivering babies), which is completely inefficient. Actually I was not interested when I started in any of the financial or administrative matters, I simply wanted to improve the way labor is managed.

ADVICE TO YOUNG ACADEMICS

Now it's networking. So you can open the door, the door will not stay open too long if you have nothing to offer it—it will close in no time. In academia in general, and more so in academic medicine, you are constantly on the run, seeing patients, teaching, doing administrative and committee work and continuing your research along the lines you started early in your career. You need to have free time to meditate, to think. In academia, you can get into a treadmill and start running and you are too busy dealing with the next step, the next month the next year, so that you don't really plan 10 years down the line. If you really want money, if money is the only thing you care about, you're not very likely to go and learn medieval history. You're going to go to banking, to business, to do your MBA. The trick is to find the balance and decide what it is. Some people, when they get tenure, they just fade away. They must have done something to get the tenure, but once they got there, all of a sudden they do nothing. This may be a result of complete exhaustion once the marathon of getting tenure is over or the lack of opportunities to reflect and develop long-term goals while 'running'.

Motto: When you're not desperate there's more freedom.

DISTINGUISHED SCHOLARS INTERVIEWED

Barry French, O.C., PhD, FRSC, FCASI, FCAE, FRSA

Professor Emeritus, University of Toronto Institute for Aerospace Studies; Officer of the Order of Canada; fellow of the Canadian Academy of Engineers, the Royal Society of Canada, the Royal Society of Art and the Canadian Aeronautics and Space Institute; co-founder and scientific advisor to SCIEX, currently a division of MDS Health Group Ltd and a world leader in mass spectroscopy instrumentation.

MOTIVE FOR CHOOSING AN ACADEMIC CAREER

I was misguided by a high school teacher. My marks in mathematics were only average, but I liked chemistry and physics. He said, well if your mathematics is only average, take engineering, don't go into arts and sciences! I was interested in combustion and so I took chemical engineering because it seemed to be the right choice—turned out to be the wrong one. I had an opportunity to go and work for Orenda engines and the thing I got assigned to do was some analysis of the combustion products.

I'd heard of liquid chromatography, but I'd never heard of gas chromatography and then I learned it was just growing so I home-built a gas-chromatograph out of glass tubes and charcoal and it worked. I had a fellowship when I went to England, and went to a gas turbine establishment. I still at that point in time hadn't any idea where I was going except I thought I might be coming back to Orenda. I talked to a colleague and he said why don't you come back to the Institute and do further work? With a Masters, they sent me into a PhD program under the Institute's Director and he was good because he encouraged my lateral thinking outside the box. The first time I really seriously thought about being an academic was when he offered me a chance to stay on here, on the staff. I literally had never considered it before.

RESEARCH CAREERS

One of the ways of bootstrapping your career and getting to the next level is working with other excellent people at other institutions.

The biggest advances often come from lateral thinking, from applying something that's an advance in one field in an entirely unexpected area.

BEING AN ENTREPRENEUR IN A UNIVERSITY ENVIRONMENT

You need to have financial connections, and you have to have an ability to be creative in marketing skills. You have to have enough business knowledge to be able to analyze markets and market trends. And then you have to be able to collectively inspire a group of people that, hey, if we do something here, this is going to change the way things are done. I was only interested in something that was really going to be a platform technology for major change. Patents—there is no sense in getting patents unless you have a realistic view that this thing is commercially useful.

You have to be a good character judge of people because you've got to build a team with the right people. Timing is everything. There are business cycles and you've got to be lucky.

I don't think some of these events in your life you can plan, that's the point. So you have to be flexible.

ADVICE TO NEW PROFESSORS

The way I looked at the future, I was beginning to realize very much what my strengths and my weaknesses were. I think one has to know yourself; you have to know what your strengths and weaknesses are and what you like and what you dislike and be brutally honest about it. That's crucial because it guides everything you do after that. If you don't do what you enjoy doing, it's not going to work.

Peter Likins, PhD, FAIAA

President, The University of Arizona and formerly President, Lehigh University; former Provost of Columbia University, where he had earlier served as a Professor and Dean of the School of Engineering and Applied Science; Fellow of the American Institute of Aeronautics and Astronautics; elected to membership of the National Academy of Engineering; former member of the White House Advisory Committee on the Health of Universities and the President's Council of Advisors on Science and Technology; he has served on the boards of six public companies, two hospitals and one university.

MOTIVE FOR CHOOSING ACADEMIC CAREER

I didn't start out with any grand plans. In fact, my background expectations educationally were quite modest. As a kid I wanted to be an engineer but I didn't understand the educational implications. I began my professional life as a development engineer at the Jet Propulsion Laboratory of the California Institute of Technology, involved in the very early years of spacecraft development. (Graduating at about the same time as Sputnik I made this a very exciting time!) My faculty advisor at MIT urged me to continue my studies and become a professor, so I knew by then that JPL was a transitional job.

ACADEMIC CAREER STRATEGIES

My teaching, my research, and my consulting projects were all mutually supportive. Each of the three was supported and fed by the other two. My fixation was not with a pre-planned series of "career moves." Instead, I would say that my obsession was really a "competitive" one. I just wanted to do the best darned job I possibly could—whatever my job was; you know, teaching, research, consulting, and some administration—and I wanted to do it better than anybody else doing similar things.

CLIMBING THE ACADEMIC LADDER TO ATTAIN A LEADERSHIP POSITION

At UCLA I had by this time developed quite a network of colleagues, through my discussions at conferences, my consulting work, my invited lectures, and I had also been developing important administrative experience during my later years at UCLA. One such colleague told me that he knew the engineering deanship at Columbia was open . . . so I let my name stand and I was successful. I then became "co-provost" for two years before moving to the Lehigh presidency.

ACADEMIC LEADERSHIP

People who go straight to the presidency of a major university cannot possibly know in any detail about major segments and divisions within that university, and that does place them at quite a disadvantage.

In arriving at important decisions, I work on three phases: (a) discuss; (b) decide; (c) explain. In Phase (a), everyone on the senior management team (and anyone else who is an important stakeholder) has an opportunity to give their input—to provide data, ideas, and reasoned responses. In Phase (b), I decide. I see that as being my job. The difficult task of integrating all the available information together with the many key considerations—to produce what is (I hope) the best decision—is up to me. In Phase (c), I announce my decision and explain my decision to all concerned. This last phase is very important because it has been my experience that, if people know that you value their concerns and have taken their views into account, they will tend to support your decision. I am a "relationship-based manager." If you don't like people; if you're suspicious and distrustful of people, how can you possibly lead them? I always say "Number 1 is integrity." If you haven't got that, there's no point in having any conversation, because that is the foundation on which everything else is built. You have to have a sense of what's "right." You can't be dogmatic or intolerant of people who have a different view. But you have to have a sense of yourself.

Donald Mackay, O.C., PhD, FCIC, PEng

Professor Emeritus Trent University and the University of Toronto; Director Emeritus Canadian Centre for Environmental Modelling and Chemistry; Officer of the Order of Canada; Order of Ontario; NSERC / Industry Research Chair; Honorary Doctor of Science Degree from the University of Toronto.

MOTIVE FOR CHOOSING ACADEMIC CAREER

I decided that doing research was enjoyable and that (university) was where I would go.

RESEARCH CAREER STRATEGIES

I don't think you can predict in advance where the big developments are going to come but you're not going to find them unless you try. I've advocated one should undertake a fairly central area of research but dabble in peripheral things as well. Sometimes they're the ones that take off.

I think a little diversity is good but not to the extent that you dabble in too many things, and do none well. There's a balance there. Attending scientific meetings and reading the scientific literature gives you a sense of what some of these areas are going to be in the future.

I found it just fascinating to go and visit people (top authorities in a field) and hear what their priorities are and how they're setting about doing things. The contact with the leaders in the field I think is very important and I think that's best done through scientific meetings . . . the more contact you have with these people the better. By forming partnerships with people and building a community of supporters is the way to go.

There is a role for turning out a few papers in the more mundane journals. Often, they'll turn out to be much more significant in the future than you thought . . . they also have the advantage that they can be published fast. That can be important.

I think from the point of view of getting a career in scientific research, administration is an annoying distraction.

ENTREPRENEURS IN A UNIVERSITY ENVIRONMENT

I thought of creating a commercial operation that would develop and sell (software) models, but I decided not to do that partly because when you develop a model and sell it to somebody, you're then on the hook for providing advice. So I gave them away free. You take a model, you use it, it's your responsibility; I'll help you if I can but I'm not on the hook. But if you want me to apply that model and slightly modify it for your purposes I will do it on a contractual basis and so I set up a company which is called D. Mackay Environmental Research Ltd., and that's been on the go for almost 20 years now, and that's provided me with a steady source of consulting income. There is a Website where you can download the models free and that's been a major activity and it's quite warmly supported by industry folks who use these models. They are downloaded, 10 per day, all over the world.

ADVICE TO YOUNG ACADEMICS

If you can establish a reputation as a good speaker, and an authority in your particular area, I think it opens up a lot of opportunities.

It would be useful to think about putting all your thoughts down in an academic book (at about the tenure stage of your career). That gets you a lot of exposure—not much royalties—but I've done a few, and it tends to clarify in my own mind, what is important, what is not, and where one should go. I've seen a number of people who just happened to have the right book at the right time and that increases their status enormously.

Heather Munroe-Blum, O.C., PhD, FRSC

Principal and Vice Chancellor of McGill University, Montreal, Quebec; Member of Faculty of Medicine and Professor, Department of Epidemiology and Biostatistics; former VP Research and International Relations, University of Toronto; Officer of the Order of Canada;Officer of the National Order of Quebec; Specially Elected Fellow of the Royal Society of Canada; Chair, the Association of Universities and Colleges of Canada's Standing Advisory Committee on University Research (SACUR); Board Member, Association of American Universities; Member, Science, Technology and Innovation Council (STIC) of Canada; Member, U.S. National Research Council's Committee on Research Universities; Co-Chair of the Private Sector Advisory Committee of the Ontario-Quebec Trade and Co-operation Agreement.

HOW TO SUCCEED

You want to use your intellect and your talents fully and to do so you must focus—nonetheless, I never have adequately managed to fully focus. My curiosity simply wouldn't let me narrow the fields. The challenge may be to manage to focus (enough) while also managing and engaging with complexity yet being thorough, disciplined, and focused on quality, in whatever you do. These three dimensions will limit what you can do at any one point in time. For me, successful leadership, academic and otherwise, has an activist dimension, not allowing oneself to be constrained by obstacles and not letting others constrain you when you have conviction about moving in a new direction. This is essential.

I'm a big believer in multi-sectoral partnerships (government, universities, industry, NGO's) as being critically important for achieving and advancing the full mission of the university. But you do have to know what your core academic mission is, and then to define the common arena of activity—where that overlapping area is what defines a common cause. I feel sometimes that we start again and again, from scratch, to create these "new" platforms of productive collaboration, instead of refining the model(s) to be mutually productive and rewarding. This is true of everything from basic research collaboration, to interdisciplinary teaching and research within a university, to managing intellectual property effectively.

The real ability to make a difference depends on using your full network and talent in any number of arenas to do interesting, important, and different kinds of things. Getting outside of the confines of your lab or your classroom is really important. It's easier to do the big transformative things in research, teaching and service than the small incremental things, so why go for a little grant? Go get a huge project!

VIEWS ON ACADEMIC LEADERSHIP

If you want to be successful and fulfilled, I urge that you not let title or rank overly influence you. The ego gratification of a position with a fancy title will last fifteen minutes, max. Then you have your life to live and your job to do, and so be guided by the "what" of your role, and whether what you are responsible to contribute to it suits your interests, talents and passions. There is biochemistry to success. In that regard, not needing much sleep and having a big appetite for work are important assets. And, as corny as it sounds, aim to have a broad impact—to make a difference to others and to your institution and your world. Finally, of course, an absolutely necessary condition to success is that you aim to be as good as you can be.

Leadership opportunities—these are special roles—are opportunities to make a difference, to work with a great team. If there's anything I think about, it's an opportunity to embrace activist leadership in a time-limited but important role. It really is what are we doing, and who we are working with, that makes these roles worthwhile and successful. The team is so important, as is the sense of esprit de corps when we're working together on something we feel is really important. Get on the team and make sure you know what's happening and who the players are—take an active role. And celebrate the success of those on the team.

To influence, you need to inspire, you need to work hard yourself, you need to be successful yourself, and you need to help others succeed—being able to mobilize people to work together while maintaining excellence, coherence and shared goals.

The role of leaders across the university in various capacities is to promote our colleagues, the benefits of the research, scholarship and teaching that we do, and to be creative in thinking about what those benefits are and getting these out to where they can have a societal impact.

OTHER VIEWS

People say there's nothing as tough as the politics in academe, and there is nothing as rewarding as the cause of universities and the people in them.

While it is a forced distinction, I think men are often more inclined and encouraged to be very focused on one domain, while women tend to lateral-task and analyze laterally and to go outside of any one sphere and engage entire systems.

SO YOU WANT TO BE A PROFESSOR?

David Naylor, O.C, MD, DPhil, FRCPC, FRSC

President, University of Toronto; former Dean of the Faculty of Medicine and Vice Provost-Relations with Health Care Institutions, University of Toronto; Fellow of the Royal Society of Canada and the Canadian Academy of Health Science; Officer of the Order of Canada; Rhodes Scholar; founding chief executive officer of the Institute for Clinical Evaluative Sciences; former Director of the Clinical Epidemiology Program, Sunnybrook Health Science Centre; served as chair of the National Advisory Committee on SARS and Public Health.

PERSONAL CAREER CHOICE

I had a longstanding interest in research, and by the middle of medical school, I had already decided that I would pursue an academic career. By late 1978, I had formulated some ideas about a career path, and followed through on these as a graduate student at Oxford and thereafter during clinical residency and post-residency Fellowship training. Before the end of my residency at the University of Western Ontario, I concluded that my eventual interest was likely to be in some form of academic administration. However, I certainly did not have any pre-specified timeline or end-point. My first goal was to find a rewarding and engaging line of research that could be coupled to a part-time clinical career.

ON LEADERSHIP AND CLIMBING THE ACADEMIC LADDER

Some people choose administration because they are second-tier researchers and decide that they will not advance further in their research careers. At the same time, universities continue to make the mistake of choosing Chairs, Deans, Vice-Presidents and Presidents on the basis of the thickness of their resumes and the number of research awards they have received, rather than demonstrated capability in management and leadership. The reason to go into administration is because there are issues that one cares about passionately.

I have doubts about Presidents who have not served time as scholars and teachers, and who lack any experience in academic administration. The academy has a unique culture where decisions are made by "power of reason rather than reasons of power", and where radically participatory decision-making and wide consultation are the norms.

No matter what discipline she or he has pursued, a junior professor should in my view focus in the first instance on developing an excellent record as a teacher and scholar. My own prejudice is that anyone who is unduly ambitious or seen to be currying favor to facilitate administrative advancement is likely to be given short shrift by colleagues on search committees. I may be naïve, but my sense is that the colleagues who make the biggest impact in administrative roles have two overriding characteristics. First, they enjoy the breadth of challenges that administrative and leadership roles bring, and are energized by the chance to work with large numbers of smart and creative people at all levels of the organization. Second, they have some burning platform, compelling vision, or overarching purpose to their pursuit of a particular position.

SO YOU WANT TO BE A PROFESSOR?

Arnold M. Noyek, MD, FRCSC, FACS, Senior Ashoka Fellow

Professor of Otolaryngology-Head and Neck Surgery, Public Health and Medical Imaging, University of Toronto; Director of International Continuing Education, Faculty of Medicine, University of Toronto; Director, Peter A. Silverman Centre for International Health, Mount Sinai Hospital; Founder, Canada International Scientific Exchange Program (CISEPO); recipient of the Canadian Red Cross Power of Humanity Award, the 2005 Lifetime Achievement Award of the Canadian Society for International Health, the Colin R. Woolf Award for Long-Term Contributions to Continuing Education, Faculty of Medicine, University of Toronto, and the Ludwik and Estelle Jus Memorial Human Rights Prize at the University of Toronto.

MOTIVE FOR CHOOSING ACADEMIC CAREER

I can remember in grade six, we had to write about what we wanted to be when you grow up– we had to fill in three choices. I remember this graphically. So I wrote down, doctor, doctor, doctor—never any question in my mind. I trained in otolaryngology because it was a depressed specialty. I picked ENT to train in because I sensed it as a potentially important specialty because it reaches into the lives of so much of the public. I decided that if we're going to move this specialty forward, we have to make it more scientific. My opening academic opportunity was to build a bridge between ENT and medical imaging to assure interactive relationships and discourse because of all the complex anatomy and pathology to be understood in effective diagnosis and in the context of new technology. All these new applications were a developmental gold mine of new knowledge. The model was always clear to me from the beginning: if you're going to be a player, you've got to find a way to play. I was very aware that in this world the only way you could be a player was to join in and to invite other people to join with you.

HUMANITARIAN ENTREPRENEUR IN A UNIVERSITY ENVIRONMENT

When we talk about entrepreneurship, we're not about money, we're about capacity-building. The capital we build is social capital. I believe that education is powerful and carries the day. It overcomes ignorance and relieves suffering.

Our team and I have carried out over 100 academic missions to the Middle East because of my initial bridge between ENT and radiology. I'm fortunate enough to be the founder of what is now a multidisciplinary organization (CISEPO) using health as a bridge to peace across the Arab and Israeli frontier. In order to lead in this kind of enterprise, first of all you have to have the courage of your own personal convictions. You have to have a large, strong network around you who believe in and who support collectively a vision of peaceful professional cooperation where all are treated with equitable respect. It's an academic model. We're about education, research and service. My idea is that you build distributive academic networks to do good, to build social capital. We start with medicine but we incorporate nursing, science, students, public health—all in a continuing health educational system and the idea is to advance society by touching the lives of ordinary people. We see the health sector—it's never been used for peace-building—as ideal.

So what we're all about at the end of the day is building peaceful professional co-operation network—health based and then moving out into and impacting on the lives of kids, women, the disabled and society at large and influencing change because you touched the lives of ordinary and needy people. When we work in the Middle East, we're doing research projects and educational projects, and cross-border training, and people-to-people activities, in spite of the constant conflict and violence. We just keep moving forward—it's using health as a bridge to peace!

ADVICE TO YOUNG ACADEMICS

When disciplines rub up against each other, real academic growth—personally and professionally—takes place. I believe if you stay within one discipline, you never realize your full growth potential. The sparks occur when you start to move into other disciplines. You need to dare enough to move into new areas; you have to really enjoy riding out there to that far horizon where no-one has gone before. You've got to really like the action. And you need to be armed with reasonable intelligence and a supportive network—you can't go in there naked. You have to look out for the team, they have to watch your back and do their thing. You have to be passionate about whatever you're doing, love the action—be a pioneer. It's the sport of contact chess!

Molly S. Shoichet, PhD, FRSC, FBSE, FAIMBE

Professor, University of Toronto, Departments of Chemical Engineering & Applied Chemistry, Chemistry, Biomaterials & Biomedical Engineering, Faculty of Medicine and the Program in Neuroscience; elected to the Mathematical and Physical Sciences Division of the Academy of Science of the Royal Society of Canada; Canada Research Chair in Tissue Engineering; Killam Research Fellowship Canada Council for the Arts; Natural Science & Engineering Research Council Steacie Fellowship; Fellow of the Biomaterials Science and Engineering and the American Institute for Medical and Biological Engineering societies; Founder of Matregen Corp., a company focused on drug delivery based on a polymer platform technology.

MOTIVE FOR CHOOSING AN ACADEMIC CAREER

I've taken a non-traditional path. I had a great job in industry, I was working in a bio-tech company and we were doing cell therapy—leading edge research. When I looked at what was going on at the University of Toronto, I was really excited about the research—and because I grew up here I wanted to come back. But I've been involved in a couple of spin-off companies and part of my motivation is to grow the bio-tech industry in Toronto.

There is nothing more satisfying, I think, than to have worked on something in the academic level and for it to be translated into a product, either through a spin-off company or through a licensing.

ON RESEARCH CAREERS & STRATEGIES IN ACADEMIA

Part of what I love about research is that it's always changing.

You realize pretty early on that you might have a great idea, but if you don't have any data to support it, you're not going to get funded. So I think it's extremely important to work on big questions. I think that's our mandate in fact because if you're working on the incremental questions—industry can do that.

But if you're looking at a big question, there's a series of smaller questions, you go from the big vision down, and it gets you into some really interesting basic science questions. It's just having your eyes open to the possibility of painting on a bigger screen or on a bigger canvas.

TEACHING

There is nothing more wonderful than to see the light bulb go on, when they say, hey I get this, I know what you're talking about.

The only thing it's never fun to teach is a class when people don't want to be there. You can either change the course to make it better or sometimes the system is set up and these just aren't good courses to teach.

LEADERSHIP

Wanting to have a position of leadership is almost reason for people not to promote you to positions of leadership.

There are leaders who tend the farm—and leaders that grow the farm.

The idea of reaching out to people and figuring out what they want is essential.

ADVICE TO NEW PROFESSORS

I don't think many people in academia think strategically about their career.

I think in university we have to remember what our mandate is and that's advancing knowledge and education.

About the Authors

Peter C Hughes, PhD, PEng, MBA, FAIAA, FCASI, CDir
A University of Toronto PhD in aeronautics and astronautics (1966), Hughes was made Full Professor at U of T in 1974. He has had visiting appointments in the Canadian Space Agency and at Purdue University. Hughes performed the complete dynamics models used in the design of the NASA space shuttle and space station remote manipulator arms (Canadarms). His text-reference book *Spacecraft Attitude Dynamics,* originally published by John Wiley in 1986, has been re-published (2004) by Dover Publications as a classic in its field.

He is a highly rated teacher and developed and taught over a dozen different undergraduate and graduate courses. Over his 38 years as a Professor of space systems engineering, he published over 242 items (refereed papers, conference papers, professional presentations, and consulting reports). He has personally supervised 48 MASc theses and 33 PhD theses. His book *Satellites Harming Other Satellites*, written for the Canadian Department of External Affairs, led to a key presentation at the U.N. *ad hoc* Committee on Outer Space in Geneva.

He obtained his MBA from York University in 1996 and became the founding Director of the Jeffrey Skoll BASc/MBA Program at U of T, 2000–2004. Hughes has served on many committees, both inside and outside the University. He is a member of the national Innovation Council. He is currently a Professor Emeritus at the University of Toronto's Institute for Aerospace Studies and a Professor Emeritus at the University of Toronto's Rotman School of Management.

Hughes has recently (2006) published *Engineers Becoming Managers— From the Classroom to the Boardroom.* Also in 2006, he won the Alouette Award, the highest award from the Canadian Aeronautics and Space Institute. In 2007, he won the John H. Chapman Award of Excellence. The

Chapman is the Canadian Space Agency's highest award; only one other individual has won both the Alouette and the Chapman during his or her career.

Dr Hughes currently serves as Chairman & CEO of Dynacon Inc. (founded by Hughes in 1975 as Dynacon Associates), a space and medical automation business. It designed and built Canada's first microsatellite and exported medical lab automation instruments to the U.S. and Europe.

ABOUT THE AUTHORS

Roderick C Tennyson, BASc, PhD, PEng, FCASI

In 2001, Dr. Rod Tennyson co-founded a Toronto-based start-up company, "Fiber Optic Systems Technology Inc (FOX-TEK)", where he currently serves as Chief Scientific Advisor. FOX-TEK designs and installs fiber optic sensor systems to monitor long-term structural integrity of civil engineering structures such as bridges and pipelines. A University of Toronto PhD in aerospace materials and structures, Tennyson was made full professor at U of T in 1974, and subsequently served as the Director of the University of Toronto's Institute of Aerospace Studies (UTIAS) for two terms from 1985–1995. In 1996, he was the first Director of the University of Toronto's Government Research Infrastructure Program (GRIP) office which played a critical role in securing over $400 million in grants and contracts over a four-year period, awarded to premiere researchers across the whole university spectrum.

Dr. Tennyson was a Founding Member of the International Space University (ISU) headquartered in Strasbourg, and served as President of the Canadian Foundation for ISU (CFISU) from its inception in 1987 to 2001.

His career as a research scientist in aerospace engineering spans 40 years, and he has published over 200 technical papers in subjects ranging from the design and testing of aerospace structures to the design of new fiber optic sensor systems. His most notable research in the past 20 years has involved studying space environmental effects on materials, with experiments on the US Space Shuttle and the NASA satellite LDEF, and currently the design of fiber optic impact detection systems for NASA spacecraft such as the International Space Station.

He is the coauthor of six patents dealing with protective coatings for spacecraft, and fiber optic sensor systems. He is a Fellow of the Canadian Aeronautics and Space Institute (CASI), and his work has been recognized with several awards, including his selection as the Turnbull Lecturer by CASI for his significant achievements in aerospace engineering, and in 1996 the G. N. Patterson Lecturer as a distinguished alumnus of UTIAS. In 1998, the Canadian Society of Mechanical Engineers recognized him with the Duggan medal for his contributions to advanced materials. In 2004, CASI honored him with their McCurdy Award for outstanding achievement in aerospace science and engineering. He received an award in 2005 from the Canadian Government's Department of Natural Resources for his "exceptional contribution to the development of a novel remote monitoring system for high-pressure oil and gas pipelines" using his fiber optic sensor system. Dr. Tennyson is currently a Professor Emeritus at the University of Toronto Institute for Aerospace Studies.